Public Relations Ethics

This book is a pragmatic, case-rich guide to how current and future public relations practitioners can apply ethical principles and the industry's codes of ethics to their day-to-day work.

Authors Trevor Morris and Simon Goldsworthy draw on their years of industry and academic experience to illustrate key ethical issues and ground them in reality, all within an international frame of reference. *Public Relations Ethics* incorporates interviews with industry practitioners, offering contrasting perspectives as well as recent examples of real-life complaints and disciplinary issues. Provocative questions and exercises help readers grapple with ethical dilemmas and review the key scenarios and challenges that PR people face.

The book is ideal at the undergraduate, postgraduate and continuing education levels as a core text for public relations ethics courses and a supplementary text for general public relations survey courses. Accompanying the text are online resources for both students and instructors, including lecture slides and links to further resources.

Trevor Morris is former CEO of Chime PR. He taught Public Relations for 14 years, first at the University of Westminster, and then at Richmond, the American International University in London, where he was Professor of Public Relations. He is currently a non-executive director, consultant and PR trainer. He is a Fellow of the Public Relations and Communications Association and the co-author of *PR – A Persuasive Industry?: Spin, Public Relations and the Shaping of the Modern Media* and *PR Today: The Authoritative Guide to Public Relations*.

Simon Goldsworthy taught Public Relations for 20 years, first at the University of Westminster, and then at Richmond, the American International University in London, where he was Professor of Public Relations and Advertising. Prior to his academic career, he was a member of the UK Government Information Service, serving in a range of government departments as a press officer. He is a Fellow of the Public Relations and Communications Association and the co-author of *PR – A Persuasive Industry?: Spin, Public Relations and the Shaping of the Modern Media* and *PR Today: The Authoritative Guide to Public Relations*.

'Morris and Goldsworthy's combination of academic and practical insight delivers another highly readable guidebook, providing hands-on advice that practitioners at all levels will turn to again and again.'

— **Sally Costerton**, *CEO of SCA Consulting and former EMEA CEO of Hill and Knowlton Strategies*

'Possibly the most comprehensive and up-to-date guide on navigating PR ethics that exists. This is a must-read for anyone serious about working in PR or public affairs.'

— **John Harrington**, *Editor*, PRWeek UK

'Undoubtedly the definitive work on ethics in public relations. In an era when ethics has never been more central to every organisation, Morris and Goldsworthy have done the PR industry a great service with this no-holds-barred analysis of where our industry is and where it needs to be.'

— **Francis Ingham**, *Director General of the Public Relations and Communications Association*

'This book achieves the rare feat of combining informed reflection on PR today with an accessible and engaging style. Morris and Goldsworthy bring deep experience and insight to bear on the most charged issues facing the industry.'

— **Paul Mylrea**, *Director of Communications, University of Cambridge and formerly of the BBC, and former President of the Chartered Institute of Public Relations*

'Morris and Goldsworthy deliver what they set out to do ... The touch is light but the insights are sharp and the issues matter to all of us.'

— **Philip Young**, *Senior Lecturer and Course Leader, Birmingham City University*

Public Relations Ethics

The Real-World Guide

Trevor Morris and
Simon Goldsworthy

Routledge
Taylor & Francis Group

NEW YORK AND LONDON

First published 2021
by Routledge
52 Vanderbilt Avenue, New York, NY 10017

and by Routledge
2 Park Square, Milton Park, Abingdon, Oxon, OX14 4RN

Routledge is an imprint of the Taylor & Francis Group, an informa business

Library of Congress Cataloging-in-Publication Data
Names: Morris, Trevor, author. | Goldsworthy, Simon, author.
Title: Public relations ethics: the real-world guide /
Trevor Morris and Simon Goldsworthy.
Description: New York, NY: Routledge, 2021. |
Includes bibliographical references and index.
Identifiers: LCCN 2020036212 (print) | LCCN 2020036213
(ebook) | ISBN 9780367620172 (hardback) | ISBN
9780367612276 (paperback) | ISBN 9781003107491 (ebook)
Subjects: LCSH: Public relations—Moral and ethical
aspects. | Public relations personnel—Professional ethics.
Classification: LCC HD59 .M6449 2021 (print) |
LCC HD59 (ebook) | DDC 174/.4—dc23
LC record available at https://lccn.loc.gov/2020036212
LC ebook record available at https://lccn.loc.gov/2020036213

ISBN: 978-0-367-62017-2 (hbk)
ISBN: 978-0-367-61227-6 (pbk)
ISBN: 978-1-003-10749-1 (ebk)

Typeset in Times New Roman
by codeMantra

Visit the eResources: www.routledge.com/9780367612276

Contents

About the Authors

Simon Goldsworthy taught Public Relations for 20 years, first at the University of Westminster, and then at Richmond, the American International University in London, where he was Professor of Public Relations and Advertising. At both universities he curated postgraduate and undergraduate programmes in PR. He has also taught at other institutions, including Johns Hopkins University, Tsinghua in Beijing and Université Paris-Sorbonne, and has acted as a consultant or external examiner at several more, in the UK and other countries.

He is a Fellow of the Public Relations and Communications Association and is a member of its Ethics Council, has acted as a judge for their awards and as an examiner on their professional programmes.

Prior to his academic career, Simon was a member of the UK Government Information Service, serving in a range of government departments as a press officer.

Trevor Morris, in over 30 years in the PR industry, has successfully built and sold a major PR consultancy with margins of over 30 per cent, been the CEO of what was then the UK's largest PR group, worked for numerous major companies and organisations and written and lectured extensively.

He taught Public Relations for 14 years, first at the University of Westminster, and then at Richmond, the American International University in London, where he was Professor of Public Relations.

A Fellow of the Public Relations and Communications Association, Trevor holds the 'Mark Mellor Award for Outstanding Contribution to the PR Industry', and was one of the three experts who reviewed the communication capability at No 10 Downing Street and the Cabinet Office, as well as having been Agony Uncle for the industry bible *PRWeek*. Today, Trevor works as a non-executive director, consultant and PR trainer. He is also an advisor to SIGWATCH, cited on pp. 209–212.

Co-authored Books

Trevor Morris and Simon Goldsworthy have collaborated on four other books, all published by Palgrave Macmillan: *PR for Asia; PR for the New Europe; PR – A Persuasive Industry?: Spin, Public Relations and the Shaping of the Modern Media*; and *PR Today: The Authoritative Guide to Public Relations*, the second edition of which was published in 2016.

Preface

At the time of writing, the world is reeling from the impact of the coronavirus COVID-19 pandemic. Whatever one thinks about how this emergency has been handled in different countries, one thing is certain. Public relations, usually under different aliases such as 'communications', has played a crucial role everywhere. There is no way in which medical professionals or health officials around the world could speak to every citizen individually, let alone update them as the situation changed. Instead the media, in every shape and form, were used by international bodies such as the World Health Organisation (WHO), by national governments and by medical authorities to pass on advice and instructions, on disease avoidance, symptoms, and what to do in the event of apparent infection, to the global population. This was closely followed by advice on the economic and other implications of this unprecedented crisis. Aside from governments, companies and charities needed to communicate vital information to their stakeholders – investors, clients and customers, worried employees, volunteers, those relying on the work of charitable organisations: the list was endless.

PR people may not have been the ultimate source of all this information and advice but they sought to ensure that it was crafted as effectively as possible and passed on to the relevant media. Those recalling the early months of the outbreak will remember the countless press conferences, media briefings and interviews around the world. These represented public relations in action, set up and arranged by PR people. PR could not solve the problem, but it was vital in attempting to ensure that vast amounts of information reached all concerned in a timely way. It was also used to counter 'Fake News' and many misleading rumours and theories. No-one else had the time, resources and expertise to perform this task.

The story of the pandemic illustrates the crucial, positive role that PR practitioners can play in our lives – but it does not in itself prove that public relations is necessarily a force for good, as the same skills can be used by all kinds of people for all kinds of purposes. It is true that the PR industry has mushroomed over the last generation, with the numbers employed in public relations surging in practically all parts of the world, but while that is evidence of the enormous importance people place on effective PR, it does not necessarily demonstrate its moral or ethical value.

In reality, PR's undoubted success story has been accompanied by a degree of critical introspection. PR people may thrive, but can still feel their role in society is not appreciated – instead they can find themselves mocked, derided or viewed as sinister in popular culture and the media, and some of this filters through to the wider public. Public Relations' own academy – the academics teaching the subject – find themselves in a similar position. The popularity of their courses does not mean that they are not viewed with suspicion or worse by colleagues in other subject areas.

Ethics lie at the heart of these problems. Many outsiders see PR as 'ethically challenged', and its practitioners as morally rather supple, too willing to do almost anything for any kind of client, including dictatorial regimes, notorious politicians, controversial businesses and fickle celebrities.

PR programmes at universities, many training courses, PR's own industry bodies and countless books and articles have tried to tackle this issue, but their counter-arguments are little read or listened to in the wider world. The problem does not go away.

Another major issue with existing approaches to public relations ethics is that PR is not practised in a sterile vacuum where moral concerns can be discussed at length and put on a pedestal. Instead PR is practised in a dynamic environment, where all kinds of decisions have to be made at speed and under pressure. Money matters. In the real world, most of us would be tempted by the offer of great deal of money, and while we might not do absolutely anything that is asked in return, it will surely influence our thinking and behaviour. And what if that – or the loss of that income – affects not just our own well-being, but that of our families, our colleagues and others? This reality has been underscored by the pandemic, as PR agencies around the world have laid off staff and struggled to survive at all, while many of their counterparts working in-house have quickly found their jobs on the line. Owning up to brutal financial and business realities is perhaps not PR's greatest strength.

Sometimes business ethics is represented too simplistically, or in a woolly way, as a win-win scenario – acting in an ethical way is a sure path to maximising financial returns. If it were that easy, even the most ruthless and immoral business person would seek to act ethically in their desire to succeed. Similar principles hold good for politics.

So, while placing the debates about PR ethics in a wider context, this book is intended to be a real-world guide, not an exercise in abstract theorising. It seeks to tackle the practical, day-to-day issues of PR ethics head-on. These include the key questions of for whom it is legitimate to work, and what it is permissible to do when you are working for them. One of the authors is the 'Agony Uncle' for *PRWeek*, the main industry magazine, and we include some examples of the questions he has tackled. When it comes to other problems, we make some suggestions, but, in the main, we seek to raise concerns and ask questions which enable you to find the answers that are right for you if you are starting or continuing careers in PR. There are real-life examples from different countries and exercises which are designed to help you think through the issues for yourself. Consider the issues that we raise and try to relate them to the world around you.

We also include interviews with a range of people well placed to give informed opinions on these issues. In most cases their expertise is self-explanatory, but there is one exception. It can be difficult, for all kinds of reasons which we explore in the book, for people to be completely open about ethical matters – and, understandably, they may want to go off the record before saying what they really think. At various points in this book we include the extremely frank comments of an anonymous senior PR insider with considerable international experience. We hope you agree that they add value.

We appreciate that many busy practitioners and would-be practitioners won't have the time to read the book straight through at once, but may wish to look at particular chapters, and with this in mind there is some reiteration (traditionally a good thing in PR terms!) of the key points throughout the text.

Remember that the ethical debates swirling around the PR industry are a sign of its importance and centrality to modern life. What could be more boring than to work in a field where ethical issues never arose?

Acknowledgements

Creating *Public Relations Ethics: The Real-World Guide* involved talking to a wide range of busy people who were kind enough to share their knowledge and experience. We are particularly grateful to the following for their contributions: Eben Black of Erudite PR; Robert Blood, founder of SIGWATCH; John Harrington, Editor of *PRWeek UK*, and to *PRWeek* for allowing us to include some material first published there; David Gallagher, President Growth and Development, International, Omnicom Public Relations Group; Jim Hawker, Founder of Three Pipe; Claire Walker, CEO of Firefly Communications; Francis Ingham, Director General of the Public Relations and Communications Association and Chief Executive of the International Communications Consultancy Organisation; Dr Sian Rees of Swansea University; Rob Smith, Editor of INFLUENCE; and Ian Wright, Chief Executive of the Food and Drink Federation.

A special mention is required for the senior PR industry insider whose comments feature throughout the book and who gave freely of their time and expertise without so much as a namecheck in return. On a subject of this nature, frankness of this kind is invaluable but sometimes comes at the price of anonymity.

Many other people, too many to name, have helped us along the way, and we are naturally indebted to our numerous students, colleagues and others in the industry for sharpening our thinking. With the kind permission of the publishers, Palgrave Macmillan, we have also drawn upon material in our earlier works, in particular the second edition of our book *PR Today: The Authoritative Guide to Public Relations* (Palgrave 2016). We are also grateful to everyone at Routledge, especially Felisa Salvago-Keyes, Grant Schatzman and Susan Dunsmore, who helped to take forward this project. Of course our views remain our own, and any faults are ours as well.

Chapter 1

Introduction

Introduction

People often invoke 'ethics' and talk about ethical and unethical behaviour. What do they mean by 'ethics'? What foundations are ethics built upon, and what are the main strands of ethical thought? In what way do they relate to PR work? How do ethics overlap with the law? PR people are not employed as philosophers, nor indeed as lawyers, but they are greatly affected by what others think, and are subject to the law, so they need a fundamental awareness of ethical thought and why the law matters. In this introductory chapter, which serves as a starting point for the rest of the book, we look at these issues.

Imagine this. You're being interviewed for a PR job that you want – and the person you hope to work for lobs a 'what would you do?' question at you, perhaps based on some current issue in the media. It's quite likely that at least part of the question involves thinking about what would be seen as the ethical thing to do in a complicated situation. You've been put on the spot.

Or, you're got the job you want and everything's going well. But suddenly something comes up – maybe it's an unexpected phone call from an important client when you can't get hold of other people (it happens!). They make an urgent demand. You could do what they want, but you have doubts about whether it would be the ethical thing to do. On the other hand, you hardly want to upset the client – that could have serious consequences (not least financial …), for you, your colleagues and perhaps the agency itself.

These kinds of things and many more happen. The luxury of PR education – and training courses, and reading what follows in this book – is that you can think about these sorts of situations and put forward and discuss your ideas about what to do without the serious consequences that can flow from the decisions you make in real life. Socrates would have approved: as one of the founding fathers of ethical thought, the ancient Greek philosopher argued that moral knowledge could be achieved through debate and discussion, and that 'virtue is knowledge'.

But in the real world you seldom have time to refer back to ethical theory, and it's likely your colleagues and those who employ you would not be too impressed if you try to do so. This book is designed to help existing and would-be PR practitioners to deal with these realities, and to confront the kind of practical problems they will face in their working lives.

Nonetheless, it is useful to be aware of some of the theoretical under-pinnings offered by academic authors, so we tackle some of the key ideas. But the emphasis of this book, as its subtitle suggests, is on real-world decision-making, the practical world of PR – an arena where complex issues are often hard to unravel and there are often downsides to any course of action – and despite that, you have to make, or contribute to, a decision and act in a particular way. To do this, we look at real cases, and speak to some of the key players.

It's worth bearing in mind the context. Public relations is very much part of the world we all inhabit. The growth of PR means more and more people work in the field (although many, perhaps most, are not formally called PR people – and thereby hangs a tale). It has become a popular, high-profile occupation. In the last generation or so, it has come of age and is now used by all kinds of organisations (unless they are very small), and even by rich or powerful individuals, from presidents and prime ministers to almost every celebrity or billionaire you've ever heard of. It's associated with all kinds of controversial issues and the rights and wrongs of PR activity are often debated by outsiders.

A library of books has been written to support PR education and training. The present authors have contributed to its shelves. Along the way we have written a little about ethics – we draw upon those writings here (we have not changed our overall thinking), but this is our first attempt to give it the full-length treatment it deserves.

While we cannot provide definitive answers to the dilemmas we all face, hopefully we can help you to think things through, be prepared, and be ready to offer good advice and better solutions to problems.

What Are Ethics?

The *Shorter Oxford English Dictionary* defines ethics as: 'The science of morals; the branch of knowledge that deals with the principles of human duty or the logic of moral discourse; the whole field of moral science.' It further defines them as: 'The moral principles or system of a particular leader or school of thought; the moral principles by which any particular person is guided; the rules of conduct recognised in a particular profession or area of human life.' The last part of this definition is probably the most useful for our purposes, as we look at what is and is not acceptable in the field of PR practice. As we shall see, PR ethics find their main public expression in the codes of PR's professional bodies which are now well established in most countries and internationally as well. These set out what is expected. The other parts of the definition highlight how important morality is to understanding what people mean by ethics. It is why PR ethics remain related to the study of moral philosophy, even if this seldom features on a day-to-day basis in the working world of public relations.

Some of the other terms in the definition are more relevant to everyday PR practice – the notion of *the principles of human duty*, for example, have a clear bearing on what PR people do and will feature in the next section. Similarly, *the moral principles by which any particular person is guided* are also highly relevant. Tellingly, the Cambridge philosopher Simon Blackburn's *Ethics: A Very Short Introduction*[1] originally appeared under the title *Being Good*. Over and above the expectations of PR professional bodies or the media industries, we all – one hopes – feel that there some moral principles each of us should adhere to as individuals.

The Relevance of Ethical Theory

How Do We Decide What Is Ethical?

> Do unto others as you would have them do unto you.
> (The Gospel according to St Luke, 6:31)

Why are we quoting the Bible in a book about PR ethics? Because for millennia the world's religions have set out ethical principles at length and with enormous claims to authority – for another version, think of the biblical Ten Commandments, most but not all of which concern ethics. The world's faith communities have always set out to answer ethical questions. Their notions of what it takes to be good often overlap, for example, the teaching that we should show consideration for others and love our fellow humans is shared by most religions. While holy scriptures and religious teaching may not be to the fore in the secular world which most western PR practitioners inhabit, they cannot simply be dismissed. First, the teachings of the world's great religions, passed down through countless generations, have cast a long shadow and remain influential even for people who are no longer adherents. Second, many PR people today work in less secular environments and belong to faith communities.

Moral principles are also set out by non-religious movements, for example, humanism, and are fundamental to major secular political ideologies, such as socialism and environmentalism. Again, they often overlap with the principles of faith communities but do not claim any supernatural authority, although they have their own books which serve as sources of authority. As is the case with religion, the influence of socialist and environmentalist thought extends well beyond those who see themselves as adherents.

Influential political statements in the constitutions and founding documents of different nations are also important ethical building blocks. They include the Magna Carta of 1215, an English charter of rights, the impact of which has been felt well beyond the UK; the US Declaration of Independence of 1776, with its famous assertion that 'life, liberty and the pursuit of happiness' are inalienable rights; and the French revolutionary Declaration of the Rights of Man and of the Citizen of 1789, which is also rooted in ideas of fundamental and universal rights and the philosophical thought of the Enlightenment (the intellectual movement which led to human reason challenging divinely-inspired teaching), and has come to be summed up in the expression 'liberty, equality, fraternity'.

In living memory these earlier statements have helped to shape major international agreements such as the UN Universal Declaration of Human Rights and the European Convention on Human Rights (1948). Article 1 of the former states that: 'All human beings are born free and equal in dignity and rights. They are endowed with reason and conscience and should act towards one another in a spirit of brotherhood.'[2]

What all these influential statements of moral thought, whether religious or secular, have in common is that they seek to answer the question of what is right and claim a special political, intellectual and/or faith-based authority for their answers. In their own more modest way that is what PR's professional bodies seek to do. Otherwise how are we to know how to be good?

Moral Relativism

Even a cursory glance at the world suggests that principles that are manmade can vary over time and in different societies. Key moral issues are viewed very differently by different groups even within the same societies – think, for example, about women's rights, abortion, homosexuality, euthanasia, veganism and attitudes to immigration. Opinions shift, and abstract principles buckle under the pressure of events. The classical Greek pioneers of much thought about ethics, Plato and his pupil Aristotle, kept slaves (as did, much later, George Washington and Thomas Jefferson). In practice, a degree of flexibility seems to apply to some religious teachings, which are interpreted differently in different communities over time – some of the things that some of the major Christian churches permit today would have been unthinkable in past generations, and vice versa (for example, two hundred years ago many Christian churches condoned slavery). The idea that there is no absolute moral truth is called *relativism*.

However unattractive it may be to many moral philosophers – not least because of the danger that people can choose their ethics to suit them – relativism probably, and perhaps rightly, plays a big part in how most PR people approach their work (even if they don't recognise or use the term). It has its philosophical basis: Aristotle thought ethics should be determined by ordinary people seeking goodness and that it involved finding a mean or compromise. Much more recently, as many of the grand moral narratives which guided people seem to have collapsed, postmodernist thought suggests that in our atomised world there is no objective moral truth.

PR is an international discipline, bringing together people from many countries and backgrounds to serve an enormous range of organisations and causes. An ability to relate to others, not least different clients and employers and journalists, is key to the job. Seeking to impose one's views on others is seldom a good look. In practice, a one-size-fits-all ethical system would be hard to square with the variety of what is required, but neither would an anything-goes approach seem acceptable to most people. Box 1.1 presents a senior PR industry insider's views of what they have encountered in different markets around the world.

Box 1.1 Different Attitudes around the World

According to a senior PR industry insider:

> So let's look at it this way. In different parts of the world there are really massively different standards and normalities and expectations. You can't openly be gay in the Middle East. You will pay for coverage in India. In Russia, you are effectively part of the state. And the idea that there are common standards is just a fallacy. And quite frankly, the people in London and New York who say this know that they're lying. They just have this worry about being seen as imperialists, saying that they know better than these other markets which is quite ironic, given the whole MeToo, diversity, liberal ethos they pedal otherwise.

In reality, the moral relativism of PR people within any country reflects the reality that they are not a cross-section of society. While it is easy to find exceptions, the PR practitioners of today tend to share a range of attributes: they have been educated to degree level, typically in an arts or humanities subject; they are relatively affluent; and most live and work in major cities. They are on average young and, especially at entry level, predominantly female (Box 1.2). In major PR centres, such as London, they come from a wide range of countries and cultures. The traits of PR work mean that they tend to be quite sociable, working and enjoying their leisure time with like-minded people and seeking social acceptance. Unsurprisingly, but often unconsciously, the characteristics we have just described play a major role in defining their ethical attitudes.[3]

Box 1.2 Characteristics of PR Practitioners

The world's largest PR body, the UK's Public Relations and Communications Association (PRCA), conducts regular censuses of PR practitioners. Its 2019 census found that the UK industry was 67 per cent female, with a median age of 33. Some 80 per cent are graduates, and 22 per cent have a master's degree, while 20 per cent had attended a fee-paying private school, well above the national average. The average salary in the industry was £42,700 – again well above the national average.

What exactly characterises the attitudes of PR people? Short of undertaking extensive research it would be hard to prove, but based on our experience of the PR industry we would say they are as follows.

- PR people generally cleave towards the political centre ground – there are relatively few at either extreme of the political divide, although of course there are outliers, with PR people serving any cause you care to think of.
- Economically, they broadly accept free markets and private enterprise, albeit with plenty of qualifications and reservations: after all, most PR people work in the commercial world.
- They see themselves as socially liberal and tolerant in matters of race, gender and sexuality, and as exponents of cosmopolitan values. To be more specific, this means that they are the sort of people who are concerned about, or even aghast at, such events as the election of Donald Trump as US President, the UK's vote to leave the European Union in 2016 (a *PRWeek* survey in the UK shortly before the referendum found that 79 per cent of PR practitioners favoured remaining in the EU),[4] (Box 1.3) and the rise of populism and nationalism in a range of other countries, while their views on the environment are greener than average. Overall. they see themselves as on the progressive side in the big debates.

Box 1.3 PR's Ability to Predict Events

According to Francis Ingham, Director General of the Public Relations and Communications Association:

> After the UK's Brexit vote in 2016, we, at the PRCA, put together a political prediction panel and piece of work to understand why so many people had got their predictions wrong. And the conclusions we came to were that we simply didn't get out of London enough. There's a certain degree of inevitability, given how London is the centre of the UK PR market. Though that is lessening all the time and you see vibrant PR communities in Manchester and in Scotland and in Wales and in Belfast and all around the UK. But I think PR was not alone in terms of established professions and industries in getting a lot of political predictions wrong. And we've been upfront about that.

These are characteristics which they share with educated youth and other members of what are often seen as the world's metropolitan elites. However, there is one special dimension. PR people are particularly attuned to whatever is popular or trending in their societies. The nature of their work means they are not normally great experts in the technical issues which confront society – matters which require scientific or financial expertise, for instance – but they are very much aware of what is being said in the media, and what looks and sounds good or bad. The ever-growing role of social media has accentuated this still further, turning people into moral *fashionistas* with a fear of missing out on the latest ethical cause. So, for example, while PR people as a group have no particular expertise in environmental matters, they often put forward ideas based on what is topical and popular. In purist terms, that is not a matter of ethics (no-one has ever suggested that being ethical is the same as being modish or popular) – but it certainly has a powerful if undeclared impact on how they see the world. But sometimes, PR practitioners are out of touch with large swathes of public opinion (Box 1.4).

Box 1.4 PR People Can Be Out of Touch

A senior PR industry insider offers this view:

> People at the top of the PR industry are overwhelmingly white, middle-class men with liberal opinions. And they employ people in their own image who just happen to be slightly younger

and less well-remunerated. I think that there were reports in *PRWeek* that the industry was four to one or five to one Remain. And that shows how out-of-touch it is. If you were a Brexit-supporting industry figure, you wouldn't tell people that because they would look at you as if you were a leper. And the shock in the PR industry when the vote was announced shows quite how out-of-touch it is. And the people who want to advise others on reputation and issues management, they know no more than the man in the street. In fact, they often know distinctly less than the man in the street.

Perhaps it's best to think about PR people applying a form of conditioned or qualified relativism. The kind of views which PR people often share have not quite hardened into a comprehensive code of ethics, and there are people who are exceptions to the rule with different views, but nor are PR people completely free to make up their own minds. Which brings us back to rules.

Deontology

The word above is seldom heard in the PR world, but as a philosophical concept it is an unacknowledged but major component in PR's ethical system. Stemming from the Greek, *deontos*, meaning duty, it concerns itself with what we must do and what is expected of us. It is fundamental to the faith-based ethical systems mentioned above which make it clear what one must and must not do.

As we shall see, it is also key to PR's own ethical codes which operate like rules, detailing the obligations of PR practitioners and what they may and may not do. As such, they play an important part in PR ethics.

How are such rules arrived at – unless you accept a supernatural authority? Can moral values be proven? Plato thought that a carefully nurtured elite – the Guardians – should establish the correct answers with mathematical certainty. It's easy to see the dangers of the tyranny which might then arise, and the question of who chooses the experts remains difficult to answer. We've probably all found ourselves tempted to dismiss 'expert' views when they're at odds with our own strongly held opinions, and, famously, experts disagree with each other (as became clear during the COVID-19 pandemic) and have not always been right, but 'leaving it to the experts', or technocracy, remains a strand of thinking which still influences many people's views of how the world should be run.

Perhaps the most famous deontologist of the modern era is the German philosopher Immanuel Kant (1724–1804). He argued that there were universal moral laws which we all must obey, even if we didn't want to.

These could be determined by considering the effects of the relevant be-haviour. So, since a society in which everyone lied would be unworkable, no-one should lie – even if, as he famously argued, it was to distract a would-be murderer from his victim. It's not hard to see the downsides of this approach. What it gains in clarity and consistency, it loses in practi-cality, flexibility and, one might well argue, humanity.

Leaving Kant to one side, a more general difficulty with rule-based systems, or ethical absolutism, is that it can involve imposing straitjack-ets on others. When we join a professional body, we accept its rules – but in some contexts it can look like an imposition. A strand of philosophical thought dating back to ancient times has argued that moral rules are simply invented by the powerful to subjugate the weak – and Marxists would argue that bourgeois morality simply furthers bourgeois interests.

In more practical terms, the major problem with rules is that they sel-dom cover all eventualities to everyone's satisfaction, and frequently leave key areas open to interpretation – as we shall see when we look at PR's ethical codes. What, for example, is 'in the public interest', a term which will keep coming up when we look at such codes? One person's view of that can be very different from another's. When we have to interpret the rules – or even disagree with them – relativism creeps back in and we also look for other moral criteria. However, a deontological approach does have the advantage of providing people with a reassuring framework for making difficult decisions – they can tell themselves and others that they were simply following established rules which separate right from wrong.

Utilitarianism

Popularly defined as *the greatest happiness of the greatest number*, util-itarianism is the brainchild of the English thinkers Jeremy Bentham (1748–1832) and John Stuart Mill (1806–1873). However, it is the heir to much older ideas of general benevolence – the supreme virtue of Confu-cianism, for example.

Again, the term may be little recognised in the PR world, but it has a subtle influence on how people see the world, providing a basis on which to make ethical judgements. Many of the organisations which PR peo-ple serve are, perhaps unconsciously, pursuing utilitarian objectives. In doing so, they can be more pragmatic than deontologists and rec-ognise human desires. For utilitarians, it is consequences that matter – a *consequentialist* or *teleological* (*telos* is Greek for the end) approach: sometimes moral rules can be broken because the ends justify the means (Kant's extreme prohibition of lying would not apply). Exactly how far the ends can justify the means remains an open question: to this day, defenders of leaders such as Stalin and Mao seek to excuse the killing of millions of people on the grounds that it was in pursuit of a praiseworthy objective.

Moreover, even if we agree that happiness is a desirable goal, defining what happiness is to everyone's satisfaction is fraught with problems: is 'happy hour' in a cocktail bar what the rather serious-minded John Stuart Mill had in mind?

The utilitarian approach can also be decried as majoritarian – something may be good for the greatest number, but what about the rights of minorities and individuals? This was something that concerned Mill. Almost two centuries later, the socially liberal milieu in which many PR people mix places great store on individualism and minority rights, so once again the principle is in practice tempered, and judgements on what to do become 'value judgements', based on our personal values.

Being Machiavellian

Citing philosophers is all very well, but they have rarely encountered the fast-moving world of contemporary PR, with its need to satisfy demanding employers who seldom want to hear a philosophical disquisition. For those realities, Niccolò Machiavelli (1469–1527) remains an authoritative guide, if not perhaps a name to cite in public. His treatise, *The Prince*, was based on his real-world experience of political life in Renaissance Italy – think White House fixer or spin doctor in any modern capital, but playing for even higher stakes (he himself was imprisoned and tortured – many others he knew or worked with were put to death).

Machiavelli identifies what he calls a 'necessary immorality'. As he puts it, 'It is necessary for a prince [for which we could read president, prime minister or chief executive] who wishes to maintain his position to learn how not to be good.' This is the world of 'dog eat dog' or the 'survival of the fittest' and its stark brutality shocked his contemporaries. To this day this kind of realism, at best a harsh form of utilitarianism. rarely makes an appearance in PR textbooks – but let us just say that Machiavelli would probably outperform Kant in a PR role, and there's more than a dash of Machiavelli's approach in successful corporate and political PR.

Ethics and the Law

> The good of the people is the greatest law.
>
> (Cicero)

Ethics and the law are closely related but are not the same. Many of the things we might regard as unethical are not necessarily illegal – and, on the other hand, many people believe that in some circumstances it is permissible, or even essential, to break the law.

For the most part, when we discuss PR ethics in this book we are talking about things where the law has no bearing. Breaches in accepted ethical standards may mean that an individual loses their job, a PR agency loses its clients, or that people or organisations are thrown out of their professional bodies. No doubt there will be damaging publicity. This is serious enough, but it does not normally involve the law – although readers should note that the authors are not lawyers and cannot offer definitive legal advice in this book.

A simple way of making the distinction between the two concepts is to say that ethics concern what we *should* do and the law is about what we *must* do. If we act unethically but not illegally, then there is no formal sanction which society as a whole can apply, although we may become unpopular and suffer informal sanctions, such as other people refusing to have anything to do with us. If, on the other hand, we act illegally, there is an established and formal process for dealing with the case and ultimately we could be punished, for example, we could be fined, or in criminal matters imprisoned (and in some jurisdictions even be executed).

Laws reflect society's ethical concerns, and the most important ethical matters are enshrined in the law, for example, murder, which is illegal in all societies. The notion that the law reflects public concerns is particularly true in democracies, where laws are made and unmade in response to ever-changing public opinion. Nor is that just a matter for legislators: the law has to be interpreted and applied to individual cases and circumstances, and the ways in which the law enforcement agencies and courts do this reflect the ebb and flow of ethical currents. If, for example, one considers the debates that have swirled around the US Supreme Court's rulings on capital punishment and abortion, one can see moral relativism at play: the judiciary in different eras (and different societies) responds in different ways as the world evolves around them.

However, public opinion often fails to affect the law as quickly as some people would like it to, and there is often plenty of scope for disagreement. At any one time, many, perhaps most, of us will disagree with some of the laws in our society and, if we break them, we may not feel we have acted unethically. Today, for example, the non-medicinal use of cannabis remains illegal in many countries – but many citizens feel entitled to buy and make use of the product.

More relevant to PR practice, campaigners who feel particularly strongly about major issues will often seek deliberately to break the law to highlight their concerns by engaging in PR stunts of various kinds. Environmental protest groups such as, in recent times, the activists of Extinction Rebellion, are good examples of this, carrying out acts of trespass and obstruction and deliberately courting arrest. The fact that they are breaking the law is a key part of their PR strategy as it helps to generate publicity. But although such actions are clearly illegal, they are seldom seen as unethical – certainly not by the perpetrators, and usually not by the media and much of the wider public.

This demonstrates how complex the relationship between ethics and the law can become. In some cases the fact that people have knowingly broken a democratic society's agreed laws is overridden by other concerns – a degree of sympathy for them and their motives, for example.

Most illegal activist activity is of course relatively harmless and benign – more about photo opportunities than violence and serious damage. This is no doubt helpful from the point of view of public perception. However, activism can shade into threats of violence, actual violence towards property and sometimes people, and even terrorism. This may be illegal, but even in such extreme cases those involved will have persuaded themselves and perhaps others that what they are doing is ethical and that the cause is so important that the ends justify the means (a utilitarian approach).

PR and the Law

Beyond activism, PR people tend to brush up against the law rather less than many other comparable occupations, for a number of reasons:

- Routine PR work has traditionally focused on media relations, a private and relatively informal process which seldom involves the legally enforceable contracts which are a staple part of many forms of business and professional activity. In the place of binding agreements, there are some sometimes loosely observed ethical principles governing the PR-journalism relationship, but if a journalist has failed to follow through on a promise to write a particular story, or writes it in a different way, that is not normally a matter for the courts.
- Traditionally PR has not had much of a public face. It operates via the media, getting journalists to say (or sometimes not say) particular things. What appears is the editorial responsibility of the publisher, not the PR person. In an era of social media, where everyone, including PR practitioners, can publish, this is changing – sometimes leaving practitioners exposed in an unfamiliar environment where they are directly and publicly responsible for the words and images they use.
- The main purpose of PR work is to promote those who pay for the service – and this is inherently low risk, certainly compared with journalism, which is often in the business of breaking bad news about people and organisations. PR practitioners are generally in the business of saying things that people want them to say and doing so with their approval.

Nonetheless, PR people are as much subject to the law as anyone else, and perhaps the main danger for them is that because they do not normally have lawyers breathing down their necks, they become blasé and get caught out.

There are some key areas of the law which have a special bearing on PR work. They are founded on ethical principles, even if our understanding of those principles and hence the law itself keeps evolving. One important feature of such laws is that they are double-edged swords: PR people not only have to obey them themselves – they can also use them to protect or otherwise help their clients and employers. As their organisations' media experts they will often be the first port of call when such issues arise and they need to know when to seek expert legal advice. However, such advice should always be tempered with an awareness of the wider context, an area where sensible PR people can make a vital contribution. There's little point in winning a small legal victory if by doing so you court lasting unpopularity or are generally seen to have done wrong. Here ethical considerations can play a vital role.

Defamation

All legal systems give individuals, and in some circumstances organisations, the right to sue anyone who has defamed them, typically in the media. PR people can be in the front line in such cases, which involve recourse to legal advice and legal action. While they are not expected to be legal experts, they are expected to consider the wider implications of legal action: would it be right for a powerful corporation potentially to crush a small media outlet over a minor error of judgement, for example?

Usually defamation takes the form of libel, when someone's reputation is seriously damaged without justification, although what exactly is libellous varies in different jurisdictions. Notwithstanding the variations, the essential issue is the same – the attempt of the law to balance a person's right to protect their reputation against the right to free speech.

Intellectual Property

Intellectual property embraces copyright, trademarks and patent law. Every PR person needs at least a basic awareness of intellectual property law as it is so fundamental to the concepts of branding and corporate identity. The general principle is that the fruits of people's intellectual endeavours – including writings, photographs, music, logos or inventions – are their property in a similar way to physical property. The use of trademarks is protected. Again the law here overlaps with ethical ideals – in addition to the idea that it is wrong to take someone's property, many would, for example, regard it as unethical to lay claim to what someone else has created.

Privacy and Data Protection

In an era of social media and e-commerce, vast amounts of information about all of us are in the hands of a wide range of organisations which can seek to use it for commercial, political or other purposes, not least medical ones. There are already laws in place – including Europe's far-reaching General Data Protection Regulation of 2018, but concerns about this have aroused an ethical storm which is raging at the time of writing and will have consequences to which PR people need to remain alert.

Summary

Ethics are recognised rules of conduct, often relating to particular occupations or professions. While practitioners are often unaware of it, the work of moral philosophers going back to the ancient world remains relevant to understanding the principles upon which PR ethics are built. There is no single system of ethics, and even within the different schools of ethical thought there is considerable scope for interpretation and disagreement. Ethics overlaps with the law. The latter – especially in democracies – is founded on commonly accepted ethical standards, but in any society there are many things which may not be illegal but are widely considered unethical. There are also actions which some individuals and groups consider ethically justified although they are illegal.

Questions

1. Describe some of the main foundations of ethical thought.
2. How do the main strands of ethical thought relate to the world of PR?
3. Compare and contrast the law and ethics.

Notes

1 Blackburn, Simon, *Ethics: A Very Short Introduction* (Oxford: Oxford University Press, 2003).
2 The Declaration was adopted by the UN General Assembly in 1948. The final wording with its masculine overtones might well be phrased differently if it were being put forward today – an example of how those who seek to be ethical are always aiming at a moving target.
3 See www.prca.org.uk/sites/default/files/PRCA_PR_Census_2019_v9-8-pdf%20%285%29.pdf
4 *PRWeek UK*, 11 April 2016.

Chapter 2

Why PR Ethics Matter

PR people often like to say they are in the reputation management business, but paradoxically they have quite a serious reputation problem themselves, which is why so many practitioners avoid using the term 'public relations' to describe what they do. A major reason for this is the ethical question marks which have hovered over PR from its earliest days. Oddly enough, for an occupation that focuses on communication, PR has a weak public voice of its own – and plenty of more vocal critics. For these reasons public relations has always struggled to shore up its moral standing, which is a major reason why PR ethics matters.

In this chapter we look at:

- PR's reputational problems.
- What others say about the industry – including the way PR is portrayed in popular culture such as TV and film, the attitude of PR's 'frenemies' in journalism, and PR's critics in academia and elsewhere.
- PR's intriguing relationship with propaganda.
- The PR industry's own debates about ethics.
- PR is not an all-conquering ethical force: what are the limits to its role? See Box 2.1.

Box 2.1 *PRWeek* Agony Uncle, November 2014: Does PR Have a Higher Purpose?

Q: I enjoy my job as an account director in a medium-sized agency. But I have real trouble when people start asking me about the 'higher purpose' of my chosen industry. What is the social (not economic) function of PR?

Good question and one best not answered with false claims to virtue. PR can serve any cause, good or bad. It is silly to pretend otherwise – though what constitutes a good or bad cause is usually a matter of opinion.

But overall PR is undoubtedly a force for good. It thrives in democracies. It is a symptom of freedom, choice, argument and debate. Politics, business, NGOs, even the media all depend on PR to help communicate their policies, sell their products and promote their ideas and beliefs. So asking if PR has a higher purpose is a bit like asking if food is good for society. Everyone needs it though too much of certain kinds of PR may sometimes make us a bit sick. The ideal is a balanced diet of PR washed down with a free and independent media. The ideal may not always be achieved, but if you took away PR, where would be choice, debate and democracy?

No-one (we hope) would want to see their livelihood as unethical. It's reasonable to suggest than in addition to the financial rewards we receive, most of us want what we do in our working lives to be seen as having some wider value and importance for society. That's at least as true of PR people as it is for any other occupational group. Indeed, there are reasons why it's particularly true. First, PR practitioners' day-to-day work means they are more aware than most of what's being said in the media, society's main shared source of information and comment. News media content is prepared by journalists, an occupational group with a troubled relationship with PR – of which more later. Second, PR people often say that public relations is about reputation – and surely it's hard to have a robust reputation if you are seen as unethical.

Public relations is about reputation – the result of what you do, what you say and what others say about you.
Public relations is the discipline which looks after reputation, with the aim of understanding and supporting and influencing opinion and behaviour. It is the planned and sustained effort to establish and maintain goodwill and mutual understanding between an organisation and its publics.

The above definition of public relations is one put forward by the UK's Chartered Institute of Public Relations (CIPR). One might quibble about it – PR people seldom if ever control their clients' or employers' reputations to the extent that this implies – but it underscores why it is reasonable to consider PR's own reputation.

The authors have taught public relations at a number of universities. At one of them, PR was being introduced as a new subject. At a meeting of other academics, a professor teaching a long-established humanities subject (now discontinued ...) protested. 'You're going to teach people to lie!'. Few people who have taught PR within a university will not have encountered similar remarks, or at least wry smiles, from colleagues in other disciplines. PR is commonly seen as ethically dodgy or at least morally lightweight. Simply protesting that it is not so – being preachy and sounding virtuous – does not cut much ice and can even backfire. On the other hand, there is a reason why public relations has sprung up as an academic discipline and why universities tolerate, if not always welcome, it: it is popular.

Reputation is a complicated thing – more complex than perhaps the CIPR definition allows. PR can have many negative associations – as we shall see – but it is a sought-after career, one which is seen as offering exciting opportunities. It is also in demand by the people who pay for PR services. Today few if any organisations of any size, or indeed individual celebrities or politicians, would be without PR. They value it, and increasingly so (the UK's PRCA Census for 2019 shows that the industry grew by almost 8 per cent in value in a year, and took on almost 10 per cent more staff).[1]

It may even be that PR's somewhat racy reputation is one of the industry's attractions. PR practitioners can be reluctant to acknowledge it, but it is certainly true that many career paths with more solid reputations can be seen as rather worthy and dull: important jobs that we want other people to do. Meanwhile, those paying for PR know, without necessarily wanting to shout about it, that its sometimes Machiavellian skillset is something that they want to have at their disposal – not least because they know their competitors, rivals and opponents will.

Journalism and PR

Journalism's relationship with public relations can be likened to a long-standing but difficult marriage. Mutual need and dependence mean that it will never end in divorce, but there's plenty of abuse, sometimes even contempt. Despite attempts to play it down, media relations – talking to journalists and trying to influence what they say, and don't say, on behalf of whoever is paying for the service – have always been central to PR work. This creates a natural tension with journalism, with its ideals of fearless independence. Journalists might prefer to be able to investigate and publish stories without relying on PR, but know that this is seldom practical. Producing high-quality news costs money – PR help makes the process quicker, cheaper and easier.

Increasingly, the news media in the developed world are starved of resources, as people are reluctant to pay for journalism, and advertising revenue has migrated to Google and Facebook and their subsidiaries. Social media may offer news but don't produce it (or certainly not in a professional way), so they pass on the fruits of other people's labours but collect the money themselves. Expectations have shifted: it's rare indeed today in a western university to find a student who pays for news – entertainment is a different matter, as followers of the fortunes of Netflix and Spotify know. So, in an era of social media, traditional news outlets such as newspapers and magazines have been shedding jobs, while traditional broadcasters also struggle. Even online news sites have found that simply being online is not a panacea.

In the UK, this trend was highlighted in the noughties in the best-selling book *Flat Earth News* by the award-winning investigative journalist Nick Davies.[2] He showed that fewer journalists have to do more work. Newspapers now have more pages and supplements than a generation ago, but not only do they have more space to fill; they also maintain constantly updated websites, featuring additional material including videos and podcasts. There has been a parallel trend on broadcast media, with ever more TV channels and radio stations operating 24/7, as well as maintaining their own websites. How were journalists squaring the circle and producing more with less? Davies commissioned research which showed that the news media were highly dependent on PR for their stories and that only a small proportion of what was published was the unaided work of journalists. Indeed, he concluded that journalism was in terminal decline – a judgement which may be too pessimistic, but highlights the angst felt by his colleagues around the world. More recently this process has been sharply exacerbated by the COVID-19 pandemic, with troubled companies greatly reducing their advertising, and paid-for circulations falling precipitously.

Their increasing reliance on PR is scarcely something for which journalists are grateful. Few of us are thankful for gifts which remind us that we are growing weak and the giver is increasingly powerful. Traditionally journalists, whose trade was in existence well before there was anything called a PR industry, have prided themselves on researching their own stories and outwitting others as they do so. They are only human and feel under-rewarded for the important role they play in society, where they have traditionally been exalted as the Fourth Estate, playing a vital role which is of comparable importance to parliaments and national assemblies. Seeing the number of PR jobs increase, with, on average, better salaries and working conditions, has caused some resentment, although many journalists have moved into PR. However, they still have an important card to play – as the people who produce media content, they have the last word. Public utterances by the PR industry reach few people – while in contrast there is a long history of journalists pillorying PR. For individual journalists, PR people are 'flacks', 'lying scum', or the 'head-lice of civilisation'. This is backed up with research which shows that the great majority of news media mentions of PR are negative.[3]

On a day-to-day basis, PR people usually shrug this off. They can and do have good working relations with individual journalists based on mutual need and advantage – they want to place stories which journalists are pleased to accept. Nevertheless what underlies journalists' critical view of PR is their sense that journalism is morally superior. Their role as fearless seekers after truth, independently holding the powerful to account, trumps PR, which is simply advocacy on behalf of its paymasters. It is a view which overlooks the fact that journalists are not free agents but work for organisations which ultimately control what is published, and which often have agendas of their own. Box 2.2 offers another perspective.

Box 2.2 Another Perspective: Eben Black, National Newspaper Journalist Turned PR Practitioner

Eben Black was a national newspaper journalist for 16 years, working for Britain's top-selling daily newspaper, *The Sun*, and the then best-selling Sunday newspaper, *The News of the World*, before finishing his journalistic career as Chief Political Correspondent of *The Sunday Times*, usually regarded as the UK's leading 'quality' Sunday newspaper, although he describes it as 'the world's largest tabloid'. Black began in journalism in the then customary way, moving on from an English Literature degree at university to a postgraduate qualification at Cardiff University's well-known journalism school and starting out at a local newspaper. In 2004 – like many journalists before and since – he transitioned to PR, becoming head of media at the world's largest law firm, DLA Piper, and going on to work as a partner at Newgate Communications, before setting up his own PR agency, Erudite PR. He is a Fellow of the Public Relations and Communications Association and has written a book drawing on his experiences, *Lies, Lobbying and Lunch: PR, Public Affairs and Political Engagement: A Guide*.[4]

As a political journalist, Black had extensive dealings with PR people – both civil servants (government employees who serve governments of all complexions) and politically partisan special advisers or spin doctors, who serve particular parties or politicians. In his view, at least when he started out, most government PR people were essentially decent people, trying to do a conscientious job as public servants by providing information about the government to the public. Few were 'bad'. However, most lacked journalistic experience and the 'rat-like cunning' of the journalists they were up against. As a result, they were not up to coping in what Black calls the 'shark-infested' waters of political journalism and their weakness could be exploited. This changed when more professional special advisers and spin doctors were brought in – most famously Alastair Campbell, the media advisor of the long-serving UK

Labour Prime Minister Tony Blair. They were more effective but also more ruthless – perhaps an indication that ethics and professionalism do not always go hand in hand.

For all the high ideals of journalism, including the sort of things taught in journalism schools, in Black's experience, 'Journalists are not particularly ethical and if they are, it is by accident.' All that matters for journalists is 'the story' – something interesting and newsworthy which may or may not be true, or not even particularly important. Today this is truer than ever. The change in the media landscape means that journalists have less time and fewer resources to produce more content and are under ever-increasing pressure to produce eye-catching headlines. They have less time to sift PR they are supplied with and hence are more easily persuaded. Instead it is increasingly a matter of what they can get away with as they seek to come up with their all-important stories.

Black's experience of working for the UK's top-selling newspapers is particularly useful in examining the realities of journalism and its relationship with PR. The UK retains one of the most vigorous and competitive national newspaper presses in the world, but within academia discussions of journalistic ethics are often framed in terms of the approach of the BBC or the ideals (and not necessarily the realities) of one or two 'quality' papers: first-hand knowledge of the practices of much of the media is often woefully thin. For Black, it is PR people who are more likely to be ethical. Drawing on his experience at the top law firm DLA Piper, he points out that PR practitioners are simply acting like lawyers, doing their best on behalf of their clients, whereas journalists are doing whatever it takes to generate a story, regardless of the story's value. Indeed, long after Black's time at *The News of the World* this led to journalists there and at other papers engaging in 'phone-hacking' – illegal eavesdropping on celebrities' and politicians' private messages – in the search for stories.

In terms of telling the truth, he comments that PR people should 'always tell the truth – but tell the truth they want to tell'. As a political journalist he expected, and accepted, that, for example, PR people would deny that ministers were in disagreement with each other, even if they were. However, lying about specific, important facts would be viewed rather differently. In other areas of PR he is aware of much more blatant and deliberate lying.

In common with this book's authors, Black has never encountered direct bribery in attempts to influence media coverage. However, beyond his political beat, he was aware that, for example, free holidays were being given to journalists by travel companies in the expectation of favourable coverage – a practice he regards as essentially corrupt. But even in the realm of hard news and political journalism, journalists could be rewarded with exclusives. Given that the story is king for journalists, this could be the making of a journalist's career – and hence be worth more than most bribes. Conversely journalists could be cut off and denied stories by senior PR people. This would leave them seeking out alternative sources of stories in a kind of information war where the PR side struggles to maintain a monopoly on access to the news while journalists seek to exploit rivalries and divisions and hence find alternative sources. Arguably, and particularly in the political field, this tough-minded PR approach may mean favouring some media audiences – and hence members of the public – over others. However, it is a never-ending and ruthless war in which ethics will often be a by-stander.

As public relations has developed, Black also notes growing resentment and envy among journalists towards their better-paid PR counterparts, who are often former colleagues.

PR's Other Critics

Journalists who are critical of PR have found plenty of allies, not least in academia and among public intellectuals. Hostile attitudinising towards PR has a long history.

Media studies, or the study of mass communications, a university and even school subject in many countries, has played a significant role in shaping people's views of all the media industries, including PR. It grew out of the work of the Frankfurt School, a group of German intellectuals with Marxist leanings who fled Germany for the USA as Hitler came to power in the 1930s. Horror at Nazism was replaced by hostility towards what they saw as the manipulative promotional culture of their adopted American homeland. For them, the relentless advertising amounted to a kind of propaganda of capitalism, fostering consumerism and instilling a false consciousness in the working classes, distracting them from their true interests and discouraging rational debate. PR might have been an infant discipline at the time, and has always had a lower profile, but it was, and is, used for similar purposes to advertising. The suspicion that the PR people are up to no good and represent corporate and other unacceptable interests in society has continued to mark academic and other criticisms of PR.

Westminster University was the first in the UK to teach media studies. One of the founders of the discipline there wrote the following: 'The rise of PR [represents] the direct control by private or state interests of the flow of public information in the interest, not of rational discourse, but of manipulation.'[5]

For all the chatter about PR people, actual public relations activity often has an iceberg-like semi-invisibility in the public mind, as few are conscious of most of the PR campaigns taking place all around them (try asking people outside the industry to talk about particular PR campaigns; aside from politics, typically they cite advertising). Partly for that reason it usually escapes the censure and calls for regulatory measures which affect its high-profile advertising cousin. However, some critics (and perhaps lovers of conspiracy theories) latch onto precisely that – the way in which PR is so often undertaken behind the scenes and in private. We have in previous books likened this view of PR to seeing at least some of its practitioners as the sinister special forces of capitalism. It is true to say that PR lacks the transparency of advertising, where at least the finished product – the ad itself – is on display. In contrast, when PR people influence media content, or otherwise seek to get involved in public debate, it is hard for outsiders to know exactly what they have done. Occasionally investigators have tried to get to the bottom of this process, making a real effort – for example, PRwatch.org, and its founders' books – most famously *Toxic Sludge Is Good For You!*,[6] and the UK's spinwatch. org – but it is difficult to strike a public chord about what PR is doing. Nonetheless the fact that it is hard to study PR activity hasn't stopped others, including academics, from condemning it.

For those on the political left, public relations will always be suspect, although quite a few have ended up working in the field. Under that name – public relations – PR is overwhelmingly undertaken by private sector for-profit organisations, although even many of them shy away from the term themselves. It is used to justify their business practices and profitability and to influence governments. Charities, NGOs and public sector organisations, viewed more sympathetically by many, use other names to describe what they do ('campaigning', 'communications', and so on). Nonetheless, call it what you like, most PR activity is furthering the interests of the private sector, with the lion's share being marketing PR, although the public and not-for-profit sectors are themselves huge. If you are hostile to, or even just suspicious of, private enterprise, and especially 'big business', then you probably won't like one of its main mouthpieces.

It's also worth noting that many academic and other accounts offer a highly selective view of the relationship between journalism and PR, contrasting their favoured forms of journalism (for example, the BBC, the *New York Times* or the UK's *Guardian* newspaper, all now successfully exported around the world online) and their least favourite kinds of PR (for example, for large corporations operating in controversial sectors). Comparing the behaviour of less favoured news outlets – popular papers and magazines, or the kind of online blogs which attract the most visitors – with PR for respected institutions and NGOs would not offer such tempting targets. Whether fair or not, such depictions of PR tend to cast it in an unfavourable light.

PR and Popular Culture

PR people often want to shrug off the way their industry features in popular culture, for example, in films and TV shows.[7] However, the television and film industries have found the PR world to be an attractive backdrop for entertaining drama and these fictional portrayals have undoubtedly had a major impact on how public relations is perceived.

One reason for this is the real PR world's surprisingly low public profile. Despite PR coming of age and being on the tip of people's tongues – 'PR stunts', 'just PR', and so on – it is still the case that, as we have mentioned, most people know surprisingly little about the actual industry. As we know from countless interviews with would-be students of public relations, questions about real-life PR practitioners (with occasional high-profile exceptions), PR consultancies and PR – as opposed to advertising – campaigns normally draw a blank. Indeed, after some big bad spin doctors began to attract adverse publicity in the 1990s and the noughties, their successors sought to draw back from the public gaze. Nor do most people have much direct contact with PR in the way they do with many other service industries. Despite the first part of its name, *public* relations, practitioners seldom have direct contact with members of the general public in the way that – for example – health care workers, teachers or people working in banks, restaurants and stores do. Nor are they visible in the way that many journalists are on TV or in newspaper and online by-lines. The numbers of PR practitioners may be growing, but are still small relative to the overall population, and dwarfed by the numbers in many other fields of work. Moreover they are concentrated in a few major urban centres.

Against this background of limited real knowledge or contact, PR academics and others writing about their industry have had grudgingly to acknowledge that it is above all TV shows and films that have shaped the public image of PR. One TV show has been particularly influential – and it's surely reasonable to conclude that a series which attracted so many people to PR has had a wider impact on how other people see the occupation:

> Students have told us they chose PR as a major because they wanted to be like Samantha on *Sex and the City*.[8]

The number of people I've spoken to that say *Sex and the City* played a part in their decisions to become a PR person is depressingly – and amusingly – high (in a *Schadenfreude* kind of way).[9]

It is fair to say that Samantha Jones, the PR protagonist of *Sex and the City*, played by Kim Cattrall, does not put ethics centre stage (it's worth checking out an episode featuring her 'PR' antics if you haven't already). On the other hand, her work seems like fun – it's varied, as she surfs the waves of fashion and celebrity with the independence of someone who runs her own business, and is able as a result to enjoy an affluent lifestyle in Manhattan.

Our own experience bears out the quotes above – PR's not-too-guilty secret. *Sex and the City* was originally aired between 1998 and 2004, and a little later in the many other territories in which it was broadcast – it was even adapted into a separate Brazilian version – with the follow-up films appearing in 2008 and 2010. Indeed, although the programmes and films are still shown worldwide, it is tempting to link some recent falls in recruitment to PR courses to the passing of this very popular series, and the fact that nothing new has emerged to match it.

Sex and the City may have led the field into the new millennium, but was and remains far from being alone. TV and movie depictions of PR (there are some versions in novels and on radio as well) tend to fall into two categories.

The first and probably the most popular is the genre to which *Sex and the City* belongs, the realm of the PR girl or woman (the leading characters are overwhelmingly female). The PR work involves such things as fashion, lifestyle and entertainment, as in *Sex and the City*'s British predecessor *Absolutely Fabulous* (also a long-running TV series which made it into film as well), or Gwyneth Paltrow's fashion PR woman in *Sliding Doors*. The fact that ethical concerns don't come to the fore is balanced by the fact that the PR activity is seen as relatively trivial – nothing very serious is at stake (although the serious-minded heirs to the Frankfurt School might deplore the cheerful acceptance of consumerism).

The other genre is the territory of the (usually male) spin doctor, seen at work in films such as *The Ides of March*, *In the Loop* and the British and American versions of *House of Cards* and the French series *Spin* (originally, and tellingly, called *Men from the Shadows*). Here the work is very different. Spin doctors hover around the seat of power and play a vital role in determining important events, such as election results, major policy initiatives or the fates of top politicians. Ethical concerns are central – but seldom to the spin doctors, who are brutal exponents of Machiavelli's 'necessary immorality', as described in Chapter 1 of this book. In the Danish television political drama *Borgen*, the generally high-minded Prime Minister actually sacks a seemingly extremely well-qualified media adviser who has too many scruples and whose head is in the clouds, replacing him with a tough but effective ex-journalist. Indeed, spin doctors' very name, derived from the way a ball can be spun to advantage in baseball (or indeed cricket), implies that they are willing to manipulate information to advantage. They are prepared to act ruthlessly and to attack opponents with no-holds-barred. Truth is not at a premium.

Aggrieved PR people do of course argue that both these versions of their occupation are unreal, and do not reflect the worthy realities of PR. However, the people who have created these dramas are generally well aware of the world of PR. What they have really done is use artistic licence to exaggerate what happens, understandably highlighting sensational aspects of the job and controversial tactics. There are few things shown which do not *ever* happen – just not that often, or not in quite so lurid a way. Paradoxically such portrayals have helped PR in many ways, not just by raising its profile, but illustrating both the ways in which it can be a fulfilling and enjoyable career choice and why it is seen as so important politically, in business and in many other organisations. Nonetheless by showcasing such things repeatedly to vast audiences around the world, these fictional accounts in popular culture have had a significant impact on perceptions of PR's ethical standards. Many PR people feel that they are swimming against that current and need to do battle to counter the reputational damage done by the kind of behaviour depicted on our screens.

The Skeleton in the Attic: PR's Embarrassing Relationship with Propaganda

When discussion gets heated about the PR undertaken for anything which people dislike or view with distaste, it's odds on that someone will start mentioning propaganda, a term which has become a dirty word associated with unacceptable forms of persuasion for unedifying causes.

The PR industry – in its official statements and literature – understandably doesn't want to be associated with such things, but doesn't much like the term 'persuasion' either – something that might surprise ordinary people at the receiving end of a consumer PR campaign or a political candidate's PR. There are many hundreds of 'official' definitions of PR – produced by trade associations, PR academics and others who write about the industry. Our own definition, explained more fully in our previous books, is as follows: 'Public relations is the planned persuasion of people to behave in ways which further its sponsor's objectives. It works primarily through the use of media relations and other forms of third-party endorsement.'

Apart from our own, the ones we have encountered – and certainly the best-known ones – sidestep 'persuasion'.

What Is Going On?

As it happens, 'propaganda' has a distinguished history – certainly for adherents of one of the world's largest faith communities, the Roman Catholic Church. The use of the term stems from the setting up of the *Sacra Congregatio de Propaganda Fide* in Rome in 1622. The Roman Catholic Church, which had enjoyed a near-monopoly over religious and intellectual life in Western Europe for more than a millennium, faced both a challenge – the threat of the Protestant Reformation which had got underway in 1517 – and an opportunity: the chance to evangelise in the territories in the Americas and elsewhere conquered by Catholic Spain and Portugal. The establishment of the Congregation for the Propagation of the Faith (to give it its English title) was a response to these circumstances. In effect, it sought to professionalise the Church's persuasive activities, with particular emphasis on the work of missionaries in both non-Christian and Protestant lands. (Since 1967, it has become the Congregation for the Evangelisation of Peoples; perhaps the term Propaganda became too tarnished to be used even by its originators.)

For Protestants, the term propaganda always had somewhat sinister overtones, but it had nothing like the prominence it has today: the otherwise comprehensive *Encyclopaedia Britannica* did not even think it merited an entry in 1911. It was from the second decade of the twentieth century that the word really leapt into public consciousness as some new and controversial causes used it openly to describe what they were doing.

The first major example was the British, who from 1914 used propaganda to vilify Germany and encourage America to enter the First World War on the side of Britain and France, hoping thereby to tip the scales in what was becoming a long-drawn-out and finely balanced struggle. Later, after the war, as the USA retreated into isolationism, propaganda, including what seemed to be exaggerated accounts of German atrocities, was blamed for dragging the country into an unnecessary war.

By 1917, the US President, Woodrow Wilson, believed America should enter the war and set out to persuade the American public to back the move. To achieve this, his government employed many of the people who became early exponents of PR. As perhaps the most famous of these, Edward Bernays, said much later, they came to see how useful and effective propaganda techniques could be and thought they could be applied in peacetime. However, as he admitted, 'propaganda' had got a bad name for itself, so he opted for the term 'public relations counsellor', although that did not prevent him later calling one of his best-known books *Propaganda*.

Following the Bolshevik revolution in Russia which took place in the same year that the USA joined the war, the new Communist regime in the Soviet Union made extensive, open use of propaganda, both to consolidate the new system at home and to spread revolution beyond Russia's borders. The regime's objectives included a total transformation of society and the economy, making mass persuasion crucial. Communist propaganda remained a key weapon throughout the Cold War which lasted for most of the rest of the century. Propaganda techniques have continued to be crucial in the regimes which sought to emulate the Soviet Union. To this day, Chinese officials use the term quite openly, and it is very publicly evident in North Korea.

But for most people, the final nail in the coffin for propaganda as a respectable term was its association with the Nazis, who used its techniques both to achieve power and to further their policies of aggression and mass murder. Hitler's propaganda chief, Dr Goebbels, will forever be synonymous with the unacceptable and immoral use of methods of mass persuasion to help Germany perpetrate some of the greatest evils of modern times.

This explains why PR people, unless they are being ironic or playfully courting controversy, don't want to be associated with propaganda. But it does not explain what the real difference is. As we shall explore later on in this book, saying that persuading people to do good things is PR while persuading people to do bad things is propaganda does not get us very far intellectually. We surely all agree that the Nazis were evil, but in most cases the balance between good and evil is much more nuanced and open to debate. Nor is it necessarily about technique – some of the approaches used by propagandists could be, and probably are, used by your favourite charity or political party.

For many, propaganda is associated with lying – including the Nazis' 'Big Lie'. Some champions of public relations might be tempted to say that this distinguishes it from PR – a vital moral difference. However, as we shall see later on in this book, it is far from clear that PR people always do tell the truth. On the other hand, not all propaganda is about telling lies – even Goebbels recognised that sometimes it was important for propagandists to tell people uncomfortable truths, not for moral reasons but because in that way they could at least exercise some control over how and when the truth was told, and because otherwise when the truth emerged from other sources, people would lose all faith in the propagandist. And, in any case, it is not always clear what the truth is. Members of the Roman Catholic Church's Sacred Congregation for the Propagation of the Faith believed they were promoting the most important truth imaginable – but others did and do disagree, and with equal vehemence might say the religious messages they proclaimed were 'fake news'.

In reality, as one of the early scholars of mass persuasion put it, propaganda is as moral or immoral as a pump handle. It can be used for any cause – just like PR. We would argue that the differences between PR and propaganda lie elsewhere:

- One of the virtues of public relations is that it is a symptom of freedom. The media matter in all societies, including those dictatorships which use propaganda, but in such regimes those in power can be sure about what's said about them: their messages will be delivered to the public, and they do not have to fear hostile headlines. In free societies, everyone, however wealthy or powerful – from presidents and prime ministers through to chief executives of the largest companies and celebrities – remains uncertain about what the media might say about them. It might be positive – but as people as wealthy and/ or powerful as Mark Zuckerberg, Harvey Weinstein, Hillary Clinton, Donald Trump, Philippe Macron and Boris Johnson know, it can also be very negative and damaging. PR exists to try and deal with this uncertainty. Even its greatest practitioners cannot guarantee positive coverage, but they can try – and perhaps, in the worst situations, make bad coverage a little more balanced.
- The main reason for this is that true propagandists always seek to exercise full powers of censorship. From the Roman Catholic Church with its index of banned books to the rigid censorship practised in Fascist and Communist regimes, critical voices are silenced. It is true that no regime has ever managed to seal itself hermetically from all criticism, and there will always be a black market in alternative views, even if those expressing them are, when caught, brutally punished, but mass media – even social media – can be, and often are, censored. In the free societies in which public relations has flourished, PR people certainly try to use whatever means they can to influence media coverage, and can act energetically and ruthlessly to seek to prevent hostile stories appearing but – and it is an important distinction – they do not have the same overarching, official powers of censorship.
- The other major difference between PR and propaganda has fewer direct ethical implications. It is that propaganda involves pulling on far more levers than PR. PR's origins as a distinct occupation can be traced back to the growth of the modern mass media, and media relations remain at the heart of PR, with the industry evolving as new forms of media emerge. The mass media, a relatively new phenomenon in historical terms, represent an important way of getting messages across to vast audiences, but they also represent a threat, by publishing unwelcome news and giving a voice to criticism. In contrast, propaganda pre-dates the modern media. While the practice

of propaganda, if not the name, may be as old as human society, the first people to coin the term, the Roman Catholic Church, sought to persuade by other means, for example, education, music, art, architecture, ritual and ceremonies, books and preaching. Later propagandists added other methods, including films and sport – a famous case in point is Hitler's involvement in the Berlin Olympic Games in 1936. Such things remain important ways of communicating and persuading in all societies, but it would be a bit of a foolish boast to claim that they are all controlled by PR people. Public relations practitioners may dabble in such matters, but they are so extensive and so specialised that they largely fall outside PR's remit.

These are important points of distinction. The implications can be observed to the full in present-day China, a country which combines a tightly controlled one-party system of government with an economy which has to a large extent become entrepreneurial and open to competition. As a dictatorship, the Chinese regime does not have to practise PR in the same way as its western democratic counterparts – because it can be sure of what the mass media will say about political matters. It can be so sure because it devotes enormous resources to propaganda, including employing an army of censors who attempt to banish hostile comments and unwelcome news and information online, as well as in more traditional forms. Where the Chinese regime has increasingly used PR (and this has involved sending officials on training courses overseas and hiring foreign PR consultancies) is to try and project its messages overseas, where – to their discomfort – China has found that the positive coverage it is used to at home is by no means guaranteed.

On the other hand, more routine marketing PR by commercial companies has increasingly flourished in China. It is not normally seen as politically threatening – but instead as a necessary part of China's economic growth and development as a competitive market economy within a one-party political system. However, as is the case for practitioners in countries with free media, there is no guarantee of the extent and nature of coverage for private companies.

These distinctions between PR and propaganda remain little discussed. Instead people often just think of propaganda as any kind of promotional activity – including PR – for causes they strongly object to: try Googling 'Trump propaganda', or 'Tory propaganda' for the UK or 'Modi propaganda' for India. The distinction may be right or wrong, but is largely subjective – and Trump, Tory and Modi supporters would be happy to turn the tables on their opponents. However, propaganda's relationship with PR will continue to bedevil the reputation of PR industry – and hence the issues underlying it matter.

The PR Industry's Own Debates about Ethics and Why They Matter

Box 2.3 presents an official view of PR ethics.

Box 2.3 Ethics in PR: An Official View

According to Francis Ingham, Director General of the PRCA:

> Ethics are certainly at the heart of the PR industry. They've been transformed in the last decade because public expectations have themselves been transformed. Expectations are higher. But also it's social media. There is simply nowhere left to hide for malpractice. And that has had the natural effect that if you want to prosper in the industry, you have to accept and embrace higher levels of ethical behaviour than was previously the case.
>
> Our belief is that an organisation's most valuable asset is its reputation. And chief executives increasingly understand that – and the people who are advising them reflect that belief. So in the PRCA and the ICCO data that we produce every year, we know that one of the top three or four factors driving the growth of the industry has been CEOs investing in corporate reputation, increasingly, year-on-year.

On a day-to-day basis, most PR practitioners get on with their lives without confronting major ethical issues. As in most other occupations, much of their work seems innocuous – they are doing familiar things for familiar organisations, although it's worth pausing to reflect that, just because someone's work is familiar does not mean it is actually ethical: we all perhaps become accustomed to practices which, on closer examination, are questionable. However, if one attends PR industry events, follows the activities of its professional bodies, or reads what the PR industry says about it itself whenever practitioners put fingers to keyboards, a different picture emerges.

Despite the industry's evident success, reflected in high rates of growth (at least until the pandemic) and the way in which its services are today sought after and valued by practically every kind of organisation – it sometimes seems as though the world of PR is consumed with anxiety. PR's own damaged reputation (see above) is something PR's spokespeople are acutely aware of – and they believe it has implications for their status and their remuneration. This is reflected in the debate about whether

PR is a profession in the full sense of the term – something we discuss in Chapter 4.

However, there is another reason why ethical issues come to the fore. As we saw in Chapter 1, the PR world is dominated by well-educated, young cosmopolitans living in big cities. Unsurprisingly they reflect the values of their 'tribe' and are understandably concerned about how they are seen by others, although seldom to the extent of losing sleep over it. They may broadly accept private enterprise – the mainstay of PR work – but will have an ever-changing set of concerns about it. All kinds of issues come up which may affect their view of their work, something we will look at in later chapters. The important point for now is that if PR employers want to attract, recruit and retain the people they need, they have to recognise these concerns – concerns which often have an ethical component.

Being Realistic

As the PR industry has grown, so have its institutions. As we see throughout this book, there are now a large number of industry bodies, and there are also many university courses and books about PR. These are supplemented by PR journals and conferences, and plenty of online activity by those who want to discuss industry issues. All of these provide forums for debate, but without denying the value of such activities and their contribution to Socratic dialogue (see p. 1), one must temper this with realism.

One of the great drawbacks of such debates is that they are inward-looking – and indeed what is discussed (perhaps thankfully) rarely reaches wider audiences. Some of the things that PR people say about themselves and their role in such forums might surprise many of the people who actually pay for PR. There is plenty of hard evidence that such people value PR – they spend ever more money on it and seek to employ top PR talent – but they want to achieve specific results, and PR is only one – important – tool in their toolbox. Beyond the PR industry itself, PR people seldom become chief executives of companies. Coming as they do from a range of different professional and business backgrounds, chief executives and their board members are not always fixated about PR issues, with other matters, not least financial indicators, coming to the fore.

It is also the case that those who are most vociferous in PR's internal debates are devoting time to activities which many leading practitioners, who are running agencies or working inhouse at a top level, cannot spare. As a result, PR's most senior people are often underrepresented in such discussions, and even when they do participate, they have to pull their punches, being wary of upsetting their clients and employers (Box 2.4).

Box 2.4 How Far Can PR People Express Views about the People They Work For?

Lord Bell, the leading UK PR practitioner (see pp. 72–77), was unusually outspoken. In an interview with the *Financial Times* he commented on bankers – many of whom were existing or potential clients of his then-PR firm:

'They're all complete criminals. The whole bloody lot,' he says. Might expressing such a caustic opinion of bankers not unnerve Bell Pottinger's financial sector clients, such as Investec and TPG? 'That's the problem, you see, you're not allowed to tell the truth. Isn't that disgusting?'[10]

His remarks were widely seen as a *faux pas*, causing embarrassment to his colleagues. Few people in PR would care to emulate his approach.

In practice, PR's role in wider ethical debates is limited by a number of factors. First, PR practitioners simply do not have the expertise required to weigh up what's right or wrong in many, often complicated, situations in business or government. They are not experts in commercial, financial, legal, technical or environmental matters, let alone epidemiology. Indeed, their special area of expertise, which includes their ability to advise on what is popular and how things will be seen by the media, may be a distraction in that it may not coincide with what is ethical. Second, they rarely have the resources or time to devote to in-depth ethical audits of their employers' activities (Box 2.5): relative to other parts of a business, PR departments are small and busy, with a range of tasks. Third, they often lack the seniority required to challenge top-level decisions effectively.

Box 2.5 How Far Can PR People Know What Organisations Are Doing?

The sudden collapse of the energy giant Enron in 2001 in the USA remains one of the most spectacular corporate collapses of our times. The vast firm had seemed to be a model corporate citizen, a sought-after employer with a strong record on corporate social responsibility. Subsequently its key executives were convicted of criminal offences.

In the documentary film, *Enron: The Smartest Guys in the Room* (2005), one of the interviewees is a former in-house PR person at the company. As he comments on what happened, there is – understandably – no suggestion that he was in any position to know about what was really going on: comprehending the extremely sophisticated financial manoeuvring and ultimately the fraud perpetrated at Enron was something that defied many seasoned business experts for a long time, let alone PR practitioners.

In another example, the former editor of the *Financial Times*, Andrew Gowers, served for two years as head of corporate communications at Lehman Brothers in London, before the bank foundered amid the global financial crisis in 2008. Again, despite his background, which should have provided him with more specialist expertise than most PR practitioners, he seems to have been in the dark about the scale of the challenges facing the company.

Gowers went on to perform a similar role at BP, where he was responsible for handling the aftermath of the *Deepwater Horizon* oil disaster in the Gulf of Mexico in 2010. Again, there is little suggestion that he could make judgements about the adequacy of health and safety arrangements at the company – any more than his successors in PR roles at BP are equipped to second-guess senior managers about the rights and wrongs of fossil fuel use.

More recently, after successfully running Donald Trump's first presidential campaign (see 87–89), Kellyanne Conway became, until her departure in August 2020, one of the longer-serving senior members of Trump's team at the White House. However, it has been suggested that since the election she has managed to survive because she 'has perfected the art of satisfying Trump while running from him ... never being in the room, understanding that the room is where Stalin kills you'.[11] Arguably her ability to dodge responsibility and hence her survival wouldn't have been as easy to accomplish if, like other senior figures, she had been responsible for a concrete area of policy as opposed to the slightly more nebulous realm of communications where what has or has not been achieved is always a little difficult to pin down.

Summary

Despite its important role in contemporary life, and its popularity as a career path, PR's troubled reputation forms the backdrop to its attempt to establish itself on secure ethical foundations. Almost since its birth the public relations industry has been the butt of criticism from journalists, academics and others. While PR work has often featured prominently in popular culture, it is usually represented in ways which practitioners find unflattering – as alternately trivial or sinister. PR is also associated with the ogre that is 'propaganda'. PR industry bodies and spokespeople agonise about these issues, although sometimes their views seem more idealistic than realistic.

Questions

1. Why does PR seem to have a troubled reputation – and does it matter?
2. What has influenced the attitudes of journalists and academics towards PR?
3. How is PR portrayed in popular culture?
4. Compare and contrast PR and propaganda.

Notes

1 PRCA Census for 2019. Available at: www.prca.org.uk/sites/default/files/ PRCA_PR_Census_2019_v9-8-pdf%20%285%29.pdf
2 Davies, Nick, *Flat Earth News: An Award-winning Reporter Exposes False-hood, Distortion and Propaganda in Global Media* (London: Chatto & Win-dus, 2008).
3 Morris, Trevor and Goldsworthy, Simon, *PR Today: The Authoritative Guide to Public Relations* (Basingstoke: Palgrave, 2016), p. 17.
4 Black, Eben, *Lies, Lobbying and Lunch: PR, Public Affairs and Political En-gagement: A Guide* (London: Bite-Sized Business Books, 2017).
5 Quoted by Simon Goldsworthy, in 'PR Ethics: forever a will o'the wisp', in R. Keeble (ed.). *Communication Ethics Now* (Leicester: Troubador, 2008), p. 210.
6 Stauber, John and Rampton, Sheldon, *Toxic Sludge Is Good For You!: Lies, Damn Lies and the Public Relations Industry* (London: Constable & Robin-son, 2004).
7 See the Appendix: Suggestions for Further Reading and Sources of Infor-mation, Stimulation and Entertainment, p. 229, for details of film, television and other portrayals of PR.
8 Emily Kinsky of West Texas A & M University, quoted in Parsons, Patricia, *Ethics in Public Relations: A Guide to Best Practice* (London: Kogan Page, 2016), p. 13.
9 Leigh, Rich, *Myths of PR: All Publicity Is Good Publicity and Other Popular Misconceptions* (London: Kogan Page, 2017), p. 79.
10 See www.ft.com/content/3d39bf02-4ae2-11e4-839a-00144feab7de
11 Wolff, Michael, *Siege: Trump under Fire*, quoted in *The Sunday Times*, Cul-ture Section, 9 June 2019, p. 28.

Chapter 3

Theory and Practice

As public relations has gradually emerged as an university discipline, a body of academic writing has taken shape, partly to secure the foundations of what is a relatively new subject. Perhaps unsurprisingly, given the issues discussed in Chapter 2, much of the work has focused on PR ethics – how far public relations is, or can be, ethical; and what would-be practitioners need to be taught in order to tackle the relevant issues.

This book, as a 'real-world' guide, focuses less on abstract theory than some other volumes, and recognises the danger that, if people dwell in ivory towers, they can lose touch with reality. Nonetheless, it is important to be aware of some of the thinking about ethical matters that has proved influential in academic circles, even if it is much less well known in the world of day-to-day PR.

In this chapter we look at:

- Some of the key ideas in academic works exploring PR ethical theory.
- How far such theorising is applicable internationally, in different cultures and contexts.

> The conscious and intelligent manipulation of the organized habits and opinions of the masses is an important element in democratic society. Those who manipulate this unseen mechanism of society constitute an invisible government which is the true ruling power of our country.

The above quotation is from the beginning of the first chapter of *Propaganda*, a provocatively-titled book first published in 1928 by Edward Bernays.[1] It describes the role he saw the then new PR industry performing and, to most modern readers, what he says surely has a sinister ring to it: few of us are happy about the notion of manipulation, especially if it is 'unseen'. The chapter is tellingly entitled 'Organizing Chaos'. It was one of the first books to be written by a PR practitioner about the industry.

Edward Bernays, whom we come across elsewhere, has often been portrayed as the 'Father of Public Relations'; it's a role he seemed more than
comfortable with – he died aged 103 in 1995. He was active in the field
from an early stage, wrote many other books on the subject and even for
a time taught PR, leaving a public legacy unequalled by most of his contemporaries (given that most PR practitioners operate outside the public
gaze). He was certainly one of PR's first theorists, writing in the abstract
about public relations as well as practising it. He took full advantage of
his relationship to Sigmund Freud (he was his nephew twice over), and
featured in Adam Curtis's four-part BBC television documentary, *Century of the Self* (now available on YouTube).

In fact, there were other, earlier practitioners of PR, and Bernays'
achievements were not perhaps as great as both he and, paradoxically,
his critics have suggested. Unlike some other contemporaries, he did
not establish a consultancy which survived his retirement – there's no
'Bernays' on the door of a major contemporary PR firm – and indeed his
clients had a habit of dispensing with his services rather abruptly. Nor
is there much evidence to back up some of the more grandiose claims
about what he achieved, not least the unsupported assertion made in
Century of the Self that he all-but-singlehandedly persuaded women to
take up smoking cigarettes. Perhaps his ideas were not so original – he
was to a large extent building on the thinking of a contemporary American intellectual, Walter Lippmann. Lippmann was afraid of the ways in
which the uneducated but enfranchised masses could cause harm, and
hence wrote about the 'manufacture of consent' as a way of preserving
a façade of democracy while ensuring that the elites continued to rule
the roost. Nonetheless, Bernays' exalted image as both a theorist and an
all-powerful practitioner of PR suited both him – his early books were
in large part a way of marketing what were then new and unfamiliar
services – and critics of PR: good stories need villains, and who could be
better than a sinister puppet-master?

For many decades, Bernays' relatively well-publicised books and other
pronouncements came perhaps as close to a body of PR academic theory
as anything else. Public relations teaching was initiated in the USA, and
spread from there – but even in the UK, probably the second most mature major PR market in the world, the first PR graduates did not emerge
from university until the early 1990s. London is a huge centre for PR, but
when one of the authors launched an MA programme with PR in the title
in 2000, it was the first such course in the UK capital.

Understandably, given that people who study PR at university level do
so wanting to enter the industry, students have always been particularly
keen on learning about PR practice, and many PR books, both for university and training purposes, continue to have a how-to-do-it focus. However, as the numbers of PR academics swelled, things began to change.

They were aware, sometimes painfully so, of PR's reputational problems, as described in Chapter 2. While PR courses were often popular with potential students, and so found favour with university management, they were less popular elsewhere in academia. Colleagues teaching media studies or mass communication who were steeped in thinking derived from the Marxist Frankfurt School found the very idea of PR troubling on moral grounds: PR, like advertising, was another tool of capitalism. In so far as they knew anything specific about PR, they mainly knew about its occasionally publicised scandals and alleged abuses. Established teachers of journalism also often harboured a resentment towards the teaching of PR, feeling, for the reasons discussed in Chapter 2, that it lacked the moral qualities that characterise their trade.

PR academics have endeavoured to rescue public relations from these perceived injustices and hostility and establish the subject on secure ethical foundations. At the same time they have sought to secure their own positions within the university world, recognising that a subject which simply rests on practical skills could never secure the serious academic credibility and status they desire. Media theorists could decry PR, but this was not a ready option for most of those involved in teaching PR. As the PR academic C. Kay Weaver puts it: 'Unlike radical and critical Media Studies scholars, Critical Public Relations theorists are far less likely to position public relations as propaganda and dismiss it as the villainous tool of neoliberalism'.[2]

This dilemma – the need to justify the subject they were teaching in terms which seem academically respectable – is surely a major factor behind the range of academic theory that has emerged over the last generation, as PR courses have started to proliferate across the university sector (Box 3.1).

Box 3.1 PR and Universities

According to Francis Ingham, Director General of the PRCA:

> We really place a high emphasis on our relationship with the universities. We've got 20-odd university partners. And one of the key deliverables of that is we talk at least once a year with each of our partner universities about ethical expectations, with case studies and guidance. And we talk about the whole black, white and grey issue. So that when the students reach their first job, they have a firm ethical grounding. They're willing and willing and able to say no to their employers. And they know what's right and wrong and what the guidelines are that they should listen to and adhere to and bear in mind.

An alternative view from a senior PR industry insider:

These PR graduates, when they enter their first job, have no idea how to write a press release. They have no care for ethics. They can't write, full stop. Their idea of PR is a mix of advertising and marketing and what they read on Twitter. And the universities that so-called teach them are just taking their money and leaving it to employers like me to do all of the hard work. And also, you've got to blame the schools. These people arrive at the universities barely literate in many cases.

The most influential example of these attempts to establish theoretical underpinnings is probably the four models theory of PR first put forward by the American scholars James Grunig and Todd Hunt in 1984:

1. *The press agentry or publicity model.* Here communications professionals seek to persuade key audiences in a one-way form of communication. Truth is not important and those using this model do not seek audience feedback or conduct audience analysis research. This is the model used by propagandists, such as those working for the North Korean regime.
2. *The public information model,* where 'the public relations person functions essentially as a journalist in residence, whose job it is to report objectively information about his [sic] organisation to the public'. Again, communication is essentially one-way, but accuracy is more important. There may not be any persuasive intent. Grunig and Hunt thought this was practised by 50 per cent of organisations.
3. *The two-way asymmetrical model.* Here, with deliberately persuasive intent, communications professionals seek to research their audiences and shape their communication accordingly, but the communication is asymmetrical because the interests of the organisation come first. This is typically found in consumer PR.
4. *The two-way symmetric model.* In this model, the communications professional is liaising between an organisation and its public in a balanced way to achieve mutual benefit, and should 'usually use theories of communication rather than theories of persuasion'. Although this is the ethical ideal, it was relatively rarely practised.

To a large extent, enjoying first-mover advantage, Grunig and Hunt set the scene for modern PR ethical theory with these four models. Although Grunig himself has since modified them and others have suggested alternative approaches, nothing else has had quite the same impact.

The last three models clearly relate, or are intended to relate, to public relations practice as we know it (the first more closely resembles propaganda, see pp. 25–29). They are intended to show how PR could and should develop in a virtuous way, shedding its questionable moral role in persuading people, and instead becoming a moral force which facilitates mutual understanding, an idea which overlaps with how some industry bodies have sought to describe public relations. As Grunig concluded elsewhere: 'Public relations ... should be ethical in that it helps build caring – even loving – relationships with other individuals and groups they affect in society.'[3] This ideal continues to be influential. In her widely-used textbook, *Ethics in Public Relations*, Patricia Parsons writes of a future 'where public relations' role truly is to develop mutually beneficial relationships between organisations and their publics whose foundation is trust – the only true foundation for mutual benefit'.[4] This closely parallels the definition of PR adopted by the first World Assembly of Public Relations Associations, also known as the Mexican Statement, which talks about PR 'implementing programmes of action which will serve both the organisation's and the public interest'.[5]

It's worth examining these influential ideas in more detail. Certainly, before there was anything called a PR industry, there were *press agents* – people who sought to get positive namechecks for their clients in the newspapers and magazines of the day. Their work was probably not as sophisticated at some of today's PR practitioners, but the concept of getting positive media coverage still forms the kernel of much PR work, and often it is a one-way process. Sometimes, it has to be acknowledged, truth is not always at a premium.

The second model, *public information*, which is what Grunig and Hunt put at the heart of PR work in countries such as the USA, is intriguing. The idea that PR people report objectively on the organisations they serve assumes that they have autonomy – a ring-fenced authority to speak in public, even if that means saying things which are detrimental to the organisation that has hired them: after all, if they kept quiet about potentially harmful information, they would not be objective. Our response to this is based on the maxim 'follow the money'. PR people are paid by the organisations they work for in order to get across their desired messages, and to maximise the positive. While there are occasions on which PR people have to acknowledge mistakes or problems and even apologise on behalf of their organisations, that is not the same thing as being balanced or objective. A PR practitioner who tried to do this – volunteering information about all kinds of difficulties and disputes affecting their organisation in a truly even-handed way – would have a short career indeed. One might also add that no-one really expects PR people to be objective – least of all, the news media. It is the job of journalists to weigh up a variety of information and views and deliver the finished product via the media: PR people, often a range of them working for different organisations on different sides of the argument, simply contribute many of the ingredients.

The second issue here is 'persuasion'. One can understand why PR people want to distance themselves from the term, but in our view there is a vital and commonsensical connection between PR and persuasion: there are few if any PR campaigns which don't seek to get people to do things, even if it's to donate money to a worthy charity, or to give up smoking. Grunig and Hunt seem uncomfortable with the word 'persuade', but perhaps the real moral issues are about which techniques are being used to persuade, and what people are being persuaded to do.

The *two-way asymmetrical model* probably comes closest to describing modern, professional PR. It is planned persuasion, with the nature of the audience very much taken into account. The two-way nature of the communications is a key feature of social media – something Grunig and Hunt can hardly have anticipated when they drew up their models. However, in view of the emphasis on two-way communication, it is worth stressing that finding out about and hearing from your audiences do not on their own make PR activity more ethical, only more efficient and effective. Even the worst dictators want to know what people think (readers of the diaries of the Nazi propaganda chief Dr Goebbels can see that he was very interested in what ordinary soldiers and civilians were saying – the censorship of letters being one key source of information); indeed, a major part of the work of secret policemen in oppressive regimes is gathering information about what we might call 'public opinion'.

Although these models represent perhaps the most influential attempt to create a theory of PR which puts it in an ethical framework, no real evidence is offered to back up the claims. Is – or was – a suspiciously rounded 'half' of PR work ever 'public information', as Grunig and Hunt define it? Is there, or will there ever be, any PR work which is truly 'symmetrical' – assuming that the people paying for the work altruistically place their own interests no higher than those of their audiences? The ideas may be idealistic but if they are not grounded in reality, they may not just be of limited value, but may actually be misleading. In their attempt to rescue PR's reputation, they may have simply created a series of suspiciously hollow-sounding claims. It may be just as well that they are not more widely known beyond PR's academic circles.

As a pioneering attempt to theorise PR, the models are now more than a generation old. They were built upon through an International Association of Business Communicators-sponsored 'Excellence' project in the last years of the last century, which sought to establish a universal framework for 'excellent' PR,[6] and since then PR academics have sought to modify them, although none of these attempts have had the same resonance.

In his critique of Grunigian-based theory, communications ethics academic Tom Bivins points out that while persuasive techniques are open to abuse, 'The reality of public relations ... is that persuasion is a recognised and respected communication technique.' Nonetheless, he maintains that an ethic of care can be incorporated into the persuasive process, and that practitioners should turn down requests which unduly harm third parties, pointing out that professional codes call for a balancing of interests, for example, by demanding that PR people tell the truth (for more on the professional codes, see Chapter 4).[7] Box 3.2 presents a view of PR as a discipline in contemporary academia.

Box 3.2 Writing about PR in Contemporary Academia

As exponents of PR theory have sought to take their theorising beyond Grunig, there is increasing interest in what are often called 'critical' perspectives on public relations, with PR academics often applying a range of theory from other fields – sociology, gender studies, psychology, and even Jungian psychoanalysis. They share the preoccupations of many other contemporary academics: perceived power imbalances, inequality, feminism and issues around diversity, identity and inclusion. They also seek to broaden understanding of PR activity, 'decolonising' PR and replacing the traditional preoccupation with US and other Anglosphere-based practitioners, not least those normally seen as the industry's founding 'fathers'.

Amid all of this activity there is a real danger of PR academics, who are often based in rather remote locations, simply talking to themselves and losing touch with the realities of the industry they are supposed to study. Another concern is that their view of the industry is one-sided, with an in-built ideological bias, a tendency described by two well-known PR scholars, writing about what they term 'Progressive PR':

> We personally welcome that trend but would be disappointed if the academy's future output is only liberal and left-leaning. If that happens, it will be, in one respect at least, a regrettable 'return' to a feature of the intellectual mood status quo ante bellum when the dominance of the Grunigian paradigm limits the academy's thinking ...

They continue: 'being PR scholars can lead to the distortions of the single perspective ... Also we can be a closed group, too disconnected from PR practice and the forces that call it up to serve them.'[8]

Although PR exists to serve whoever pays for it, few would go so far as to say that they would do absolutely anything, regardless of the wider repercussions of their work. Nor does accepting that PR has a persuasive purpose mean that practitioners are engaged in a free-for-all contest, although one reason for this is not strictly ethical – it is, as we argue elsewhere, that PR people need a degree of social acceptance to carry on their work. The major problem is, of course, that it's often hard to come to categoric judgements on what will and will not cause the 'undue harm' mentioned above, and assessment of this can simply reflect one's personal prejudices and be self-serving. Even the arguments for telling the truth are more nuanced than it might at first seem (see pp. 54–55 and 113–117). When it comes to applying rules – a deontological approach (see p. 8) – to PR ethics, Parsons points out that rules cannot cover every eventuality; that there are always loopholes; and that rules are open to interpretation and can be in conflict with each other.

This notion of PR's duty of care also comes to the fore in *Ethics in Public Relations: Responsible Advocacy*, a volume edited by Kathy Fitzpatrick and Carolyn Bronstein.[9] As the title suggests, they assign a particular role to public relations. While they accept that some deprecate the term advocacy, and prefer 'consensus builder' as a descriptor, 'the majority of practitioners seem to have embraced advocacy as a primary function'. They note that in 2000 the Public Relations Society of America, then the world's largest professional body in the field, acknowledged advocacy as one of public relations' core values, stating that professionals should be 'responsible advocates', but, underlining the point about rules in the previous paragraph, without defining what exactly 'responsibility' means. The authors of the individual chapters of the book go on to try to explore what responsible advocacy is and how it can be achieved in different contexts.[10]

Bivins also points out that that Grunig's emphasis on mutual understanding, as opposed to persuasion, seeks to position PR as the corporate conscience of the organisation, as PR, with its range of communication with all kinds of audiences, is in a unique position to understand the views of others. He cites academic research showing a divergence of views among practitioners as to whether this is justified.[11]

It would perhaps be more enlightening to step outside the PR world and ask other people in organisations whether they see their PR teams (let alone the agencies they hire) as their corporate consciences. PR is not always seen as it might like to be. It is certainly true that PR people can and do have a range of relationships with external audiences which can give them a better perspective than many other employees – but does that necessarily mean that they are better qualified to exercise their consciences? And what about others? Depending on the nature of the organisation, other codes of professional ethics can have a strong bearing on the corporate conscience, as can the roles of those involved in compliance and regulatory affairs, while senior management might also be said to have an overarching role as a conscience itself. All in all, such debates in PR literature can come to sound like half-empty boasts: insular and little unreal (Box 3.3).

Box 3.3 The Dangers of Overcomplication

As Lord Tim Bell put it:

> I think there are people who try and make PR sound fantastically complicated when it's really quite simple – why try and use long words to make it sound more important than it actually is, and I don't like people who demonstrate their ignorance by trying to sound like they're highly intelligent when they're not.[12]

A final thought. PR academia has sought to show it is grown-up by developing theories. Perhaps researching and writing more proper histories – of PR departments and agencies, and campaigns as well as biographies of PR people – would be more useful and certainly more interesting. Properly considered, such stories could also serve as moral tales. It would require more effort, but if done properly, it might trigger a fuller discussion of the realities within which decisions are made.

Think Globally, Act Locally: The Applicability of PR Theory Internationally

Public relations – at least with that moniker – may have been born in the USA and have spread first and most vigorously to other English-speaking countries, but is now practised worldwide. The world's largest PR agencies may be American, but most public relations is undertaken in-house, by organisations' own employees, and PR has adapted itself to some very different cultures and contexts around the globe. As we have said before, effective public relations depends upon social acceptability and so tends to adapt to what is considered appropriate in different societies. Nor is PR founded upon the same absolute and universal principles, like, for example, science or engineering; it is ultimately an art which depends greatly on how it is viewed by its users and its audiences.

Guanxi: Relationship Building in Chinese Public Relations

> In China ... it is still common for agencies to pay reporters and media outlets for favourable coverage. The going rate for a flattering interview with the chief executive in Chinese media is about 7,000 renminbi. Companies and their agencies also pay 'taxi money' for reporters to attend press conferences.[13]

The emergence of modern public relations in China can be dated back to the early 1980s, as the country opened up in the post-Mao era and introduced economic reforms. In fits and starts the industry has grown and today most of the large international PR agencies are represented in the country.

Guanxi is a long-established concept which is fundamental to Chinese society and which is associated with Confucianism and the ideals of harmonious relationships. It has been defined as 'the exchange of gifts, favours, and banquets; the cultivation of personal relationships and networks of mutual dependence; and the manufacture of obligation and indebtedness'.

American academic Katerina Tsetsura undertook the first study to collect data first-hand in mainland China on the implications of *guanxi*, and specifically gift-giving, for public relations.[14] She describes the prevalence of 'paid news', whereby journalists are paid by PR people in the expectation of coverage. This is disguised, so consumers of the news are unaware of what has happened, and so there is a lack of media transparency. The payments take various forms, direct and indirect:

- money ('lunch money', 'bus fare') or other gifts to reporters in return for attending PR events such as launches;
- payment to journalists for the time spent preparing longer stories or features;
- buying a regular column in a newspaper;
- journalists soliciting advertising or offering other services, or offering to self-censor in return for money or other favours.

Tsetsura's attempts to research this by surveying people in China ran into difficulties. The response was very limited, with some respondents citing the sensitivity of the subject, thus highlighting the perennial problem of researching the informal, private relationships which are typical of so much PR activity. Nonetheless, she ascribes the prevalence of gift-giving to a number of factors, including the low pay received by journalists, problems with journalistic education and codes of ethics – and low levels of PR professionalism. 'Paid news' may in theory be forbidden, but few are upholding the rules.

Payment and gift-giving of this kind raise a number of interesting issues. It is common in many societies – in addition to the vast Chinese media market, Tsetsura cites Russia and Ukraine and mentions Poland, and there are surely many other societies where it is prevalent. Nonetheless, while the practice is sometimes mentioned in western PR textbooks, it is usually shrugged off and not properly tackled. Clearly appearing to trample upon another country's customs can appear insensitive – a subject best avoided – and the assumption of ethical superiority can have unpleasant overtones of cultural imperialism.

The ethical guilt in the cases Tsetsura describes is of course shared – between the PR person seeking to influence coverage and the journalist (and indeed their editors, people who have final responsibility for what appears). Arguably, the moral guilt is greater on the part of the media which are, in some sense, betraying their audiences – whereas the PR people are simply serving those who pay them, albeit in a dubious way. Tsetsura suggests such behaviour reflects the Chinese media's competing loyalties – allegiance to government and party versus the interests of their audiences. In such circumstances PR people will also have competing loyalties.

Nonetheless, a practice can only be so prevalent because it is largely acceptable to both parties – and perhaps the ultimate audiences suspect what is going on and are not too concerned. One common defence in tackling ethical dilemmas is to say 'everybody else is doing it' and, by extension, 'if I don't do it, somebody else will'. This may not hold up in terms of moral philosophy, but is much more understandable in everyday life and in business, where people have to make a living and don't want to end up as virtuous paupers. We are social animals and probably all feel better about guilty feelings if we share them – and perhaps, if the custom is well enough established, we cease to feel guilty altogether.

Of course, in societies such as those of the USA, the UK or Australasia, payments to journalists in return for coverage are a taboo – for journalists just as much as PR practitioners. However, the situation is not quite as clear-cut as people think (see p. 195). It is true that direct payments are not made – but there are a range of indirect alternatives, and different kinds of journalists view this in different ways. Fashion and lifestyle journalists quite often receive gifts or loans of sought-after items, while travel journalists and others often receive valuable flights and holidays in the expectation of favourable coverage. Nothing is written down, but there are clear expectations which, if betrayed, could lead to broken or damaged relations.

Even 'hard news' journalism focusing on politics and business is potentially susceptible to influence of this kind. Cash payments might be off limits, but lavish hospitality isn't. More importantly, journalists can be rewarded with exclusive stories. This may not be regarded as bribery and is seldom seen as ethically troubling – but a supply of major exclusive stories can be worth much more to a journalist in terms of their future pay and promotion than an envelope full of banknotes.

What do western PR practitioners do when confronted with such practices as 'paid news'? After all, as mentioned, all the major global consultancies are represented in China and in many other countries where such things happen. Do they leave it to locally recruited staff and subsidiaries and avoid the subject, pretending such things don't happen or happen only rarely, or that they will be eliminated as levels of PR professionalism rise? None of these solutions tackles the ethical issues, and the fact that involvement in such activities could be deemed to be a form of bribery for which they could be prosecuted in their home countries. No-one wants to be party to the dirty work, but perhaps it can be passed on into other hands with few questions asked. In Box 3.4, Dr Sian Rees discusses ethics in PR education.

Box 3.4 Interview with Dr Sian Rees, Swansea University, UK

Another academic perspective: an interview with Dr Sian Rees, Associate Professor and Head of the Department of Media and Communication, Swansea University, UK.

Dr Rees teaches on a full range of undergraduate and postgraduate courses covering different aspects of public relations at Swansea University. In common with most PR academics, she has a background in PR practice, having worked both in-house and for PR agencies, including Countrywide Porter Novelli, working for clients such as Gillette, BT and Danish Bacon, and later setting up her own PR and marketing consultancy where clients included the charity The Suzy Lamplugh Trust, *Gramophone* magazine, Wembley Arena and the London Arena. She then worked part-time for Swansea University as a Strategic Marketing Manager while developing a lecturing career.

Rees explains that, at Swansea, PR ethics are not taught in a separate course or module, but are instead embedded throughout the curriculum. During their studies, students are introduced to the principles and practices of modern PR, alongside a historical overview, together with subjects such as PR and journalism, PR and democracy, corporate social responsibility, crisis management, digital PR, propaganda and corporate public relations, all of which have ethical dimensions. The aim is to produce graduates who are able to evaluate PR activity critically and consider its implications for society. However, the decision not to teach ethics separately also reflects staffing and resource issues. (The authors have adopted both approaches in their teaching. While timetabling and resources are always live issues, one could also argue that if ethics are – or should be – integral to all PR activity, singling the subject out and placing it in a ring-fenced module or course has its own drawbacks.)

Rees agrees that universities often view the teaching of PR with some suspicion. She points out that as an academic discipline, it is relatively new, lacking the credentials of established subjects, and is associated with the corporate world and big business. However, these suspicions aren't shared by students, including students from other disciplines who often take her PR courses. As a generation, they are used to the idea of self-publicity, and PR simply seems like a natural extension of that. She adds that the subject fits in well with other media-related subjects.

Students' ethical concerns are often reflected in their project choices during their studies, but when it comes to choosing internships and jobs, the desire to gain experience often comes to the fore. Rees recalls a lengthy discussion with one student who was offered a position at a tobacco company and went on to work there. The university is in South Wales, a long-standing centre for the steel industry, and given concerns about climate change and pollution, she notes that a somewhat similar debate can be had about the ethics of that industry.

Asked about books and resources, Rees says the following:

> We tend to rely on broad-based public relations texts which cover a wide range of topics including ethics and responsibility. Examples would be Tench and Yeoman's *Exploring Public Relations*, which has a chapter on Public Relations' professionalism and ethics by Fawkes. Morris and Goldsworthy's *PR Today*, which has a chapter on PR ethics, and Theaker's *The Public Relations Handbook*, which has a chapter from Somerville on business ethics, public relations and corporate social responsibility.
>
> These texts tend to be accessible for all levels of students, including those whose first language is not English. They provide a clear and easily understandable introduction to the concepts of ethics and how they are applied in the industry. I also find that many students have very little if any experience of working in organisations, so their understanding of organisational situations and challenges needs context and explanation. While the very positive views of PR found in some PR textbooks may be a little simplistic and unrealistic, some more recent books looking at PR history offer a more balanced and critical alternative,

such as *The Routledge Handbook of Critical Public Relations*, edited by L'Etang, McKie, Snow and Xifra.[15]

In terms of other resources, I keep an eye on the news media and other sources such as *PRWeek*, to identify contemporary case study examples.

Rees's responses to further questions are given below.

Q: Do you find any particular theoretical approaches helpful or illuminating?

I find it useful when I can use theoretical models as a structure for getting students to apply principles of ethics themselves to organisational settings. As an example, I undertake an exercise where I get students to apply Peach's Business Impact model to decide whether organisations are operating at a Basic level (paying taxes and observing the law), an Organisational Level (minimising negative effects and acting in the spirit of the law) or a Societal level (taking responsibility for a healthy society and alleviating society's ills). I find this helps students to see beyond organisational and public relations rhetoric to challenge the intentions and ethical decisions behind organisational behaviours.

Using Somerville's chapter in Theaker's *The Handbook of Public Relations* as a source, in the second year, I introduce students to some quite complex philosophical ideas about ethics, such as cognitivism, non-cognitivism, cultural relativism, consequentionalism, and non-consequentionalism. Whilst they find these ideas challenging, I believe it is important to show students that public relations' ethical ideas are connected to historical academic discussions about what is right and wrong and how such principles are navigated and agreed upon by societies and cultures.

Q: How does your professional background help you with teaching ethics?

Using specific examples, case studies and scenarios is a great way to bring the notion of ethics and ethical decision-making to life for students. I certainly take the opportunity to share stories about decisions I have had to make during my professional life and I think this helps students to realise that ethics are a serious business, which have personal and professional consequences. This included choosing not to work for particular clients, and on the other hand undertaking unpaid or *pro bono* work for others. I then use practical, real-life scenarios to get students to debate the decisions they would make, given different sets of circumstances. Overall critical thinking is key: students who are often uncritical about relevant ideas on arrival need to become conscious of the power of PR – for good and for ill [Rees shares with the authors the view that PR is inherently *amoral* and that its techniques can be used for any purpose] – and have the confidence to contest the thoughts of others.

Q: How do you find students respond to teaching about ethics?

I find that modern-day students are generally very interested in concepts and ideas about ethics, particularly if it is addressed in terms of decision-making, who they might work for, and notions of social responsibility. They are acutely aware of the impact human and organisational activity is having both on the natural environment, but also in terms of the impact on people. They are keen to be part of a future which finds solutions to society's problems, but they are also motivated and want to find good, generally well-paid jobs. I find they have very rarely considered that some professional communications programmes might be counter to their own values and beliefs and they enjoy being challenged on this.

Q: What about the relevance of such theories for students coming from different cultures?

What is particularly appealing about twenty-first-century university teaching is that most lecture rooms these days are filled with a variety of students from different countries and cultures. This makes for fascinating and insightful discussions about culture and ethics. Interestingly when we debate scenarios in class, students often come up with different solutions and opinions, depending on where they come from. However, I often start off with an exercise where students discuss in small groups their own sets of values and beliefs and they are often amazed that their fundamental beliefs about human behavioural norms are often the same. Nonetheless, there are different attitudes and expectations – discovering and debating these are enriching. The important thing is to challenge students and open their minds up to the consciousness that they can make choices.

Q: Where's it all heading?

I think we are facing some fascinating times with regard to public relations ethics for two reasons. Firstly, the growing social consciousness about corporate social responsibility is ensuring that most organisations, whether commercial, governmental or not-for-profit, are being challenged about the way the behaviour of their organisation and their employees affect the planet and the human population. Secondly, the rise of social and digitally empowered media has given voice to this social consciousness and forced organisations to respond in real time to concerns. This means that the next generation of young public relations executives has to be ready to understand and respond to ethical challenges. They need to be empowered and confident enough to act responsibly when in communications roles and to challenge, if necessary, entrenched views about organisational behaviour. This means we have to educate them to understand the principles and practice of public relations ethics, but we also have to facilitate confidence and resilience in our future generation to enable them to act appropriately when facing difficult choices.

Summary

As an emerging academic discipline PR has sought to create its own body of theory. This in part represents an attempt at self-justification, given the scepticism with which the subject is often viewed in universities. PR academics understandably want higher salaries, better job titles and improved status. It is not altogether clear how far such theorising is based on the realities of PR work – and how far it is useful to practitioners.

Questions

1. What are some of the main academic approaches to the study of PR ethics?
2. How valid and realistic are these when considering the day-to-day practice of PR?
3. How far does academic theory take into account different cultures and international differences?

Notes

1 Bernays, Edward L., *Propaganda* (New York: Horace Liveright, 1928).
2 L'Etang, Jacquie, McKie, David, Snow, Nancy and Xifra, Jordi (eds) *The Routledge Handbook of Critical Public Relations* (London: Routledge, 2016), p. 268.
3 Morris, Trevor and Goldsworthy, Simon, *PR – A Persuasive Industry: Spin, Public Relations and the Shaping of the Modern Media* (Basingstoke: Palgrave 2008), p. 101.
4 Parsons Patricia, *Ethics in Public Relations* (London: Kogan Page, 2008).

5 Ibid., p. 98.
6 Fawkes, Johanna, *Public Relations Ethics and Professionalism: The Shadow of Excellence* (London: Routledge, 2017), p. 15.
7 Bivins, Tom, *Mixed Media: Moral Distinctions in Advertising, Public Relations, and Journalism* (London: Routledge 2018), pp. 96–98.
8 Moloney, Kevin, and McKie, David, 'Radical turns in PR theorisation', in Jacquie L'Etang, David McKie, Nancy Snow, and Jordi Xifra (eds), *The Routledge Handbook of Critical Public Relations* (London: Routledge, 2016), p. 154.
9 Fitzpatrick, Kathy and Bronstein, Carolyn (eds) *Ethics in Public Relations: Responsible Advocacy* (London: Sage, 2006).
10 Ibid, pp. ix–x.
11 Bivins, op. cit., p. 196.
12 Quoted in Morris, Trevor, and Goldsworthy, Simon, *PR Today: The Authoritative Guide to Public Relations* (Basingstoke: Palgrave, 2016), p. 21.
13 Burt, Tim, *Dark Art: The Changing Face of Public Relations* (London: Elliott and Thompson, 2012), p. 121.
14 Tsetsura, Katerina, 'Guanxi, Gift-Giving, or Bribery: Ethical Considerations of Paid News in China', *Public Relations Journal*, col. 9, no. 2 (Summer 2015).
15 Details of these books can be found in the Appendix.

Chapter 4

PR's Own Codes of Ethics

Like any occupation which takes itself seriously – and indeed occasionally has aspirations to be considered a profession in the fullest sense of the word – PR has generated its own codes of ethics, intended to set out what is expected of practitioners. There are now many such codes, as PR bodies in most countries have adopted their own versions, and there are also international codes – although the content usually overlaps. Existing and would-be practitioners need to know what such codes have to say, even if they leave quite a lot to interpretation.

In this chapter we look at:

*   What a typical international PR code of ethics says, and how it can be applied to day-to-day realities.
*   How far PR's codes of ethics can be enforced.
*   How these codes relate to wider thinking about ethics.
*   How far PR can – or indeed should – become a profession, comparable to law, medicine or accountancy.

The numerous public relations bodies around the world – most countries have them – have generated their own codes of ethics – and there are also specialist codes for particular areas of PR work (see Chapters 7 and 8). In practice, through individual membership and/or through their agency or in-house PR department's membership of a PR trade body, a large proportion of PR practitioners have signed up to such codes – often more than one. The detailed content of such codes varies, although they have common themes. It is worth bearing in mind that as more and more PR is conducted across borders, practitioners also have to familiarise themselves with different ethical notions in different societies. What may seem to be in keeping with the public interest and individual dignity at home can look very different in another country.

Rather than focus on one country, we have taken one general example, the International Public Relations Association (IPRA, www.ipra.org) and looked at the current Code of Conduct, adopted in 2011, which represents the outcome of prolonged deliberation within this body, consolidating its 1961 Code of Venice, the 1965 Code of Athens and the 2007 Code of Brussels. It is available in 31 languages with the following preamble:

> Throughout its existence IPRA has always sought to provide intellectual leadership for the public relations profession.
>
> A key part of this has been the development of a number of Codes and Charters seeking to provide an ethical framework for the activities of the profession. Upon joining IPRA all members undertake to uphold these Codes and in doing so benefit from the ethical climate that they create.
>
> In 2011 these Codes were consolidated into a single document updated to reflect the age in which we now live.[1]

We have paraphrased the Code's points, adding our own commentary on their implications.

We have also interspersed some points from another international organisation, the International Communications Consultants Organisation (ICCO) (iccopr.com), which brings together PR associations from some 66 countries around the world, themselves representing over 3,000 PR firms. Their guidelines are laid out in the Stockholm Charter.

The IPRA's Code of Conduct

Observe the principles of the UN Charter and the Universal Declaration of Human Rights

This may sound praiseworthy and unexceptional and takes us back to the foundations of ethical thought discussed in Chapter 1. PR is hardly alone in citing the UN Charter and the Universal Declaration of Human Rights as a basis for judging what is permissible behaviour, not least because the United Nations, by bringing together just about all the world's governments, has a strong claim to be the world's most authoritative body.

In reality, much of what is covered by such documents is already enshrined in the laws of most countries – and PR people are just as much subject to the law as anyone else, so these are to a large extent areas where PR has no discretion and are not simply ethical matters. The Declaration's broader principles concerning freedom of thought and expression, especially through the media, are of course particularly relevant to public relations – after all, PR only exists in the form we know it because of the media's freedom to decide what they cover and how they cover it. Nevertheless the principles are themselves open to interpretation: in practice, all societies accept restrictions on freedom of expression, for example, relating to privacy, commercial confidentiality, incitement to violence and hatred, defamation, national security and obscenity, but exactly where such boundaries lie is ever-changing, making it an example of how deontology or rules-based ethics are tempered by the relativism described in Chapter 1.

Amid these shifting sands, and over and above obeying the law, it is usually counterproductive for PR people to flout the accepted rules of the community in which they operate (not least because it makes it difficult to find other people prepared to work with or for you in future), so, for pragmatic as well as ethical reasons, a knowledge of what is and is not considered acceptable is important (Box 4.1). This is one reason why, when operating internationally, local PR experience is so often crucial.

Box 4.1 PR and the Open Society

The ICCO's Stockholm Charter expresses broadly similar thinking to the IPRA:

> An open society, freedom of speech and a free press create the context for the profession of PR. Consultants operate within the scope of this open society. They comply with its rules and they work with clients that share the same approach.

Act with honesty and integrity at all times so as to secure and retain the confidence of those with whom the practitioner comes into contact.

Take all reasonable steps to ensure the truth and accuracy of all information provided.

Make every effort to not intentionally disseminate false or misleading information, exercise proper care to avoid doing so unintentionally and correct any such act promptly.

These clauses referring to truth and honesty might seem simple and uncontroversial at first glance, but need to be stressed as they lie close to the heart of the ethical debate about PR. They relate to ethics but also have practical implications, as passing on untrustworthy information can be counterproductive. If it comes to be known that a PR person is not a source of reliable information, then journalists and others will look elsewhere for facts and comment. Providing accurate information is important, but the key word in the Code is 'reasonable'. For more discussion of how this works in practice, see pp. 113–119.

The issue continues to be hotly contested – not least because it is seen as having a critical bearing on the reputation of PR. Unlike many of the ethical issues outlined in this chapter, it directly concerns PR's relationship with journalists. In 2007, following a major debate in London organised by us and sponsored by *PRWeek* magazine, the audience – made up of PR practitioners and students – voted by a small majority that PR people did not have a duty to tell the truth. When we restaged the debate at the Sorbonne in Paris, the vote went the same way – but much more decisively. One irony was that while many PR practitioners were prepared to vote discreetly with the majority, we had much more difficulty getting PR people to speak in the debate and admit publicly to the need, on occasion, to tell lies (Box 4.2). Nor do these dilemmas only apply to relations with the outside world. A senior internal communications person might be aware of possible redundancies long before they become general knowledge, but might be under instructions to deny that they might take place if asked. Refusing to comment could simply lead to even more suspicion.

Box 4.2 PR and Telling the Truth

The ICCO's Stockholm Charter states:

> PR consultancies should not knowingly mislead an audience about factual information or about the interests a client represents. Consultancies must make their best efforts to strive for accuracy.

Seek to establish the moral, cultural and intellectual conditions for dialogue, and recognise the rights of all parties involved to state their case and express their views.

In many ways, this clause overlaps with the praiseworthy but rather general and vague principles of the Universal Declaration of Human Rights. However, while PR people should certainly respect the rights of others to express their views, it is surely naïve or unrealistic to expect them to play a decisive role in establishing conditions for dialogue: that is for others, not least the media, to do.

For example, it is not feasible for PR people to insist that journalists contact their opponents or to help them to do so – and PR's paymasters would not thank them for acting in that way. PR people seek to put across the views of those they serve as effectively as possible, not help those whom they oppose to argue their case. In practice, since today almost all everyone uses PR, it is normally possible for the media to seek out different views by contacting a range of PR people themselves, and this is standard practice for journalists who should be perfectly capable of seeking out alternative voices. In any case, few of us think that everyone has the right to state their case – what about extremists, racists and others who are deemed to be inciting hatred? Views on what is acceptable vary.

> *Be open and transparent in declaring their name, organisation and the interest they represent.*

In most cases, this requirement will be straightforward. Declaring personal and organisational names is simple enough, and other than for reasons of safety or security, there should be little reason not to state them. The difficulty really arises over the vaguer notion of 'interest'. All organisations can have a wide range of interests, financial and otherwise. Exactly how open should PR people be? Organisations usually have many stakeholders. Charities may campaign for worthy causes, but may be heavily dependent on government funding or particular wealthy donors – a clear 'interest'. Controversial businesses often come together with others in their sector to form what are often called 'front groups' (see Box 4.7 on p. 60). Today all businesses have a stake in the climate change debate, but identifying exactly what those interests are can be difficult – what are the environmental policies of all their suppliers, and how far do they make use of aviation and independent road transport, to give just some examples? To what extent is it practicable for PR people to give a full account of the interests they represent?

> *Avoid any professional conflicts of interest and disclose such conflicts to affected parties when they occur.*

This generally accepted principle is one PR shares with the advertising industry. It would clearly be difficult – if not impossible – for a PR practitioner to do their utmost for two rivals, and there would be a risk of sensitive information passing into the wrong hands. Historically, both PR consultancies and advertising agencies have resigned profitable accounts in order to take on even more lucrative business for rivals. Indeed, one reason the big international marketing services groups such as Omnicom or WPP include more than one PR consultancy or advertising firm is so that they can serve competing businesses. Since it is hard to hide the identity of clients (and publishing one's client list is often a requirement), this principle is generally adhered to. Some larger agencies think that they can cater for competing clients by setting up wholly separate teams to serve them, although at the very least the clients concerned should be informed. Problems may arise if the conflict of interest is not obvious, or the competition is indirect (representing fossil fuel and renewable energy firms simultaneously, for example). Here common sense and a sense of judgement are required, while a degree of transparency enables clients to form their own judgement on whether there's a conflict of interest and hence to decide whether they're happy with the arrangement (see Box 4.3 and Box 4.4).

Box 4.3 Right or Wrong?

In his memoirs, *Right or Wrong*, Lord Tim Bell describes being encouraged by a prominent businessman whom he was advising to act simultaneously for him and the company he was hoping to acquire in a major takeover battle:

> He was hoping, of course, that I would be able and willing to keep him informed of what they were doing that might thwart his takeover bid. It's neither the first nor the last time in my life when I've worked on both sides of an argument.[2]

Box 4.4 PR and Conflicting Interests

The ICCO Stockholm Charter states:

> PR consultancies may not have interests that might compromise their role as independent consultants. They should approach their clients with objectivity in order to help the client adopt the optimum communications strategy and behaviour.
> Consultancies may represent clients with conflicting interests. Work may not start for a conflicting interest without the current client first being offered the opportunity to exercise the rights under any contract between them and the consultancy.

Honour confidential information.

Confidentiality is an important feature of most professional codes (Box 4.5) and goes well beyond PR – it is, for example, what we expect of doctors or lawyers when we turn to them for professional advice. PR people cannot expect clients or employers to speak to them frankly about what are often sensitive matters, or discuss risky new ideas which may be ultimately rejected, unless they know their confidence will be respected. However, an issue might arise if there were legal or regulatory reasons for revealing what a client or employer is doing, or planning to do – or if the PR practitioner felt that it conflicted with another part of the Code (for example, the Universal Declaration on Human Rights – see above), perhaps because of potential harm to the public interest. More generally, there is always going to be a potential conflict between, on the one hand, legitimate concerns about confidentiality and privacy and, on the other, contemporary ideals of transparency; in practice, no organisation can afford to be fully transparent but there's no agreed way to draw the line.

Box 4.5 PR and Trust

The ICCO Stockholm Charter states:

> Trust is at the heart of the relationship between a client and a PR consultancy. Information that has been provided in confidence by a client and that is not publicly known should not be shared with other parties without the consent of the client.

Not obtain information by deceptive or dishonest means.

Once again, this might seem straightforward, and in some cases would also be illegal. However, as we have seen, it should be borne in mind that investigative journalists may be quite prepared to use deception to acquire information if they feel the potential story merits it – and that they justify this in terms of the greater good: the public interest. Activists may also use deception as they seek to expose the wrongdoings of companies, for example, by posing as ordinary members of the public or becoming employees – and that is in itself a form of PR for their cause. If that is deemed to be ethical, would it always be illegitimate for a commercial PR person to do the equivalent – perhaps by posing as an activist to attend events – if they felt it was for the greater good and that thereby they could gather information which would protect their organisation (and the livelihoods of its employees) from unjustified attacks? See Box 4.6 on the ethics of gathering information.

Box 4.6 Bayer and Allegations of Unethical Behaviour

In 2019, a PR agency, Fleishman Hillard, working for the agro-chemicals company Monsanto, was revealed to be behind a dossier containing details of critics of chemicals and genetically modified crops. French officials were investigating possible illegality as national law apparently prohibits the creation of databases 'revealing the political and philosophical opinions of a person without their consent'. Bayer, Monsanto's parent company apologised, saying, 'This is not the way Bayer seeks dialogue with society and stakeholders' and dropped the PR firm.

Without commenting on the legal position, it is easy to see why this caused embarrassment to Bayer, not least because individuals in the dossier included well-known figures in French public life. It looked like an intrusive and sinister use of corporate power. Understandably the company undertook a swift climb-down and therefore minimised the adverse publicity.

However, it is less clear how far such behaviour is unethical. While it might be immoral and potentially illegal to obtain such information by clandestine means, many of us, and public figures especially, leave a trail of publicly available evidence of our views on a range of issues. Is it not legitimate to research that? It's certainly something many of us do informally and is a standard practice in journalism, not to mention academia. One way of testing the general validity of such ideas is to turn them round, perhaps against one's natural sympathies. What if an environmentalist group was compiling a dossier on public statements made by champions of genetically modified crops?[3]

Not create or use any organisation to serve an announced cause but which actually serves an undisclosed interest.

Businesses often have an interest in issues which can affect their ability to carry on or develop their activities. This might include permission to build new plant, regulations affecting their workforce, environmental controls, or their ability to promote and sell controversial products.

Businesses have long realised that their voice in such debates will be undermined if they are seen simply to be furthering their commercial interests. To counter this, many business organisations have set up, or contribute towards, what are called *front groups* – business-sponsored lobbying groups which sometimes disguise (or do not publicise) their business links.

One of the key issues here is whether any deception is used. If an organisation is clear about how it is funded and controlled, it is for the media and others to take that into account. Certainly, the media should ask searching questions about every organisation which contributes to public debate: How many people does it represent? What are its decision-making processes? How is it funded? What are its qualifications for offering a view? Do its ideas make sense? Does it have any ulterior motives? Much of this information is normally available for commercial organisations, but the fact that the media place more trust in not-for-profit organisations makes it irresistible for some companies facing controversy to imitate them by adopting some of the characteristics of NGOs (even though NGOs' sources of funding and interests may themselves be worthy of closer examination).

However, while in the past there have been clear examples of what is called *astroturfing* (fake grassroots movements, Box 4.7), exposure of such practices seems to have led to a decline in their use – or perhaps they are just better concealed.

Box 4.7 Front Groups in Fact and Fiction

In the 1950s, faced with mounting evidence that cigarette smoking can cause cancer, the American tobacco industry sponsored the establishment of the Tobacco Industry Research Committee (TIRC), which later became the Committee for Tobacco Research. The TIRC hired Dr Clarence Little, a respected former managing director of the American Society for the Control of Cancer, as its director. The Committees focused on publicising inconclusive or contradictory information about the harmful effects of tobacco smoking, producing a booklet entitled 'A Scientific Perspective on the Cigarette Controversy' which was mailed to doctors, politicians and the media. However, despite a promise to sponsor independent research, less than 10 per cent of the two Committees' budget was spent on scientific projects.

Another important voice in the debate was the National Smokers' Alliance, which sought to protect the rights of smokers. Ostensibly a grassroots organisation bringing together millions of smokers from across America, it received millions of dollars from the tobacco giant Philip Morris.

These organisations illustrate how front groups can work – by claiming or implying academic or scientific expertise and independence (in the case of the Committees); or asserting that they represent the views of ordinary people (in the case of the Alliance, a classic 'Astroturf movement'). In all cases, front groups seek to put some distance between themselves and the business sector which funds them, while putting a positive gloss on the sector's activities, and playing down any problems. They choose their titles and their spokespeople carefully, and thereby hope to achieve greater credibility.

An excellent fictional example of this is the Academy of Tobacco Studies, for which the main character of Christopher Buckley's humorous novel (also a feature film), *Thank You for Smoking*,[4] Nick

Naylor, acts as spokesman (or *smokes*man). Buckley brilliantly satirises the world of front groups: Naylor's friends and acquaintances include spokespeople from the Society for the Humane Treatment of Calves (representing the veal industry); the Friends of Dolphins (formerly the Pacific Tuna Fisherman's Association); and the Land Enrichment Foundation (formerly the Coalition for the Responsible Disposal of Radioactive Waste).

For more on this, see also Robert Jackall and Janice M. Hirota's excellent *Image Makers: Advertising, Public Relations, and the Ethos of Advocacy.*[5]

Today PR people may face a particular temptation to pose as disinterested parties on social media and even when preparing entries on Wikipedia. The temptation arises because, by appearing to be ordinary members of the public, they have much more independent authority than company employees would have, while the nature of social media makes it easy to do. However, aside from issues of PR ethics, such practices are contrary to the dominant views of the online community and, if uncovered, may well cause outrage and adverse publicity. In many countries contributing to online media to promote a product without declaring an interest may also be illegal.

Not sell for profit to third parties copies of documents obtained from public authorities

A niche problem? Simply charging more for that which is available anyway (sometimes for free) sounds disreputable. However, in the lobbying and public affairs field, one of the services which many clients pay for is the monitoring of the work of countless, often obscure, decision-making bodies at local, national and international levels. This is time-consuming and painstaking work. Major companies, which are often affected by the decisions such bodies make, may find it cost effective to pay specialists with expertise in the machinery of government to keep an eye on such matters. Even if they cannot, or do not wish to, influence the particular decision, it may be important for them to have as much prior notice as possible. Charging a finder's fee for such a service seems perfectly reasonable – often in practice the public affairs company will simply provide a summary of what is going on.

Whilst providing professional services, not accept any form of payment in connection with those services from anyone other than the principal.

Not observing this would clearly create a conflict of interest. PR people often buy in services, such as research and expert technical advice, and must do so with the best interests of their client in mind.

Similarly, clients must know that their PR firm is serving their interests and not being tempted by payments – or indeed the prospect of payments or other benefits – from another source. However, organisations which are not competitors may sometimes collaborate on campaigns, and in such circumstances a PR company could work for two or more organisations on the same campaign. Sometimes it would be hard to say which client was benefiting more, but so long as the relationships and interests are open and above board, this does not seem in principle wrong. See Box 4.8 for a true case and two hypothetical situations.

Box 4.8 Real Life, and Two Hypothetical Situations

The late Lord Melchett, then a Director of Greenpeace, and 27 other Greenpeace activists appeared in court in the UK charged with criminal damage to a field of genetically modified maize. Melchett told the court he felt a 'strong moral obligation' to act as he did, although he was later acquitted.

Melchett later severed his connections with Greenpeace and undertook work for the corporate social responsibility practice of the PR giant Burson-Marsteller.[6]

Hypothetical Situation I

You work for The Explosive Vodka Company. In your own country the company is careful to abide by the regulations on promoting alcohol. These forbid portraying it in a glamorous way. The company is now entering new less regulated markets and is offering you a sizeable pay increase to manage the PR. The promotions they plan to use include highly sexualised images of young women and wet T-shirt competitions in night clubs. What do you do and why?

Hypothetical Situation 2

You are working for an environmental NGO which is strongly opposed to genetically modified foods. They plan to break into a warehouse belonging to a well-known supermarket chain and spray a consignment of GM food with paint. They want you to participate and help publicise this activity. What do you do and why?

Neither directly nor indirectly offer nor give any financial or other inducement to public representatives or the media, or other stakeholders.

Neither propose nor undertake any action which would constitute an improper influence on public representatives, the media, or other stakeholders.

Making payments or gifts to journalists or others in the media in return for coverage is traditionally a taboo area for PR people in countries such as the USA, the UK and Australia (see pp. 44–46). While journalists set great store by their independence and objectivity, PR people pride themselves on their ability to secure the right kind of coverage without money changing hands (this represents the traditional boundary line between PR and advertising, where content is paid for). However, there is ample evidence that in many societies corrupt practices do exist, and it is difficult for a lone practitioner to buck the trend. Anti-bribery legislation in the UK and other jurisdictions means this is not just a matter of ethics – individuals can potentially face criminal prosecution.

Within the same country, the approaches of different sectors of the PR industry may vary. In political or high-level corporate PR in most western democracies, the very notion of gifts for journalists – beyond meals, hospitality and entertainment (although of course these can become lavish and questionable in themselves) – may be unthinkable (it would, or should be, unthinkable for journalists as well). Nor is that restricted to cash or presents: most would consider the idea of media workers and their families being given privileged access to government services, such as healthcare, housing or education, outrageous. But in other areas of PR, accepted practice is different. Free holidays for journalists are a staple of travel PR, and free samples and gifts are often offered in fashion and lifestyle PR. Indeed, these and other valuable and sought-after perks have become essential elements of modern media production. While such benefits may not be explicitly tied to media coverage, it would be foolish to deny that the relationships thus cultivated (not least the prospects of future benefits) can help to tip the scales.

The treating of journalists in sectors such as fashion and lifestyle may involve giving them goods and services of considerable value but this tends to be regarded as socially acceptable, whereas if they were given a lesser amount in cash, it would be seen as blatant corruption (Box 4.9). Even if journalists are not 'bribed' in this sense, they can be, and are, provided with exclusive stories. These are valuable in their own right as they can lead to promotion and salary increases for the journalists involved. Similarly advertisers may exert direct or more subtle pressure over editorial coverage in the media outlets in which they advertise, a process in which PR can become involved.

Box 4.9 Allegations of Media Corruption in India

According to the Press Council of India:

> In recent years, corruption in the Indian media has gone way
> beyond the corruption of individual journalists and specific
> media organizations – from 'planting' information and views
> in lieu of favours received in cash or kind, to more institution-
> alized and organized forms of corruption wherein newspapers
> and television channels receive funds for publishing or broad-
> casting information in favour of particular individuals, corpo-
> rate entities, representatives of political parties and candidates
> contesting elections, that is sought to be disguised as 'news'.[7]

Beyond media relations, lobbying and public affairs tend to be in the
spotlight most often over suggestions of bribery and corruption. The relationships between protagonists in this field are private and subtle and it
is particularly hard to prove or disprove what influences decision-makers.
This is one of the reasons why lobbyists have their own codes of conduct
and – unlike most other areas of PR – are subject to specific regulation
(see Chapter 7).

Using the PR ethics map in Figure 4.1, consider the ethical issues for
each of the four groups on the map when related to:

1. manufacture of alcohol;
2. manufacture of arms;
3. manufacture of cheap clothing.

Sometimes it can be difficult to satisfy the conflicting ethical requirements of all 4 groups.

> *Not intentionally injure the professional reputation of another*
> *practitioner.*

This is clearly intended to stop unseemly attempts to undermine rivals
in a way which would run counter to the behaviour expected of a proper
profession and could damage the overall standing of the PR industry –
just as we would not normally expect one doctor to disparage another.
Of course, attacks on business rivals can circumvent this by using a little
subtlety: other people's ways of doing business can be belittled without
naming the practitioners concerned. It might also be argued that this
part of the Code is anti-competitive, serving the industry's own interests
and clashing with the injunction to respect the public interest: what if a

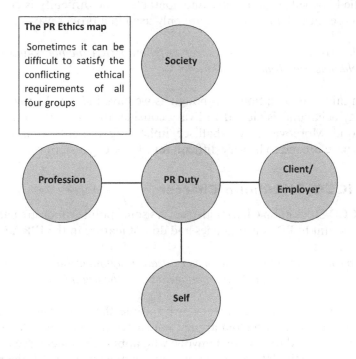

Figure 4.1 The PR ethics map.

PR practitioner felt that he or she could offer a better service, or that the work of another had serious shortcomings?

Not seek to secure another practitioner's client by deceptive means.

Again, this has much to do with PR's desire to achieve professional status, making it more similar to medicine or law than commerce. Most PR people would avoid doing this in too obvious a way – it would be unattractive and often counterproductive – but, as suggested above, the supplanting of rivals can be achieved in subtle ways that are hard to stop, and the term 'deceptive' is open to interpretation. Once again, it could be argued that this restriction is more about protecting the interests of the PR industry than the public interest: it is in the interests of users of PR to be made fully aware of the options available to them and then to choose.

When employing personnel from public authorities or competitors, take care to follow the rules and confidentiality requirements of those organisations.

This seems self-explanatory and hard to argue with – unless public interest arguments come into it. Of course, PR people are often hired for their specific knowledge, experience and contacts – the difficulty is ensuring that those special qualifications are only used in a proper way.

> *Observe this Code with respect to fellow IPRA members and public relations practitioners worldwide.*

Again this is unexceptional, although as we have indicated above, often the way behaviour is viewed will vary considerably in different parts of the world. Moreover, as we shall see, upholding and enforcing codes of ethics have proved to be very difficult for all PR organisations.

The ICCO Stockholm Charter

The ICCO Stockholm Charter also covers some points which are particularly relevant to PR consultancies and do not feature in the IPRA Code:

> *Consultancies may refuse or accept an assignment based on the personal opinions of the firm's management or the organisation's focus.*

This sounds sensible – even those who argue that everyone is entitled to PR representation seldom argue the reverse, namely, that PR people should be obliged to represent anyone who approaches them (see below). However, this stipulation only applies at a management level: the rights of individual employees are not spelt out. Clearly consultancies may offer some leeway for employees with strongly held views – but this has to be balanced against the practical needs of the business.

> *Consultancies must work with clients to establish clear expectations in advance about the output of their efforts. They must define specific goals and then work to deliver on their promises. Consultancies must not offer guarantees which are not supportable or which compromise the integrity of the channels of communication.*

Understandably there can be a temptation for PR consultancies to over-promise, especially when seeking to win or retain business. This point in the ICCO Charter makes clear the ethical dangers of such an approach: first, the client has the right to the realistic, expert, professional advice of their PR consultants; and, second, unrealistic promises may tempt PR practitioners to 'compromise the integrity of the channels of communication'.

Ethical Codes and Digital Communication

While most of the points above apply equally to digital media and communication via social media, digital and social media have created their own ethical challenges. The ICCO recommends the following principles based on the 'Online Code of Conduct' of the Austrian Ethics Council for Public Relations (*PR Ethik Rat*):[8]

1. Fairness – Use the power of communication with care.
2. Respect – Respect the users' personalities and opinions.
3. Responsibility – Assume responsibility for the content of a statement as a communicator.
4. Moderation – Define clear rules for discourse.
5. Clarity – Define rules and guidelines as orientation for the employees of a company.
6. Transparency – Disclose role as communicator and the motivation.
7. Courtesy – Use the right tone.
8. Privacy – Treat personal matters personally, and confidential matters as confidential.

These guidelines are a response to the rapidly changing media landscape. One of the underlying ethical challenges posed by online and social media to PR is that practitioners now have easy, direct and instantaneous means of communicating with their publics. Hitherto most of their messages were filtered by the media through journalists and editors who had their own professional ethics, and took responsibility for what the public actually saw and heard. Paid-for messages were the responsibility of advertising agencies.

Today, PR people operating via digital media are increasingly in the front line. They are often called upon to produce large amounts of content for direct public consumption, and to do so very quickly. They do so while working alongside an enormous number of other people – real or potential competitors, including advertising and digital marketing practitioners – who are trying to do the same thing. Historically, PR people have been unaccustomed to the rules and regulations which have long governed advertising, and so are operating in ethically less familiar territory. Some of the specific issues identified in the Code documents are as follows:

• *Labelling.* Clearly paid-for online content needs to be identified as such, as it constitutes advertising. In most jurisdictions that we know of, this is actually a legal requirement. But given the enormous volumes of online promotion, these laws are not always easy to enforce, and in any case there is an obvious temptation to make product endorsements appear spontaneous and genuine. As this Code makes clear, there is an important ethical issue at stake and identifying promotional work as such is important – even if the actual payment or benefit may be indirect or in kind (for example, sample goods supplied to a popular blogger or influencer).

- *Author transparency.* For similar reasons to the previous point, when posting online, actual names should be used – and, where appropriate, the identity of the third party principal who is paying for the communication.
- *Online editorial.* The possibilities of online communication make it easier than ever for organisations to create online journalistic material. If they do so, it should comply with journalistic principles such as accuracy and balance and making a distinction between news and views. Similar principles apply to pictures. So, for example, product reviews should comply with these principles and be independent and objective unless they are advertisements and clearly labelled as such. In practice, it is surely quite difficult for an organisation which is paying for the content to live up to these ideals.
- *Fairness and respectfulness.* Practitioners should avoid denigration, humiliation and false assertions. As PR people can now speak directly to their publics, it can be tempting to be disrespectful, and to do so without due thought. Thus, the new opportunity clearly creates a challenge. However, people will never quite agree on where the line between inappropriate and disrespectful words and robust, hard-hitting communication lies, not least in the world of politics.
- *Corporate responsibility.* Individuals create online content, and can do so very quickly and without editorial control, but the corporation remains responsible for the content its employees and contractors, including PR firms, create. Hence organisations need their own guidelines or netiquette.

Box 4.10 presents the story of how one firm used Big Data for its own purposes.

Box 4.10 *The Great Hack*: Political Campaigning in the Era of Social Media

The (2019) Netflix documentary *The Great Hack* focuses on the work of Cambridge Analytica, a political consulting firm, and its role in the Brexit campaign in the UK's EU referendum in 2016. The company ceased operations in 2018, but during its five-year life was involved in elections in countries as diverse as the USA (where they were involved in Donald Trump's successful campaign for the presidency), Australia, India and Kenya, running some ten campaigns around the world each year.

The Great Hack's starting point is that social media have made it possible to accumulate vast amounts of data – 'Big Data' – about almost all individuals based on the information we voluntarily, and perhaps unwittingly, supply when using Facebook and similar companies. Cambridge Analytica was to claim that, at the time of the 2016 presidential election, it had 5,000 data points on every US voter, and during the documentary, data is described as the most valuable asset on Earth. The company was secretly recorded arguing that it could use this information to build psychological profiles of millions of individuals, and then target them with personalised communications designed to influence their voting behaviour. The suggestion is clear: given the narrow victory for the Leave campaign in the UK in 2016, and the even narrower victory for the Trump campaign later the same year, this use of Big Data might have been enough to determine these important national votes. The former Cambridge Analytica employee Chris Wylie who spoke out against the company describes it as a 'full service propaganda machine'. The Brexit campaign is described as a petri-dish for the Trump campaign.

Complex legal issues are at stake here, not least because of differing approaches in different jurisdictions and the struggle of legal systems to catch up with changes in the media and technology. These remain to be fully examined. Clearly anyone using Big Data needs to be aware of the legal position and know when to seek advice. However, our particular concern here is with the ethical issues. These are perhaps more complex than the documentary allows.

Political campaigning is, and always has been, a brutal business (see pp. 157–161). One might add it to the list of when 'all's fair', alongside love and war. It is far more negative and personality laden than almost all commercial campaigns, not least because, unlike in most business scenarios, there are often no prizes for coming second: the runner-up in a US presidential election normally fades into relative obscurity, while the number two brands in most business sectors usually perform quite respectably. Political communicators have always tried to find out what they can about their target audiences and tailor their messages accordingly. New media have created new possibilities for doing this – but that has always been the case as communications have evolved. In the end, there are legal limits to what is allowed – again, this is not new – and these have been and are being tested in the case of Cambridge Analytica. But are there ethical issues about what is permissible even if one is obeying the law?

Although all sides in political campaigns do all kinds of things, there is a temptation to highlight one's opponents' ruthlessness, particularly if one has lost, and gloss over one's own tactics. It is noteworthy that one of the key players at Cambridge Analytica at the time of Brexit, Brittany Kaiser, had formerly worked for Barack Obama's successful presidential campaign, focusing on exploiting

Facebook to get Obama elected. It was that experience that seems to have got her the job in London. Obama's campaigning is briefly referred to – it was often seen as praiseworthy for its cutting-edge use of social media, although the potentially intrusive use of Big Data and targeting are fundamental to all social media campaigns.

The potentially scary notion of psychological manipulation always requires some scrutiny. It is a notion which certainly suited Cambridge Analytica – the documentary makes it clear that this was part of their sales pitch, positioning them as all-but -omnipotent and able to determine election results. Paradoxically, the same notion suits their critics – it sounds sinister, the antithesis of rational discourse and debate. But do not all campaigns – including the ones we support – use what could be called 'psychological manipulation'? Is that not what slogans and rhetoric are for? Is it only illegitimate if we oppose the cause?

Cambridge Analytica were surely overclaiming when they were selling their services – hyping your capabilities is not unusual in the PR world. In a polarised political environment, it is tempting to blame democratic results that one struggles to understand on such techniques. It is much easier to blame a company such as Cambridge Analytica than to attack millions of one's fellow citizens for making decisions one deplores. However, such an approach is also rather patronising and elitist. It implies that there is little scope for free will and that such techniques can work on some people but not on others – critics of companies such as Cambridge Analytica always seem to assume that *they* are immune to such persuasive techniques.

All political campaigners use similar techniques to those described in *The Great Hack* – and not a few brush up against what is legally permissible, which is why there are prosecutions for electoral matters in many countries. Traditionally PR people mainly operated via traditional mass media – print and broadcast – but today their ability to reach people directly via social media means that all the legal and ethical challenges of using Big Data, new terrain for PR practitioners, are something they have to deal with more and more – and not just in political campaigns.

Two footnotes to the Cambridge Analytica saga.

In the documentary, a former senior executive at the company claims that as the company entered its terminal crisis, facing '35,000' overwhelmingly hostile media stories a day, it couldn't find a PR firm prepared to help them. Was this because what they had done was deemed indefensible, or did PR firms wish to avoid tarnishing their own reputations – or was it a bit of both?

In the wake of this and other negative publicity, Facebook itself decided to hire the former British Deputy Prime Minister – and keen opponent of Brexit – Sir Nick Clegg to oversee its communications efforts.

Problems with Enforcing Codes of PR Ethics

There are many codes of PR ethics and they are occasionally revised and added to. However, it has proved very difficult to enforce such codes. There are various reasons for this.

One major problem for any would-be PR regulators is that much of the most controversial and important PR work takes place behind the scenes and involves private conversations and meetings between protagonists who know each other well. The process can be a subtle one, with many things hinted at and left unsaid. Moreover, journalists have a long tradition of protecting their sources. There is therefore seldom any documentation to prove or disprove what exactly happened – which makes public relations different from many other walks of life, where people sign off on important decisions. This means it is peculiarly difficult to prove beyond doubt that someone has breached a PR code. So PR scandals often revolve around PR people's conversations being tape-recorded without their knowledge (Box 4.11); misunderstandings about whether they were speaking off the record to journalists; or their failure to realise that emails and social media, despite their convenience as a means of communication, leave a permanent record. In contrast, it is much rarer for the more public face of PR – press releases and press conferences – to be called into question on ethical grounds.

Box 4.11 PR Practitioners Can Be Caught Out

In the UK, the Queen's daughter-in-law, Sophie Wessex, who ran a PR consultancy, was forced to step down after an embarrassing conversation with a newspaper journalist posing as a potential client was tape-recorded and published (and, for the same reason, her business partner became a rare example of someone who was forced to leave the UK's Institute of Public Relations).

Another problem is that membership of PR organisations in nearly all countries is voluntary. In most societies anyone is free to practise PR (whether they will succeed is of course quite another matter), and organisations of all kinds are free to employ whomsoever they wish to carry out public relations duties; quite often they hire people without PR backgrounds (most typically, ex-journalists). This openness is likely to remain the case and is arguably one of PR's positive characteristics, enabling the industry to grow and adapt itself to changing circumstances by taking on talented individuals with a range of experience.

Attempts to impose statutory regulation would not only be restrictive and undermine PR's essential dynamism but would be difficult to put into practice (Box 4.12). What exactly would be regulated? There is no universally accepted definition of public relations and those which are in widest circulation are both general and vague (for example, saying PR is about reputation management) and hence would not be of much value to a regulator. Moreover the duties of PR people can overlap with those of other communication and management disciplines.

Box 4.12 The Public Relations Society of America

One of the world's largest public relations bodies, the Public Relations Society of America (PRSA), the main industry body for the world's largest single PR market, has a Code of Ethics which members pledge to uphold. However, after decades of attempting to enforce the Code, in 2000, after much debate, the Society abandoned enforcement, while retaining the right 'to bar from membership or expel from the Society any individual who has been or is sanctioned by a government agency or convicted in a court of law of an action that is in violation of the code'. As the PRSA said at the time:

> The mission of the Board of Ethics and Professional Standards has now been substantially altered to focus primarily on education and training, collaborating with other major professional societies, and serving in an advisory role to the Board when considering ethical matters of major importance.[9]

Box 4.13 and Box 4.14 present the story of the downfall of Bell Pottinger and the PRCA's response.

Box 4.13 The Strange Case of Bell Pottinger's Downfall

A rare example of disciplinary action against a major PR firm: a "smelly" piece of business in South Africa and the strange case of Bell Pottinger's downfall

PR people normally like to stay out of the headlines, but September 2017 witnessed an unsought-for exception to the rule. Bell

Pottinger, one of London's highest profile PR firms, was thrown out of the Public Relations and Communications Association and almost simultaneously the business collapsed, leaving its employees out of work and its shareholders out of pocket. The events made headline news, and not just in the UK: one newspaper's headline summed it up: 'Bell Rottinger'. Later on, as the dust settled, the now extinct PR firm was the subject of a lengthy article by Ed Caesar in *The New Yorker* magazine, entitled 'The reputation-laundering firm that ruined its own reputation'.[10] What follows draws upon Caesar's work, as well as the other media coverage and the recollections of people who worked there. What had happened?

Bell Pottinger had been around for almost 20 years at the time of its demise (although it could trace its origins to the earlier firm Lowe Bell, founded in 1985), and, until just before the end, its co-founder, Lord Tim Bell, played a key role. Bell, whose PR career dated back to the 1980s, when he famously advised UK Prime Minister Margaret Thatcher, had worked for a range of highly controversial clients, including the Pinochet Foundation, named after the former Chilean military ruler; Alexander Lukashenko, the dictator ruling Belarus; Asma Al-Assad, the wife of the Syrian president Bashar Al-Assad; and government bodies in Bahrain. Ironically, in view of the fate that was to befall the firm he founded, he was particularly proud of having worked for the then South African President and Nobel Peace Prize laureate F. W. de Klerk at the time when de Klerk orchestrated South Africa's peaceful transition from apartheid to multi-racial democracy. In 2011, senior Bell Pottinger executives – but not Bell personally – triggered a public scandal when they were secretly recorded expressing a potential willingness to act for state interests in Uzbekistan.

According to Caesar, PR competitors, when debating whether to take on a questionable client, used to joke that the answer was either 'Yes', 'No', or 'one for Bell Pottinger'. To a substantial extent, Bell's success and high profile were built upon his willingness to undertake such work and to do so enthusiastically: for decades his firm became a go-to destination for a certain kind of regime or business interest with a troubled reputation – regimes and businesses which were happy to pay handsomely for his help. When he died in August 2019 at the age of 77, he was the subject of lengthy obituaries which detailed many of the controversies in which he was involved.

In 2012, Bell Pottinger became a private company, taking on substantial bank debt, but continued to pay its most senior people large salaries. The company was naturally anxious to secure new, lucrative business.

It was against this background that four Bell Pottinger employees, including Bell, flew to South Africa in January 2016 to meet a potential client – a company controlled by the three Gupta brothers, some of the country's top businessmen, with interests spanning the economy, from minerals to media. The introduction was made by Chris Geoghegan, a UK-based businessman. who was to receive a monthly fee in return. His daughter, Victoria Geoghegan, a Bell Pottinger employee, went on to run the account.

The Gupta brothers had close ties to the South African President, Jacob Zuma – indeed, three members of his family had worked for Gupta-owned businesses. The previous year there had been large protests against Zuma and the Guptas had been accused of running a shadow government. The term 'Zupta' came to be used to describe the relationship.

At the meeting with Bell Pottinger, Tony Gupta said that they were seeking a PR campaign which would highlight the damaging role of South Africa's large white-owned corporations. The Guptas would then be recast as outsiders who were countering white supremacy. Competing against another PR firm, Bell Pottinger won the business – for a fee of $130,000 a month for a trial period, a useful addition to the company's revenue stream.

Although Bell Pottinger's work for the Guptas included more routine PR duties, they went on to spread articles, cartoons and social media posts covertly, popularising the term 'white monopoly capital' and implying that the Guptas' opponents were sustaining the racist economic system left over from the apartheid era – 'economic apartheid'. One cartoon, for example, depicted fat, wealthy-looking white people feasting while malnourished black people ate crumbs from the floor. A South African newspaper editor claimed that 'Bell Pottinger literally stole the page from Goebbels and applied it to twenty-first century South Africa'.

Bell Pottinger's work for the Guptas soon became controversial. As early as March 2016, a South African bank ended its contract with Bell Pottinger on account of it – and indeed the top accountancy and consultancy group KPMG and other banks began to sever their ties with the Guptas themselves. Another important and long-standing Bell Pottinger client was Richemont, the Swiss-based luxury goods business controlled by Johann Rupert, the second richest man in South Africa. Caesar suggests that Rupert bore a physical resemblance to one of the white men in the cartoon described above. Richemont was to drop Bell Pottinger as its PR agency.

Bell claimed that he wished to stop working for the Guptas but was unable to get his way. He resigned from Bell Pottinger in

August 2016, saying that he did so voluntarily, and cited the 'smelly' business as the reason for his departure. Former colleagues dispute how far that is the case. There were certainly other issues at stake. He retained financial links with the company which meant he retained some liability when Bell Pottinger finally collapsed.

Bell Pottinger did not finally resign the Gupta account until April 2017. In the meantime, there was a storm of protest. Bell Pottinger's activity was depicted as colonial, and #bellpottingermustfall became a popular hashtag. Bell Pottinger's Chief Executive was to commission a review of the account from a leading law firm, fire the executive directly responsible, and go on to issue an absolute apology for work that was 'inappropriate and offensive'.

In September 2017, the Public Relations and Communications Association, of which Bell Pottinger was a member firm, acted, making headline news as it expelled the agency, ruling that it could not reapply for five years, the harshest sanction it could apply. As Bell, now ensconced in a new PR firm which he had just set up, continued to attack Bell Pottinger, more clients – who themselves came under great pressure from activists – deserted the firm and it quickly became insolvent.

What conclusions can be drawn from this high profile case? At one level, it was an example of a PR body fearlessly taking prompt, decisive action against a prominent member – although the UK PR practitioner-turned-priest the Reverend George Pitcher likened it to 'a bunch of pimps throwing up their hands in horror at the moral turpitude of their highest-earning whore'. In that sense the exercise of exemplary discipline against its top UK-based member firm was good PR for the PRCA, the British-based trade body which now claims to be the world's largest PR professional organisation. However – like all PR firms – Bell Pottinger was not obliged to be a member of any PR body.

The final straw for the firm, as it would be for any agency, was the loss of more and more of its clients, finally rendering it insolvent. In theory at least, the clients could have withstood considerable activist pressure and chosen to remain with Bell Pottinger – how far the actions of the PRCA influenced their decisions is something that it is impossible to know for certain, although the moves to expel it certainly gave Bell Pottinger a great deal of unwelcome publicity. It is a good example of PR practitioners' need to ensure that their work is generally, if not universally, acceptable: it was perhaps also asking too much to expect clients to keep paying for PR services from a PR firm which itself had such a badly damaged reputation.

It is also the case that none of those involved at Bell Pottinger, including the most senior executives, were precluded from working in PR: they were able to – and many did – seek employment elsewhere or set up new agencies.

How exactly was Bell Pottinger at fault? The law firm which reviewed the account concluded that campaigning for economic emancipation was not illegitimate in itself, but extreme care was required, given the danger of giving offence. Given the volatile situation in South Africa, it is reasonable to argue that the consequences could be serious. Arguably the motives behind the campaign were impure – it was really about supporting the Guptas' interests rather than securing any public good – and the methods used were extreme.

However, as it happens, many critics of the prevailing system in South Africa have said similar things to those featured in the campaign messages – the term 'white monopoly capital' was already in use among academics. Ironically, Lord Bell, firmly associated with the right-wing in UK and indeed international politics, found that he and his then firm were singing from the same hymn-sheet as their traditional opponents – but, given its track record, Bell Pottinger could expect little support in such quarters as things went fatally wrong.

Box 4.14 The PRCA and the Expulsion of Bell Pottinger

Francis Ingham, Director General of the PRCA, comments on his organisation's expulsion of Bell Pottinger:

> We've expelled only two companies in the time I've been in the PRCA. Bell Pottinger and Fuel PR [see p. 120], and that's testimony to how rare these incidences of unethical behaviour are. And I would repeat what I've said before, that I think that expectations have moved on in a very positive way and things that were in the margins a decade ago have now vanished entirely and things that were the norm are now at the margins with people who are not our members. And as those expectations continue to rise, the margins will shrink even further.
>
> We've always said that PR is an incredibly powerful tool for good or for ill. The Bell Pottinger case showed the veracity of that statement, particularly in a social media setting. And at the heart of the PRCA professional charter is the duty to tell

the truth and not to stir up racial hatred. And sadly, Bell Pottinger fell short on both of those by quite a long way. And they paid the ultimate price for doing so.

It wasn't a matter of the client, it was a matter of the work they were doing for them. There can be very controversial clients and you're doing very boring work for them and that's fine. We would just say that you stand by the clients you work for so long as it's legal and adhere to our code of conduct.

I think our expulsion of Bell Pottinger was a turning point for the industry because it showed we have rigorous standards and we enforce them regardless of the risk of doing so, regardless of the financial cost of doing so and, frankly, regardless of the threats that were conveyed at the time both personally and corporately. And the very fact that on the day we expelled Bell Pottinger, 27 agencies applied to join the PRCA, shows that people have embraced the highest standards in the world, even when they see that opting to be governed by those standards can destroy the company. So that shows quite how firmly people in our industry believe in self-regulation and in embracing those high standards.

An alternative view of what happened from a senior PR industry insider:

Tim Bell doomed his own company when he signed up to the PRCA. And it was, I understand, his personal decision. Because they could never meet the code of conduct the PRCA had. Now, quite frankly, one might ask why the PRCA welcomed them as a member in the first place. Because certainly their reputation and probably the reality of their work, at the point they were admitted, should have made them ineligible to be a member of any organisation that believed in telling the truth. And some critics might say, looking at their actions, PRCA probably acted out of self-interest. Because if it hadn't expelled Bell Pottinger, it would have had a massive exodus of members from it and then complete destruction of belief that anything it said about ethics was true.

And some have said that the Director General of the PRCA showed a certain glee in the way that he enjoyed the demise of an agency and the loss of 300 people's livelihoods. You've also got to wonder, the people who confirmed the decision were the PRCA board. And they were the competitors of Bell Pottinger. They picked up more or less all of their staff. So did they have a self-interest in doing what they did? Quite possibly.

Is PR a 'Profession'?

According to the PRCA's PR and Communications Census 2019, 50 per cent of practitioners believe theirs is a profession, although that represented a fall from 56 per cent the previous year.[11]

In contrast, 42 per cent believed that PR is an industry – an increase from 35 per cent the previous years. Interestingly almost two-thirds of in-house employees and a clear majority of freelancers thought they worked in a profession, whereas a slim majority of agency PR people thought they worked in an industry – something with which only 28 per cent of in-house PRs agreed.

Younger PR practitioners were more likely to believe that PR was an industry – 52 per cent in the 18–34 age group – versus 61 per cent of those in the 35–65 age range who believe they work in a profession.

One of the debates which hovers in the air at gatherings of PR people is whether PR is a profession. What is meant by this and why is it important (Box 4.15)?

Box 4.15 PR: Profession or Industry?

Francis Ingham, Director General of the PRCA, says:

> Our most recent PR census shows that people are pretty evenly split on whether PR is a profession or an industry. Neither I nor we have a view on this, really. All we care about is, is PR professional? And I believe it is professional. It has standards like the communications management standard – CMS. It has ethics, as in our code that we enforce so publicly and so rigorously. And actually, we shouldn't be debating this because it is a distraction from bigger issues about social mobility and diversity, effectiveness, evaluation, the blending of disciplines. All around the industry, there are much bigger issues than around which word we use to describe PR.

In a very loose sense, one's profession is how one makes one's living. Of course, in that sense, PR would be a profession, employing as it does a growing number of people. However, that doesn't get us very far. Nor does saying that it is about being 'professional' in the sense of being skilled and committed to one's work help us very much either – there are, after all, professional criminals, professional gamblers and, perhaps more positively, professional footballers.

When people talk about 'professions' in a more definite sense, they are normally referring to specific kinds of occupation, such as medicine, the law or accountancy. What do the professions of this kind have in common? First, prolonged study and training, which together with closely supervised work experience in the early years of work, are not just a good thing – they are an absolute requirement. Second, membership of a professional body is not just advantageous, but compulsory. Third, members of the professions can and do lose their licence to operate: a doctor or lawyer who is struck off can no longer practise.

How does public relations measure up to these tests?

Education and training

While it is true that an increasing number of PR practitioners have now studied public relations at undergraduate and postgraduate level, many have not – and many people entering PR continue to have studied completely different subjects. They may go on to attend courses in aspects of PR – for example, those organised by PR's trade bodies – but there is no requirement for them to do so, or – if they do so – any need to attain any particular professional standard. Similarly, while PR people will – one hopes – be closely supervised as they begin their careers, this is a matter for their employers: there is no equivalent of the prolonged, formally supervised work experience which is a requirement for established professions.

There is also another dimension. One characteristic of the PR industry that has been around from its earliest days is its ability to absorb talent from elsewhere at mid-career – especially by taking on board journalists switching careers, sometimes at a very senior level. These are people who have no formal training in PR but, because their journalistic skills and knowledge of the media are valued, are expected to practise at a high level from day one. Similarly, public affairs or lobbying firms often recruit former politicians and officials. It is difficult to square this reality with PR being a profession in an accepted sense: imagine if your heart surgeon had no medical qualifications but had been working successfully as a dentist and hence was recruited by your hospital ...

Professional bodies and regulation

There is a plethora of PR organisations – most countries have a least one PR body and there are also international organisations. However, in most cases – certainly those of the most mature PR markets, such as the USA and Europe – there is no requirement for a practitioner to be a member. Joining a PR body may offer many advantages – including opportunities for networking, training and sharing knowledge – but many PR people, including some agencies and in-house PR departments, choose not to take advantage of this.

Examples of PR Organisations

International

International Association of Business Communicators (www.iabc.com)
International Communication Consultants Organisation (www.iccopr. com)
International Public Relations Association (www.ipra.org)

Country-specific

Australia: Public Relations Institute of Australia (www.pria.com.au)
Brazil: Brazilian Public Relations Association (www.conrerp4.org.br)
China: China International Public Relations Association (www.cipra. org.cn)
France: Information, Presse and Communications (www.infopressecom. org)
Germany: Deutsche Public Relations Gesellschaft (www.dprg-online.de)
India: Public Relations Consultants Association of India (www.prcai. org)
Italy: Federazione Relazioni Pubbliche Italiana (www.ferpi.it)
Nigeria: Nigerian Institute of Public Relations (www.nipr.org.ng)
Poland: Polish Public Relations Consultancies Association (https://zfpr. pl)
Russia: Russian Public Relations Organisation (www.raso.ru/)
Spain: Asociación de Empresas Consultoras en Relaciones Publicas (www.adecec.com)
UK: Chartered Institute of Public Relations (www.cipr.co.uk)
Public Relations and Communications Association (www.prca.org.uk)
USA: Public Relations Society of America (www.prsa.org)

Nor are there statutory regulatory bodies of the kind to be found in established professions – bodies with the power to strip people of their right to practise their profession. Whereas doctors, lawyers and accountants can and do lose their right to work in their field, PR people, in contrast, may only be reprimanded or even expelled from their industry body: no-one can stop them practising PR.

Why Is Professional Status Important?

Compared with established professions, PR is a newcomer – under that name it barely dates back 100 years. It emerged in a rather piecemeal fashion as individuals spotted opportunities and/or were hired by employers who saw a need. The increasing importance and value of PR have, however, been accompanied by plenty of criticism and disparagement (see Chapter 2). It is perhaps understandable that, facing reputational problem of that kind, PR people should envy the status and standing of professions which are seen as playing an important role in society while upholding high standards. The requirement to look after the interests of others distinguishes professions from general commercial activity. As a result, professional bodies are very much concerned with maintaining high ethical standards. Commonly, professionals are thrown out of such bodies and denied the right to practise because they have done something that is deemed to be a breach of professional ethics, even if it is not illegal – a doctor taking advantage of a patient, or a lawyer persuading a client to do something which is not in their best interests. This demonstrates how professional ethics seek to set a higher standard than the law.

Nor is it simply a matter of prestige and dignity, although some might be jealous of the way people defer to doctors and lawyers with their special knowledge. By operating monopolies in their particular fields, professions restrict access and competition and thereby exert control over the pricing of their services, arguably becoming what the British playwright George Bernard Shaw famously called 'conspiracies against the laity'. PR's inability to police entry to its field is a major factor behind one of the industry's persistent gripes, namely, that it cannot charge as much for its services as lawyers or accountants. And while there are sizeable PR agencies, there is nothing to compare with the grip the handful of major international law and accountancy firms have on professional practice in their fields.

For champions of the idea of PR as a profession, the kind of status it confers would be fair reward for the undoubted ways in which PR has professionalised itself: more and better education and training; and bigger and more effective PR industry bodies with their own codes of ethics; together with wider recognition of PR's value in all kinds of situations. But to say PR is increasingly professional is not the same thing as saying it's a profession in the strict sense.

Could PR Be a Profession?

As we have seen, regulating entry to a profession is key to establishing it as just that, a 'profession'. In practice, there are two main ways in which that can be achieved. Often some combination of them is used.

First, certain duties can be specified as ones only members of a professional body can perform, giving them special rights. For example, only a doctor may prescribe certain drugs, or only a lawyer may have the right to represent others in a court of law. The wider range of work that those professionals carry out flows from those specific responsibilities.

It is hard to know which exact duties could be reserved for PR people. Offering advice on reputation management is too vague and general – it is something all kinds of people are involved in. On the other hand, more specific tasks undertaken by PR people are often performed by others – we all may speak to journalists, on our own behalf, on behalf of friends, or for the organisations for which we work. Saying that only PR people can contact, or be contacted by, the media would certainly not be acceptable to journalists, would be all but impossible to enforce, and would indeed flout most generally accepted ideas – and laws – concerning individual freedom (including surely the Universal Declaration on Human Rights, see p. 4). Similar problems apply to other areas of PR work. In the case of lobbying or public affairs, citizens in many societies enjoy a cherished right to approach politicians and administrators directly with their concerns – and to get other people to help them to do so. Most would consider restricting that right to registered lobbyists outrageous – and certainly in breach of accepted international norms.

Second, people can be denied the right to use the profession's name and job title to describe what they do – just as an ordinary person cannot set up a lawyer's office or doctor's surgery. If this approach was applied to PR, PR people would have to be members of a professional body before they could use the term 'public relations' or 'PR' in their job titles and company names, or on their stationery or websites. In theory, this could be quite straightforward: transgressors could be readily spotted and dealt with. The difficulty with applying this to public relations is that many PR people already prefer to use other job titles and descriptions and often avoid using the term: for them, being forced to drop references to PR would not be a problem. However, it does mean that anyone can call themselves a PR practitioner, however disreputable their activities – a source of embarrassment to the industry.

> Molleda and Athaydes' (2003) work on [PR] licensing in Brazil, Nigeria and Panama found that the licensing process was bureaucratic and that practitioners used other titles to avoid regulation. The law tended to be violated without punishment and there was still a problem of 'quacks' giving the profession a bad name. Even Bernays (1992) had admitted that licensing did not ensure competence.[12]

The upshot of this is that membership of professional organisations is likely to remain optional for PR practitioners (or that, if attempts are made to make it compulsory, they will prove impractical and unworkable). Minimal attempts to regulate lobbying in the UK have proved fraught with difficulty. Charities were particularly upset to find that the proposed controls applied to them and not just to businesses. In consequence, PR's trade bodies, although sometimes styling themselves as professional bodies, have only limited powers to police standards in the industry: members are free to leave and carry on their business as before (Box 4.16). This is one of the reasons the codes of ethics are rarely enforced: voluntary organisations which depend on their members' subscriptions are loath to expel them and in any case have found the processes for doing so fraught with difficulty.

Box 4.16 Advantages of Not Being a Member of a Trade Body

A senior PR industry insider highlighted the advantages for firms avoiding membership of trade bodies:

> *PRWeek* published its rankings of income by director and profitability by agency. And it was remarkable that I think the second-highest paid director in UK PR is Andrew Grant at Tulchan. The company that the PRCA says is beyond the pale because it tried to employ Ruth Davidson [the high-profile former Conservative Leader in Scotland and a Member of the Scottish Parliament, who, according to the PRCA, should not simultaneously be employed as a lobbyist]. And one of the highest rates of growth in the industry, in the big agencies, was Tulchan. So, so what? These guys are outside of regulation, probably accepting clients they couldn't do if they were being regulated and making shitloads of money on the back of that.
>
> They don't declare their clients. So there is a route to becoming rich. Some might say, some bad people might say, that the fact that more and more of the industry is coalescing around one set of standards, makes it easier if you're on the margin to pick up the clients who will always exist, who are dodgy and to make yourself rich on the back of that.

The Case for Not Being a Profession

For many in the PR world, the exalted ideal of professional status so clearly represents a well-earned coming of age that it is hard for them to see the counter-arguments.

However, the same PR practitioners are often justifiably proud of their creativity, overlooking the fact that the scope for creativity in traditional professions is in most cases highly restricted. Instead, people like lawyers and doctors apply rather rigid rules and principles based on their extensive training in what is established knowledge and must minimise risk. Unsurprisingly their scope to use their imaginations is circumscribed.

In contrast, much of PR's success arguably arises from the fact that it's not a hidebound profession. Instead it's open-ended and flexible. It has grown rapidly and taken on people with new expertise able to perform new tasks in new areas in ways which would be difficult for traditional 'professions'. Whatever their strengths, such professions can be seen as rather stuffy and stodgy. The prolonged training, professional exams, close supervision and adherence to established procedure are not for everyone.

In weighing up the pros and cons of professional status, PR people should also look close to home. Many of the people they work most closely with – in marketing, advertising, and journalism and the media – do not belong to true 'professions' either (neither do society's 'pure' creatives – film-makers, artists, writers, musicians). Yes, such people are often skilled, experienced and dedicated and do important and valuable work, but like PR people, it's not compulsory for them to acquire qualifications or be members of professional bodies. Perhaps the greater support for the idea of professional status among in-house PR people which features in the PRCA census arises from the fact that, more than agency staff, they need to hold their heads up alongside the other employees within the organisations they serve, and emphasise their professional skills.

It is noteworthy that whenever the authors have put the notion of PR becoming a profession to PR students – people who might have a vested interest in turning PR into a profession – they don't back it, preferring the ideas of dynamic opportunity, workplaces comprising a variety of people of different backgrounds, and a career open to talents (Box 4.17). This seems to tie in with the PR census finding that fewer young people regarded themselves as working in a profession.

Box 4.17 PR: Trade or Profession?

The senior PR industry insider's view:

> I'm a tradesman. I just do a piece of work for clients and I do it with skill and then I move onto the next piece of work. No PR person wakes up in the morning and says, 'Oh, am I part of an industry? Am I part of a profession?' Nobody cares.

How Is PR Controlled or Regulated?

Formal systems for policing PR work may be doomed, but that does not mean that PR work is a free-for-all. The urgings of, and occasional enforcement actions by, trade bodies do some good, as may the attempts of PR educators to get students to consider ethical issues, but the use of controversial techniques is more effectively tempered by social pressure and the expectations of individual marketplaces in different countries. This recognises that PR people have to respond to a range of competing pressures – as our commentary on the IPRA Code indicates – and have to make swift decisions in difficult circumstances: their working environment is not that of an academic seminar. Those who overstep the boundaries of what is deemed acceptable in a particular society or working environment risk losing the standing they need to operate effectively, as Bell Pottinger found (see pp. 72–77). PR is a profoundly social activity, and lack of social acceptance – at least within the desired circles – renders the PR person useless. In this way, the ethics of the PR business are placed ultimately in the hands of non-PR people – their employers.

PR people also face particular vigilance from the media, and from some other external sources. The fact that identifying and monitoring the subtleties of PR require knowledge and effort means that it is not an obvious target in the way that advertising is, but this makes it particularly appealing to the critical cognoscenti and those who believe in conspiracy theories. The machinations of corporate and political PR – but seldom NGOs' PR – are the subject of specialist websites, such as PR Watch, the extensive, professionally staffed PR monitoring service run by the Center for Media and Democracy in the United States, including its website www.prwatch.org and www.spinwatch.org, a newer UK equivalent.

Summary

PR has generated many codes of ethics and many – but by no means all – PR practitioners have signed up to one or more of them. The codes tend to be similar, but all leave considerable scope for interpretation. Their very existence reflects PR's yearning for respectability – even, in some quarters, professional status. However, it has always proved difficult to enforce PR's codes of ethics, not least because in most cases practitioners do not have to be subject to them, and it is unlikely that this will change. Instead PR is informally regulated by its need to be socially acceptable.

Questions

1. Look back over the ethical codes described in this chapter and summarise in three to five points the key underlying principles.

2. Examine a PR ethical code relating to your country. Does it differ from the codes mentioned above? How far does it reflect the realities of PR work?

3. What are the pros and cons of PR becoming an established profession?

Notes

1 See www.ipra.org/member-services/code-of-conduct/#:~:-text=Launched%20in%202011%20the%20IPRA,the%202007%20Code%20 of%20Brussels.
2 Quoted in Morris, Trevor, and Goldsworthy, Simon, *PR Today: The Authoritative Guide to Public Relations* (Basingstoke: Palgrave, 2016), p. 46.
3 See www.bbc.co.uk/news/world-europe-48253577
4 Christopher Buckley, *Thank You for Smoking* (London: Allison & Busby, 2003).
5 Jackall, Robert and Hirota, Janice M., *Image Makers: Advertising, Public Relations, and the Ethos of Advocacy* (Chicago: University of Chicago Press, 2000).
6 See https://en.wikipedia.org/wiki/Peter_Mond,_4th_Baron_Melchett
7 Thakurta, Paranjoy G. and Reddy, Kalimekolan S., Press Council of India, April 2010. See https://dataspace.princeton.edu/jspui/bitstream/88435/dsp-019k41zd56n/1/Press-Council-of-India-Sub-CommitteeReport_on_Paid-News.pdf
8 See www.prethikrat.at/wp-content/uploads/2015/09/Code-of-Conduct_ Digital-Communication.pdf
9 See www.prsa.org/wp-content/uploads/2019/01/BEPS_Handbook_2018.pdf
10 Ed Caesar, 'The reputation-laundering firm that ruined its own reputation', *The New Yorker*, 25 June 2018.
11 See www.prca.org.uk/sites/default/files/PRCA_PR_Census_2019_v9-8-pdf%20%285%29.pdf
12 Quoted in Morris and Goldsworthy, *PR Today*, p. 54.

Chapter 5

Who Wouldn't, or Shouldn't, You Work For?

One of the starting points for any consideration of PR ethics is the vital question of for whom you would – or wouldn't – work. Most of us would draw the line somewhere, and once we've drawn that line, the other issues fall away – we would simply have nothing to do with that individual or organisation. The problem is that no two people will ever agree on the full list of who is acceptable and who isn't – and even individual PR practitioners could legitimately claim that their view could change as circumstances change. As the great economist John Maynard Keynes was alleged to have said: 'When the facts change, I change my mind. What do you do, sir?' How can PR people chart their way through these difficult waters?

In this chapter we look at:

- How far is there an ethical basis for deciding whom you would and wouldn't work for – and how far can ethical theory be a guide?
- How far PR advice can be compared to legal advice – something everyone is entitled to.
- How far is the not-for-profit sector a special case – and how far do the same issues apply to campaigning groups and charities as they do to commercial organisations?
- Whether PR people need to be passionate about causes they serve – and whether that can be counterproductive.

Are PR prized awarded fairly? See Box 5.1.

Box 5.1 No PR Prizes for Kellyanne Conway

No prizes for masterminding the most seismic PR campaign of the twenty-first century (so far).

In November 2016, Donald Trump was elected as the 45th President of the United States of America. It was a shock result – a political earthquake which turned conventional thinking about political communications on its head: despite some valiant attempts at post-rationalisation, most experts and journalists had not seen it coming.

The final months of Trump's campaign were overseen by Kellyanne Conway, the first woman to run a successful presidential campaign and the first woman to run any Republican presidential campaign.

The world of public relations is awash with prizes and awards – presented by trade bodies, PR publications and others. But Conway was not so lucky when it came to PR's myriad awards, although, as the headline above suggests, and against the odds, she helped win what is arguably the world's most important election, and indeed was appointed to a key position at the White House afterwards. Why was this – could distaste at what she achieved more than outweigh her undoubted success?

Conway had a formidable track record. A background in polling – early on in her career she founded her own polling company, demonstrating a particular interest in what women think (she co-authored a book called *What Women Really Think*) – segued into a career as political pundit (or pundette, as they were called in 1990s' Washington) on TV and radio. She worked as an advisor to a range of politicians and in 2004 did receive an award – from the *Washington Post* – for forecasting the outcome of the 2004 presidential election.

In the 2016 campaign, she originally backed Trump's Republican rival, Ted Cruz, at that stage even describing Trump as 'a man who seems to be offending his way to the nomination'. She joined the Trump campaign in July 2016, and was originally expected to focus on women voters, but the following month became overall campaign manager, a position she retained up to the election.

When Trump took office, she joined the White House as his spokeswoman, or 'Trump whisperer', and became embroiled in many controversies – including her use of the term 'alternative facts' about the disputed claims about the number of people who attended the presidential inauguration. She has outlived many of the president's other appointees. When her own husband, George T. Conway III, suggested that Trump had a mental disorder, she defended the President – who himself described her husband as a 'stone cold LOSER & husband from hell'.

What lessons can be drawn from this example? Steering Trump's campaign to success and enabling him to secure the most powerful position in world politics in a huge contest were clearly not enough to win Conway acclaim in the PR world. While it is true that PR awards often steer clear of political campaigning because it is seen as divisive, Conway's achievement was particular significant from a PR perspective – after all, Hillary Clinton's campaign spent around twice as much on advertising, while Trump relied much more on 'earned media', with outraged responses to his tweets generating enormous amounts of free publicity. Nor did Conway win the informal plaudits given to the architects of Barack Obama's two successful presidential campaigns. Obama's campaign team was seen as capturing the zeitgeist of social media and was in keeping with the 'coolness' of his campaign – Trump's mastery (for good or ill) of Twitter was not viewed so positively.

Since the election, Conway has been the subject of controversy for the way she practises her craft (she finally stepped dwn from her White House role in August 2020), but political communication has always been a tough, even brutal, trade, and even the most highly esteemed politicians are aided by people prepared to do unpleasant things behind the scenes. Her unconventional approach has undoubtedly achieved results. Some of the techniques which people hold against her are to some degree part of any political campaign, but– if we are honest with ourselves – perhaps we are willing to overlook them when we support the candidate or the party. It is hard to deny that the PR professionals' view of her achievements has been affected by their view of the cause she has served: she and the man she serves are a long way from the PR industry's centre of political gravity (see Chapter 1). She is not alone in this: something similar could be said of Dominic Cummings, the maestro behind the pro-Brexit campaign in the EU referendum in the UK in 2016, who went on to become a key adviser to the UK Prime Minister Boris Johnson, and about a number of other effective campaigners working for causes which others – including many in the PR world – disdain.

We asked a senior PR industry insider about Conway's failure to win an award:

> She didn't get a PR award for the same reason as Nigel Farage, leader of the Brexit Party in the UK, and his PR people won't get a PR award – which is, the people who judge PR awards are, as Nixon might have put it, liberal, left-wing intelligentsia, who just hate the people they disagree with. And they will never get those awards, no matter how good their work is, they will never get it. If it had been done

by somebody for a Communist Party or if UK Labour leader Jeremy Corbyn had happened to win, his guys would have got plenty of awards. You'd never get them for Nigel Farage or Kellyanne Conway.

We put the suggestion that PR industry awards are skewed to Francis Ingham, Director General of the PRCA:

> We have a very, very rigorous awards process that involves judges from the very top of our industry who exercise their judgement and give the benefit of their experience. And what I've always prided ourselves on is the independence and the seniority of our judging panels. Always non-conflicting judges, just looking at the work on display and judging it on its creativity and its effectiveness, regardless of any personal views at all.

In the authors' view, public relations, in itself, is *amoral*. It comprises an approach and a set of techniques which can be applied to any cause and can be, and is, used by both heroes and villains (even if most of the time it is used for rather innocuous, even dull purposes – to inform you about central and local government services, utilities, insurance, pensions, and so on). Admitting it is amoral may be difficult – understandably, people tend to like to claim the moral high ground – but it is easy to illustrate from the early days of PR onwards. PR pioneers such as Ivy Lee and Carl Byoir worked for the Nazis before the Second World War,[1] and Hitler's propaganda chief Dr Goebbels consulted the writings of Edward Bernays, who is sometimes called the 'father of public relations'. To this day, PR firms continue to be hired by repressive regimes, particularly when they need to cultivate opinion beyond their borders and can no longer rely on the more brutal forms of persuasion they are free to use at home. This has always been controversial: indeed, the UK's Public Relations and Communications Association, which has since grown to become the world's largest PR body, operating both in the UK and in a range of other countries, was formed in 1969 in response to concerns about a British public relations consultancy which had been retained by the then military dictatorship in Greece.[2]

Few would now seek to defend Lee and Byoir's decisions to work for Nazi interests – although of course we have the benefit of hindsight – but often there are more difficult judgement calls. Is it realistic to refuse to work for *any* government or its state-owned companies (in many countries with questionable regimes, there may be little true distinction between the state and business) unless the country is fully democratic and has an impeccable human rights record? Such things are difficult to determine and indeed any country and its government can be criticised in some respects (would vehement critics of Donald Trump want to forgo any opportunities associated with US government contracts?). Similarly, companies can be criticised and are not necessarily paragons of virtue. In general, the more controversial the sector they work in, the more likely they are to need high-powered PR advice. In practice, PR people cannot expect to find moral perfection, and to a large extent have to take the world as they find it (Box 5.2). They can legitimately argue that good PR can play a part in opening a country – or indeed a company – up to external influences, new ways of thinking and better patterns of behaviour, but even that argument can be self-serving and it is not always true – it failed to work in the case of Lee and Byoir and the Nazis, for example.

Box 5.2 Undertaking PR in China

Today all the world's largest PR firms are well represented in China, and compete for Chinese business. This has been the case for over a generation, since the Chinese economy first opened up in the post-Mao era. Few companies seem to have any scruples about operating in the Chinese market or serving Chinese state interests, whereas criticism has often been levelled at PR firms which are apparently prepared to engage with other dictatorships – in Central Asia, the Middle East and elsewhere.

Why is this? After all, the western PR industry in China continued its work during periods of repression – the bloody crackdown at Tiananmen Square in 1989; the continuing human rights abuses in Tibet and Xinjiang; the maltreatment of the Falun Gong and other dissidents; and the events in Hong Kong. China's controversial role in the COVID-19 crisis has underlined these concerns for many. It could doubtless be argued that PR firms are helping to prepare China for a more open, prosperous future, but at the time of writing that does not appear to be the case (arguably the direction of travel is the opposite one) – and, in any case, the same could be said for PR in any dictatorship.

The positive attitude of PR firms to contemporary China is surely connected to the sheer scale and dynamic growth of the Chinese market (after all, they frequently have misgivings about doing business with regimes with poor records in other parts of the world). This very tempting 'cake' is huge and expanding, and everyone wants more and larger slices of it as China increasingly seems to represent the economic future. But the understandable fear of missing out does not make this an ethically-based decision: indeed, without wishing to go as far as comparing China with the Nazi regime in other respects, Germany in the 1930s looked like a land of opportunity for PR practitioners... There are perhaps other factors which come into play. Many activists in the West are perhaps a little more comfortable with the ostensibly Communist Chinese regime than with other kinds of authoritarian and right-wing dictatorship. China may be doing some of the wrong things, but is doing so for the right, or at least understandable, reasons, and as a country which experienced western interference and violence in its recent history, it should not be so readily criticised. Such criticism might smack of neo-colonialism or racism. This may help to explain why activists who have protested against PR firms' involvement in other countries do not focus with the same intensity on PR for China and Chinese state interests. All of this means that PR practitioners looking to the Chinese market are perhaps less prone to self-examination and are less likely to be troubled or criticised, even as they do business with the world's largest dictatorship.

According to Francis Ingham, the Director-General of the PRCA:

> The PRCA and ICCO are very clear that there is a need for basic principles of behaviour, freedom of the press, respect for the truth, regard to the public interest and a firm commitment at all times to avoid anything that sows disunity amongst people. And that's something our members take very seriously. Now, is it legitimate to do work in China? Of course it is. It's a country with whom the UK has long-standing and cordial diplomatic and business relations. And plenty of PRCA members operate there. I remember Martin Sorrell saying that China was the future for the PR industry. One might question if that prediction has proved true, but it's certainly the case that it would be ridiculous to ignore the fastest-growing part of the world when the UK and the US are the dominant players in the global PR market. And I think we're bringing our values to that market as well in a very positive, internationalist way.

The view of a senior PR industry insider:

> China's too good an opportunity to miss. Massive amounts of money. Massive population. A burgeoning middle class wanting all the nice things that PR can help to sell. And the hypocrisy is incredibly obvious. You get all these agencies, particularly the American-owned ones, banging on and on and on about multiculturalism and about purpose-driven values and then as soon as the Chinese lift their skirts, they're right up

there because of the massive amount of money. They don't care if people are persecuted for religious beliefs or political beliefs. They don't care that they're not working in a democracy. You get these agencies that bang on about their liberal credentials. They work in Saudi, they work in Qatar, they work in Oman, they work in Russia. And if there is a dollar sign attached to it, their scruples disappear overnight.

If you had a right-wing dictatorship – and China is, after all, a dictatorship – then liberal companies in America wouldn't go anywhere near it. But because it's a left-wing dictatorship, they feel different rules apply. And I'd also say this about all the industry banging on about female empowerment, MeToo, etc., they'll still pitch in Saudi. Their senior women can't go there unaccompanied. They still need to have chaperones. But they'll still pitch in Saudi. And yet when they get back to New York, it's all MeToo, MeToo, MeToo. It's like DollarToo, DollarToo, DollarToo when you go to Saudi.

And if the People's Liberation Army goes in hard in Hong Kong? If more and more people are imprisoned in China? You know what they will do? They will virtue signal. They'll be very upset personally. They'll continue talking about the things they bang on about at the moment. And then they'll still take the Chinese money. If they could do work in Iran, they'd ignore the stonings as well, because if the mullahs can pay, they'd take their money too.

Not-For-Profit Vs Commercial PR: Held to Different Standards?

Public relations is also used by everyone's favourite charities and campaigning groups (even though they shun the term PR), but that can create its own moral hazards. Users of PR among not-for-profit NGOs (non-governmental organisations) include what may be one's least favourite causes, for instance, one cannot simultaneously support pro- and anti-abortion groups, be in favour of or opposed to animal testing for medical purposes, or be pro- and anti-gun control. Once again, PR is available to heroes and villains, even if we often disagree on who is who. Just because such groups are not-for-profit does not necessarily make them morally perfect. NGOs compete with each other, individual careers and incomes are at stake, and the imperative of fund-raising means that there is always a temptation for them to do the *popular* rather than the *right* thing:

> [H]umanitarian organisations are making use of professional com-
> munication to turn the suffering of others into a spectacle/commod-
> ity to be exchanged for donations, support and political leverage.
> This is, in our view, both ethically wrong and operationally counter-
> productive in the long run.[3]

Even if one broadly supports the *cause* espoused by an NGO, one may
think that its specific campaigning objectives are wrong-headed and even
dangerous. For example, anxiety about feeding the world's growing population is a shared concern of not only the leading environment groups
which oppose genetically modified foods, but also of many people who
support the development of genetically modified foods and believe they
are the only realistic way of supplying the future nutritional needs of
the Earth's inhabitants. Neither side is necessarily more 'moral' than the
other.

Many critics of PR focus on its associations with big business. After all,
public relations in its current form in large part came into being around
a century ago to manage the relationship between major corporations
and the emerging mass media – and through that, the public. It follows
that people who do not like or are suspicious of business and capitalism
do not like, or are at the very least suspicious of, PR. Indeed, many attacks on PR are really thinly disguised attacks on the business world. If
advertising is frequently pilloried as the public face of capitalism and the
main motor behind consumerism, PR practitioners and lobbyists are often depicted as the sinister special forces of the big corporations and their
allies in government, operating behind enemy lines and using a variety of
unfair, clandestine tricks. Yet the same critics tend to remain silent about
the vigorous and ingenious campaigns of NGOs such as Greenpeace or
its brasher new competitor, Extinction Rebellion.

So attacks on public relations and depictions of the industry as being
immoral and unethical tend to focus on the worlds of business and politics. The former tends to be viewed with suspicion because it is for-profit,
while the aims of politicians are forever controversial, not least because
of their desire to wield power over other people's lives. And when business interests and politics come together, as they do in the world of lobbying and public affairs, it is doubly controversial and suspicious. This
is underpinned by the fact that commercial sector PR people, and particularly PR agencies, are almost the only people actually to use the term
'public relations' to describe what they do.

In contrast, PR for the not-for-profit sector has, at least until recently,
evaded sustained criticism of this kind, despite its extensive use (usually
under other names, such as campaigning or communications). The apparent altruism of people working for charities and campaigning organisations means that their work has been viewed with less suspicion, and

certainly not with the ideologically motivated anti-capitalist motives behind some of the attacks on PR for business.

But perhaps close scrutiny is a good thing. In recent times, some of the top global brands in the not-for-profit sector have found themselves facing serious criticism for abuses and misjudgements (Box 5.3). Their PR response has often been slow, hesitant and inadequate. Arguably they were not on their guard and were complacent.

Box 5.3 Some Not-For-Profit Sector PR Headaches

In 2018, the hitherto seemingly unimpeachable UK-based global charity Oxfam featured in *PRWeek*'s 'guide to crisis mismanagement' as their flop of the month as the organisation struggled to respond to stories emerging from Haiti and beyond about Oxfam staff using local sex workers. As *PRWeek* put it:

> When it transpires that senior execs working for a charity focused on humanitarian aid are sexually exploiting a crisis-struck population, it's clearly very bad news. But when it also comes to light that the charity actively sought to cover up transgressions, it becomes a comms disaster beyond reparation.[4]

The following year, the Communications Director of another major charity, Save the Children, which had been hit by a similar scandal, told a *PRWeek* conference that too many people working for large charities believe their larger mission excuses damaging behaviour.[5]

Even the Roman Catholic Church has been criticised for its PR handling of sexual abuse stories.[6]

Objecting to PR on the basis of the causes it serves leads to a cul-de-sac. To go back to the business world for a moment, PR can serve the interests of any company, large or small, from the most hated multinational to innocuous local businesses, or indeed wholesalers and others who have little contact with the public. Unless one repudiates business altogether, it is hard to object to the use of PR as such. Typically, therefore, people object to the use of PR in particular, unpopular business sectors. The problem with this is that no two people can agree on which businesses are acceptable and which are not – different societies often view these issues in different lights, and even one's individual perceptions alter over time or in response to particular events.

This can be readily illustrated. Some might object to the arms trade altogether on pacifist grounds. More might object to the sale of particular kinds of weapons, or arms sales to particular regimes, but it would be impossible to reach a consensus on which weapons and which regimes are acceptable. Some might see providing arms, for example, to fight someone *they* view as a tyrannical dictator or brutal aggressor, as deeply moral. Even those who object outright to arms sales are caught in a trap, due to the interconnected nature of the business world: companies which do not make weapons themselves may be supplying goods and services to those that do. Leading IT companies work closely with the defence industries, for example, and while their products may not include bullets and explosives, they contribute far more to the military capabilities of modern armed forces than many traditional arms manufacturers.

Alternatively, take the growing consensus about climate change and the threat of global warming or heating (Box 5.4). As we have seen with NGOs, general agreement about the problem does not mean that there is necessarily common ground about solutions. Some emphasise the need for people drastically to change their behaviour and lifestyles, while others put more emphasis on technological solutions. Some urge more use of nuclear power, others strongly oppose it. Some favour wind farms, others disagree. Some back the use of biofuels, while others see this as counterproductive. Tree planting to offset air travel has been fashionable in some circles, but is not backed by some of the largest environmental NGOs. Encouraging food exports from developing countries may seem positive and uncontroversial – a valuable source of income for impoverished societies, but what about the air miles used up when they are flown to marketplaces in the developed world? And what about the environmental impact of intensive agriculture versus the need to produce affordable food? How far and how fast should the world move towards vegetarianism or even veganism, for environmental as well as other reasons? In the case of the environment, even if people can agree on a destination, they rarely agree on the route to it.

Box 5.4 PR for Australian Coal

In March 2019, an investigation by *The Guardian Australia* (an online version of the UK newspaper) claimed that Glencore, a large multinational mining firm, had sought to further its commercial interests by undermining environmental activists, influencing politicians and spreading its messages on social media.

The exploitation of Australia's massive coal reserves has become particularly controversial amid the growing debate about climate change and the role of fossil fuels. Glencore, with major interests in Australia, as well as other countries, used the services of the

C|T Group, the research and corporate strategy firm founded by Sir Lynton Crosby and Mark Textor, to further its interests. C|T Group has worked in political campaigns in countries as far apart as Australia, Sri Lanka and Canada, as well as for the current UK Prime Minister Boris Johnson's earlier successful London mayoral campaigns. Crosby's protégé Isaac Levido spearheaded Johnson's successful UK general election campaign in December 2019. Its commercial clients have included Philip Morris International, the cigarette company.

From 2017, using teams in Sydney and London, C|T ran what was called Project Caesar on behalf of Glencore. *The Guardian* claims that the annual budget for what they describe as a secretive campaign was between £4 million and £7 million. C|T researched politicians' views and sought to convince them of the continuing value of coal. It also gathered intelligence on opponents, including Greenpeace. Its digital campaign aimed to shift public sentiment, blaming alternative, renewable energy sources for power blackouts and higher prices. Project Caesar also involved an online 'grass-roots' campaign – but, given that this was sponsored by C|T on behalf of Glencore, *The Guardian* describes this as 'astroturfing'. The mainstream media were also targeted.

The Guardian admits that Glencore and C|T did nothing illegal. However, Glencore told *The Guardian* it abandoned the project in early 2019 to 'ensure alignment' with its recent decision to limit coal production for environmental reasons. The newspaper suggests that pressure from investors may have been a factor here. The move earned it the following headline in *The Sydney Morning Herald*: 'Mining rivals deride Glencore's coal pledge as "brilliant PR exercise"'. C|T declined to comment on its work for Glencore, emphasising client confidentiality.[7] (See also pp. 152–153.)

With limited time and expertise at our disposal, we all try and find our own way through the shifting sands of ethical debate, sometimes – it must surely be admitted – placing more weight on the evidence which suits our prejudices and interests. And yet the environment is but one example: the list of controversial businesses and moral dilemmas is endless. From gambling to tobacco, from alcohol to 'unhealthy' foods, from pornography, the 'exploitation' of those working in the gig economy, animal testing and the use of fur, to ever-present social media marketing directed at children and much more besides, most people have ethical qualms about some legal forms of business activity.

In their role as the messengers for the world of business, PR people are sucked into all these and other debates. The public and media appetite for bad news and controversy means that, disproportionately, top PR 'muscle' is hired by companies in controversial sectors which encounter disputes and difficulties and are therefore in the firing line. It is in such fields, not more routine marketing work, that PR people can command the highest fees and salaries.

The reality is that, just like PR, business itself is ultimately amoral. It may create the wealth and products which we all need to survive – it is worth bearing in mind that those who attack the business world tend to sidestep the fact that people's jobs and livelihoods depend on it; pensioners and others depend on the performance of business investments; society depends upon tax payments from it; and, in a competitive market, companies depend upon us as their willing customers. However, successfully meeting human needs and, especially, desires, is not in itself a moral activity (just think back to some of those ever-changing controversial business sectors), and so individual areas of business are not necessarily moral.

There can also be a temptation to attempt to align one's morals with business advantage. For example, one's point of view on whether biofuels are a good thing might be influenced by the prospect of well-rewarded work for a biofuel company, even if one tries hard to convince oneself that one has reached the decision independently! Moreover, some decisions which are trumpeted as moral ones may not be all they seem at first glance: a PR firm which refuses to work for tobacco companies may be doing so because of fears it might upset existing or potential clients or employees rather than for purely ethical reasons.

Should everyone be entitled to PR? See Box 5.5.

Box 5.5 The Right to Seek Help from an Advocate

According to Francis Ingham, Director General of the PRCA:

> No, not everyone has the right to representation. Because there's a difference here with lawyers, where you're saying everyone has the right, and the next taxi in the rank and you take on whoever comes along. And you can have clients who are completely in conflict with one another. And your reputation is not influenced by the kind of people you work with, but whether you are good or bad as with barristers. Whereas with our members, we expect them to stand by the clients they work for, to have some sort of public view of who they are willing

to work for. And just because somebody comes to them and says we'd like you to represent us, they don't have to say yes. They need to make a moral judgement about the kind of people they want to work with. Let's continue the cab rank analogy. We would say you don't have to work for the next person who comes along. In fact, you shouldn't just work for the next person that comes along. You need to make a judgement. Imagine that your taxi is a convertible, with a soft roof, and you're driving round the streets of London and everyone can see who it is you're driving around and judge you accordingly.

It is very subjective and personal morality is very subjective. And that's how one ought to decide which clients one is willing to work for and with. What we think's important is that having chosen which of those clients you're working for (assuming the work's legal), you have certain values that shape the work you do for and with them. So telling the truth, regard for the public interest, not stirring up discord or hatred or disharmony. So long as you adhere to those basic principles and so long as you're willing to say who it is you're working for and take the consequences, both in terms of who will work for you as employees and which clients you will attract and which you will deter, then you're perfectly at liberty to do that sort of work. Just make it clear for whom you're working.

Our membership embraces people who are in favour of smoking or nicotine inhalation, as Philip Morris International would put it, and members like the Department of Health who publicly advocate that you don't smoke. Our members are companies who build cars and environmental campaigners who say you shouldn't drive a car. Our members include environmental campaigners and airlines. So we don't judge who is eligible to be a member depending on the clients they had or the fields in which they operate. We judge membership on the basis of, are you an ethical, professional practitioner who wants to be held accountable to the highest standards of behaviour?

Lawyers, who, like PR people, also act as professional persuaders, have traditionally seen acting for the most disreputable of clients as part of their professional duty. This duty continues even if clients accept that they are in the wrong, as lawyers can seek to make pleas in mitigation. By and large, the need for this is accepted by society, and lawyers who defend unpopular individuals or companies have not traditionally been pilloried for it (although perhaps in these polarised times, this is changing: Harvard Law Professor Ronald S. Sullivan faced protests and criticism and lost his position as dean of an undergraduate house over his initial willingness to join the defence team of Harvey Weinstein).[8] This principle is enshrined in the famous 'cab-rank' principle of the English bar, whereby, if they were available, barristers have traditionally been obliged to act for anyone, regardless of their personal views and feelings – although no-one has ever suggested a similar obligation for PR practitioners.

In some ways, PR people perform a similar advocacy function to legal counsel, albeit in the more informal court of public opinion. All people surely have a right to put their case, and therefore to seek advice and help on how best to do so. That cannot be a right granted only to 'popular' people, whoever they may be. And if a client comes under attack, at what point is it legitimate to abandon them (Box 5.6)? Are they innocent until proven guilty? If you were happy to take their money in good times, is it right to desert them when they need you most? In practice, the implications for the standing of the PR consultancy concerned would come to the fore – but that's a business, not an ethical, matter.

Box 5.6 The Ethics of Abandoning a Client

At what point could or should you abandon a client, for example, and hypothetically, Harvey Weinstein who until recently would have been a sought-after client for many PR firms?

According to Francis Ingham, Director General of the Public Relations and Communications Association:

> Accusations aren't truths. They're just that. But when there are accusations of the magnitude that was clearly the case with Weinstein, it would be your absolute duty as an ethical practitioner to ask the right questions and, if you don't receive the right answers, to walk away from that work, both because it is the right thing to do and also it is in your own self-interest. And one might say that the PR advisor who walked away from Prince Andrew recently was probably doing both of those things as well. Feeling that their advice wasn't going to be listened to and not wanting to be associated with the consequences.
>
> You shouldn't act as a court but you certainly should act as an inquisitor in asking them for serious answers to serious questions.

In the end, there is no right to have PR representation, and the stakes are lower – losing a PR battle does not in itself lead to punishment, although it can have other potentially serious repercussions. For all these reasons, coupled perhaps with a little prejudice against PR, particularly on the part of journalists, there is little comparable acceptance of the right of PR people to represent all comers, although the criteria on which such decisions are made are never clear.

A senior PR industry insider observes:

> Well, I've heard it said by some that PR ethics are probably lower than most other business ethics. At one end of the industry, certainly, we are like barristers. Just defend any client. And I think the industry is full of hypocrites, frankly, when they talk about their belief in only working for clients whom they believe in. The reality is, they desperately would like to work for tobacco and clients like that but they feel that their public reputation would suffer if they do, so they shy away from it. Equally, I've heard it said that there are agencies that say in public, no, no, we can't do this. All they do is pass the work on to another part of the network or to a conflict shop. So they're taking the money but virtue signalling by taking it in a different way.
>
> PR is, by definition, about things that are difficult and/or controversial. The reality is that everybody who runs their own agency needs to make money. And everybody who runs an agency owned by somebody else is under enormous pressure to make money. So while people say that they have very rigorous criteria about who to work for, the reality is often quite the opposite. Let's not forget, Bell Pottinger (see pp. 72–77) had an ethics committee. An ethics committee that approved running a white minority capital campaign. So a lot of these companies set up these veneers of ethics and say they turn away clients who aren't in tune with their values. And the phrase of the moment is about purpose. Well, purpose is often just greenwashing or whitewashing or pretending or making your personal views the views of your company. You have all these companies taking a really violent stand on politics. What they're really saying is they're just compelling their employees to live the values that the owner has.
>
> The growing trend for companies to adopt controversial political stances runs the risk of making us look like a complete bunch of lying hypocrites. I reckon that if you said to an agency owner, 'Oh, how do you feel about your employees taking part in politics?' They would say, 'Oh, we encourage it. It's a societal debt that must be paid.' You say, 'Great. If they were stood as a candidate for the Green

Party, how would you feel?' 'Absolutely supportive.' 'Lib Dems?'
'Right. Got their back.' 'How about the Brexit Party?' 'Absolutely
unacceptable.' What you're really saying is you're just intruding into
your staff's private lives. So you either stop them from doing what
they want to do and what their conscience dictates is proper or you
employ people who are basically you. And for all of the talk of diversity in the industry, that's the reality. People more and more are
employing people who more and more resemble them and are giving
out virtue signalling at the same time. Worst type of hypocrisy.

Lord Bell, the controversial UK PR man who acted for a range of different governments (see pp. 72–77) was once asked about this issue.

'Is there anyone he wouldn't represent? 'The Labour Party', he says,
before adding: 'Contrary to the illusion that people have, I wouldn't represent Saddam Hussein or Hitler.'

'I have represented people who are thought to be evil but I only represented them because they promised me they were going to stop being evil
and when they carried on being evil, I walked away.'[9]

Can it be ethical to undertake PR for a convicted criminal? See Box 5.7.

Box 5.7 PR for a Convicted Criminal

The parents of a UK teenager cleared of murdering a classmate
have been labelled 'shameless' for hiring Manchester PR firm MC2
Communications to handle media relations around the controversial case.[10]

Joshua Molnar, 18, who fatally stabbed Manchester Grammar
student Yousef Makki with an illegal flick-knife in March, was cleared
of murder and manslaughter, but handed a 16-month detention order
for possessing an offensive weapon and perverting the course of justice
by lying to police. The court ruled Molnar had acted in self-defence, in
what has been described as a contentious ruling.

His parents hired crisis management firm MC2 Communications
to handle media relations in the wake of the controversial ruling,
which included an interview with *The Sunday Times*.

The move angered Makki's family, with his mother Debbie telling
the media: 'Who do the Molnars think they are, having a publicist?
They're hardly Posh and Becks. They are shameless. They have
shown no remorse to us during or since the trial.

'We've never heard anything from them. Surely, as human beings they should sympathise with us losing such a huge part of our
lives. Instead, they seem to be more worried about tainting their
reputations.'

MC2 released a statement defending its appointment, pointing out that: 'Our role is to help articulate clear communications and to manage the sheer logistical challenge of national and international media demands.

'As one of the largest independent agencies in the North and one of the leading crisis management consultancies, MC2 is often at the centre of some of the most emotive and sensitive issues affecting both businesses and individuals.'

The case raises questions about where PR agencies should draw the line in choosing to represent clients in contentious and sensitive circumstances.[11]

Questions to consider:

1. Was it unethical for the Molnar family to hire PR advisors?
2. Was it unethical for MC2 to take the work?
3. What do you think of the MC2 statement above?
4. Why do people think it is acceptable or even vital to hire a lawyer for a court case but controversial to hire a PR for a case in the court of public opinion?

Can PR People Be Passionate About Their Work All the Time?

It is often said that PR people should only work for purposes in which they passionately believe. Superficially, this sounds good and hence hard to dispute – but the concept deserves a little scrutiny.

In theory, a PR person could work exclusively for organisations and products about which they are passionate, but in reality that is rarely the case. When working for a PR consultancy, no one can be sure that the brands they are working on will be their favourite products, and, even if that were true at the outset, products change and new decisions are made about which not everyone can be enthusiastic. The same is true working in-house; it would be impossible for any individual honestly to agree with – let alone be passionate about – everything that a big organisation does and says.

It is certainly difficult to do PR work for something you are passionately opposed to – in such circumstances it might well be time to reconsider your position. However, the real world of PR is usually about compromise: working for people and purposes about which one may occasionally be enthusiastic, but which are at least bearable.

In any case, there are real advantages to being *dis*passionate. PR people need to retain some objectivity to work effectively. Their work is seldom about simply preaching to the converted. They need to empathise with their target audiences, not least, people who may be indifferent or even a little hostile to the message – something which is hard to do if PR practitioners are swept away by their own feelings. Why does this point need stressing? Because too much talk about 'passion' sounds implausible and does PR a disservice: it makes PR people sound as though they are morally supple, can push aside the realities described above and express passion to order.

The Fashion Industry: What's Not to Like?

Working in fashion PR has long been a popular career choice for PR students – and indeed for others seeking to enter the world of PR. It seems neatly to bring together many people's personal interests and the world of work. It's also an aspect of PR which is well represented in popular culture – something that has doubtless contributed to the number of people willing to undertake lengthy unpaid internships in the hope of breaking into this part of the industry.

Traditionally, the challenge in fashion PR has been to get coverage – negative coverage is relatively rare – so fashion PRs exist in a more positive bubble than many other PR people who are tackling controversial issues as part of their day-to-day work. But a little thought and examination reveal that fashion PR, far from just being about nice clothes and footwear, is beset by ethical issues. Fashion PRs may not be able to resolve these issues but they are being debated more often and growing in salience.

In economic terms, the purpose of fashion is to create contrived demand – to make people want to buy things not because what they own has worn out, no longer fits them or doesn't keep them warm or dry, but because it is no longer *fashionable*. Those who attack consumerism have always taken issue with this aspect of fashion, but this concern has been sharpened by growing anxiety about the impact of 'fast fashion' and the environmental effects of producing enormous quantities of clothing which are sold relatively cheaply and then discarded after being barely worn. Is it ethical to promote such behaviour? On the other hand, one might argue that the affordability of such fashion items simply makes available to ordinary people something that was once restricted to the privileged few – and that is a good thing.

Whatever the rights and wrongs of that, all fashion items are made of something, and that creates its own blizzard of problems. Veganism is on the rise in many countries, and has allied itself to environmental causes. Those subscribing to vegan views could surely play no part in promoting anything made of fur, leather, wool – even silk. Sidestepping those products often takes vegan fashion into the territory of manmade fibres and materials – but many of these are essentially plastics, and are themselves the source of mounting concern about their far-reaching and damaging environmental impact. Even plant-based natural fibres, such as cotton, raise concerns, since producing them affordably and in the enormous quantities the global economy requires raises issues about sustainability and the effects of intensive farming, including pollution and poor labour conditions. Proponents of ethical fashion often deal rather glibly with these issues – frequently focusing on niche producers supplying small quantities at high prices, which, while it may be a good business model, hardly answers the wider ethical question, as it leaves most people excluded.

And so it continues. The raw materials may be controversial – but manufacture of fashion items may be as well: are they produced in sweatshops by poorly paid workers in unsafe conditions? Who decides what are tolerable working conditions and fair rates of pay? After all, poorly paid work in a sweatshop may be better than no job at all. And what about affordability? As we have mentioned, should fashion only be for the rich?

When the clothing has been made, the ethical issues do not go away. What about the use of unhealthily thin models to promote fashion collections? What about labour conditions at fashion retailers – and do they pay fair amounts of tax?

These and many more dilemmas show how just one kind of business has to tackle many ethical issues. Indeed, given a little time, one could find moral concerns hovering over every kind of organisation. It's a little implausible to suggest that PR people will always have the right answers.

Exercises

1. Who would you work for and what are you prepared to do?
   Imagine you have just successfully completed a PR course. You are looking for job, but the situation is bleak: there is nothing available and you are starting to get worried. Then suddenly you are offered a very well-paid, permanent position. It involves doing PR work for a large tobacco company.

2. Would you take the job? Whatever you decide, explain your reasoning.
   If you have taken the job, you are called in for a chat before you start. The good news is that the pay is even better than you thought: you'll be better off than all your contemporaries and can also look forward to lots of first-class international travel.
   They also tell you more about your duties. Their fastest-growing markets are among young people in the developing world, and they

want you to use PR to promote their products among school-aged teenagers in such countries.

3. Explain what you would do now and why.

If you haven't taken the job – either at first or after the chat with the company – imagine that instead you've found unpaid work experience with an anti-tobacco campaigning organisation. Although the placement is coming to an end, you enjoy the work enormously, and would really like to be offered a paid position. You know you need to do something to impress them soon.

You meet socially with an old friend from university, who is doing the job described above for the tobacco company. They tell you everything, in lurid detail. You realise that revealing this is exactly what will impress your employers and kick-start your career. But it is also clear that to make the story stick, you will have to reveal your old friend's identity and end their career – something they make clear to you in a subsequent, tearful phone call.

4. Explain what you would do and why.

Follow-up assignment

You work for a PR agency which is offered a big business-to-business contract by a large but low-profile paper company. A significant and growing part of their business is supplying special paper to the tobacco industry. Your CEO has asked you to prepare a one-page document considering this from an ethical standpoint.

Summary

Give us a few minutes and access to a search engine and we'll be able find some reasons why it could be considered unethical to work for just about any organisation. Increasingly, that includes charities and campaigning organisations as well as companies.

PR people have to balance this reality against the need to do business and make their living in an imperfect world where many others are competing for business. While the idea that anyone is entitled to representation may be hard to stomach, few agree on exactly who should be refused it. In practice, personal views and beliefs always come to the fore – but of course those vary and are subjective. Nor do PR people have the specialist knowledge required to weigh up rights and wrongs of most important technical matters. PR people do have some expertise in assessing popularity, including how something will play with the media – but being popular or supporting fashionable causes is not the same as being ethical.

Questions

1. What, if any, lawful activities would you not be prepared to undertake PR work for on ethical grounds – and why?
2. List some controversial areas of business activity. Are they viewed differently in different societies around the world, and, if so, why?
3. You are working for a PR agency which is offered the opportunity to work for a large state-owned company from a foreign country. The country is not generally regarded as a democracy and has faced criticism over its human rights record. What – if any – ethical considerations would you need to weigh up before accepting or declining the potentially very profitable account? (You may choose to relate this to one or more actual countries.)
4. Consider depictions of PR in films, on television or in novels (see Chapter 1 and the Appendix at the end of the book), or news stories involving PR. What, if any, ethical issues do they raise?

Notes

1 See Morris, Trevor, and Goldsworthy, Simon, *PR Today: The Authoritative Guide to Public Relations* (Basingstoke: Palgrave, 2016), p. 38.
2 Grant, Wyn, *Business and Politics in Britain* (London: Macmillan, 1993), p. 102.
3 Lugo-Ocando, Jairo, and Hernandez-Toro, Manuel, 'PR and humanitarian communication', in Jacquie L'Etang, David McKie, Nancy Snow, and Jordi Xifra (eds), *The Routledge Handbook of Critical Public Relations* (London: Routledge, 2016), p. 228.
4 Bold, Ben, 'Flop of the month: the Oxfam guide to crisis mismanagement', *PRWeek*, 28 February 2018. Available at. www.prweek.com/article/1457796/flop-month-oxfam-guide-crisis-mismanagement
5 Burt, Emily, 'Charity sector must be accountable for crises, says Save the Children comms director', *PRWeek*, 27 June 2019. Available at: www.prweek.com/article/1589276/charity-sector-accountable-crises-says-save-children-comms-director
6 Jennings, Hayley, 'Pope's late response to abuse scandal leaves Catholic Church open to further controversy', *PR News*, 20 August 2018. Available at: www.prnewsonline.com/pope-response-catholic-church-abuse-scandal
7 *The Guardian*, 'Revealed: Glencore bankrolled covert campaign to prop up coal'. Available at: www.theguardian.com/business/2019/mar/07/revealed-glencore-bankrolled-covert-campaign-to-prop-up-coal; Latimer, Cole, 'Mining rivals deride Glencore's coal pledge as "brilliant PR exercise"', *The Sydney Morning Herald*, 22 February 2019. Available at: www.smh.com.au/business/the-economy/mining-rivals-deride-glencore-s-coal-pledge-as-brilliant-pr-exercise-20190221-p50zac.html
8 Joseph, Elisabeth and Hanna, Jason, 'Harvard law professor Ronald Sullivan withdraws from Harvey Weinstein's defense team', CNN, 14 May 2019. Available at: https://edition.cnn.com/2019/05/14/us/harvard-law-professor-ronald-sullivan-harvey-weinstein/index.html

9 Stadlen, Matthew, 'The Tories should have fired Nick Clegg and made Boris Johnson deputy prime minister: we'd be 15 points ahead', *The Telegraph*, 28 April 2015. Available at: www.telegraph.co.uk/news/general-election-2015/11565838/The-Tories-should-have-fired-Nick-Clegg-and-made-Boris-Johnson-deputy-prime-minister.-Wed-be-15-points-ahead.html

10 *PRWeek UK*, 8 October 2019.

11 Hickman, Arvind, 'Cleared murder suspect's parents "shameless" for using PR firm', *PRWeek*. Available at: www.prweek.com/article/1661753/cleared-murder-suspects-parents-shameless-using-pr-firm

Chapter 6

The Ethical Issues in Dealing with the Media

Media relations remains the core skill of public relations. It is what differentiates it from all the other communications disciplines, many of which offer some similar services to PR, such as digital communications, events management, promotions and advertising. But it is the PR person who is left to pitch the story to the sceptical journalist, or to take that difficult call when the media have uncovered damaging information. Take away media relations from the PR equation and what is left? Among the possible exceptions are lobbying or public affairs and corporate social responsibility (CSR), but even these tend to boast of their media relations prowess.

Moreover, PR is vital to the media. Without it, journalists, reporters and bloggers would struggle to find stories and fill their pages and airtime. We are including here in the term media, not just journalists from 'conventional' or 'mainstream media' where PR has traditionally 'earned' media coverage by selling in stories, but bloggers and 'influencers' on social media and also organisations' 'owned and shared media' such as websites, Facebook pages, Twitter feeds or Instagram accounts, where the PR does not have to deal through a third party like a journalist or blogger but can speak directly to its audience.

In this chapter we are going to look at how PR people can deal with the media while navigating a minefield of issues relating to truth and transparency. We'll examine:

1. PR's relationship with the media – the good, the bad and the ugly.
2. Is it ever OK to tell a lie to a journalist? Is it possible never to tell a lie? And whether PR can ever really be transparent about the much-used term 'transparency'.
3. PR's role in suppressing bad news and its use of the 'Dark Arts'.
4. How the growth in owned and shared media creates new ethical issues.

A Fraught Relationship

The relationship between PR people and journalists and bloggers can be fraught. The two sides can look like people in a fractious and argumentative relationship. They stay together because they need each other, but sometimes they don't seem to much like each other. In the morning, a PR may find themselves trying to sell in a positive news story to a sceptical journalist. In the afternoon, they may find themselves fending off awkward and intrusive questions from the same journalist about a story they would rather didn't surface. It is not really surprising that sometimes PR people find journalists annoying – and vice versa.

But despite this tension, PRs and journalists have to trade with each other – even if in many countries no money actually changes hands – as each wants and needs something out of the bargain. PR people want the best possible coverage for their organisations and to get their messages across, and journalists want a supply of the best quality news.

These two desires are frequently in conflict. PR people often want coverage for things which the media do not deem newsworthy – if, for example, every new product received the kind of coverage in the media that PR people seek, then we would read and hear about little else and the media would be monotonous and dull. On the other hand, what journalists consider to be newsworthy is often exactly what PR people want to suppress or minimise: 'bad news', stories about arguments, problems, scandals and even disasters: as the journalistic saying puts it, 'If it bleeds, it leads.'

Sometimes the crisis is real and the media interest is legitimate – there are clear dangers, failures or wrongdoings that imperil people's lives or well-being – but in other cases the media's claim of wanting to publish in the 'public interest' is less clear-cut. It could be that the journalist wants to reveal commercial secrets relating to a new product or service development, or publish disclosures about the private life of a senior figure in the organisation. In such situations there is often a strong difference of opinion between the organisation and the media. The latter will claim that what they are doing is legitimate journalism and in the public interest, while the organisation will claim that they have some right to confidentiality for commercial reasons or that their staff have some right to personal privacy (Box 6.1).

Box 6.1 When Does Media Interest Become Media Intrusion?

Prince Harry, Duke of Sussex, the Queen's grandson, and his American-born wife Meghan Markle, the Duchess of Sussex, have been in the media spotlight since their wedding in 2018, and have faced considerable criticism in the media, as well as what they see as unacceptable breaches of privacy at the hands of the press. In response, they supplemented their in-house royal PR with independent advice from the consultancy world.

How legitimate is the media's behaviour? On the one hand, the couple are newly-weds with a young child and are surely entitled to live as normally as possible. On the other hand, they have been in receipt of public funds and have chosen to adopt a high profile when it suits them. They can certainly afford PR help and use it to defend themselves. Arguably, like all celebrities, they depend on publicity and have to take the rough with the smooth – but there will always be a tension between what either side in a media story of this kind sees as acceptable.

The tension in this relationship has been further exacerbated by the huge growth in social media and its impact on the amount of money available to employ journalists and researchers. In the world's two biggest PR markets – the USA and the UK – there are now more PR people than journalists.[1,2] So the volume of media needing content has increased, but the number of journalists has not.

Three things seem to have happened. First, mainstream media now have to produce more copy or 'airtime' – including webcasts, podcasts, blogs and separate copy for online versions of their print and broadcast media brands – with fewer people. Second, they have to do this at a time when traditional media's main source of revenue – advertising – has fallen rapidly as advertising spend has moved online, especially to social media, depriving news media organisations of the money needed to increase or even maintain their staff numbers. At the same time, circulations for newspapers in many countries have slumped, causing a fall in subscription income, and in countries such as the USA and the UK many smaller newspapers have ceased publication or shifted from daily to weekly editions. These trends accelerated as a result of the COVID-19 lockdowns which further suppressed print media circulations and advertising.

This decline in revenue might not matter so much if newer online media were highly profitable and able to employ thousands of journalists, but online media, just like their older relations traditional media, are struggling to make money in an incredibly competitive market. Online media have found it very difficult to get people to pay for news as people have become accustomed to finding what they want for free, and yet journalism costs money. With the exception of publicly owned corporations, such as the UK's BBC, the media are businesses. They need to spend less than they earn to make a profit. One way of ensuring that is by using pre-cooked PR material, and PR sources, rather than trying to gather fresh ingredients and prepare all their content themselves.

But not just any oven-ready PR material will do. Journalists may be hungry, even desperate, for content, but they still have standards, their own ethical codes and editors who demand a good story which is well presented. The best PR people understand this. They know that they need to inform, educate and entertain (the original BBC mission). They also know they need a compelling narrative and to be truthful and honest.

In the UK, the Public Relations and Communications Association has produced a 'Media Spamming Charter' designed to help smooth the relationship between PRs and journalists.[3] However, while it offers excellent guidance on best practice – research your media targets, don't promise what you can't deliver, make it relevant – it doesn't cover the ethical issues such as truth and honesty as they are covered in the PRCA's main code of conduct (Box 6.2).

Box 6.2 Media Ethics

Media organisations set great store by ethics. The UK's *Guardian* newspaper uses the words of a famous former editor as a strapline: 'Comment is free, but the facts are sacred.' Other examples of ethical tablets of stone are below:

> The goal of *The New York Times* is to cover the news as impartially as possible — 'without fear or favor,'— and to treat readers, news sources, advertisers and others fairly and openly, and to be seen to be doing so. The reputation of *The Times* rests upon such perceptions, and so do the professional reputations of its staff members. Thus *The Times* and members of its news department and editorial page staff share an interest in avoiding conflicts of interest or an appearance of a conflict...[4]
>
> The BBC's Mission specifies that we must 'act in the public interest'. It is in the public interest to fulfil our mission to produce output to inform, educate and entertain ...[5]

These ideals are undoubtedly hard-wired into would-be journalists through their training regimes, and are bolstered by professional bodies, such as the UK's National Union of Journalists, which have their own codes.[6]

It is important for PR practitioners to be aware of journalists' ethical aspirations, but they can also sense, and sometimes exploit, journalistic realities in what is a troubled industry. The need for stories is so fundamental than journalists sometimes trample on all kinds of conventions and even break the law. They also have to satisfy their paymasters just as much as PR practitioners do. Their proprietors and editors have agendas and political views of their own, and have to keep costs down and sales and ratings up. Providing entertainment rather than properly produced hard news is often seen as the route to success.

Truth and Honesty

Truth and honesty might seem simple and uncontroversial at first glance, but need to be examined closely as they lie near to the heart of the ethical debate about PR (Box 6.3). They relate to ethics, but also have practical implications, as passing on untrustworthy information can be counterproductive. If it comes to be known that a PR person is not a source of reliable information, then journalists and others will look elsewhere for facts and comment (see pp. 54–55 for more on the workability of the requirement to tell the truth as enshrined in PR's ethical codes).

Box 6.3 John Harrington, Editor of *PRWeek UK*, on PR Ethics and the Media

John Harrington is Editor of *PRWeek UK*, the main PR industry trade magazine, and has over 15 years' experience as a journalist. Here he gives his views on some of the ethical issues that confront PR people and journalists.

'Unethical but Understandable'

My starting point is that it is never ethical to tell a lie … unless it is a lie to protect a life or national security. A PR person should always seek an alternative route, though I accept few alternatives are perfect.

Let's take the example of the PR who denies to a journalist that their client, a high-profile footballer, is gay, knowing full well that they are gay. I can understand the desire to protect the privacy of the footballer, particularly if they are not 'out' to their families, but an outright denial is still a lie.

The alternatives might be to either reply 'we never comment on the private lives of our clients' or negotiate with the journalist, explaining that the footballer needs time to tell his family but promising an exclusive interview when he is ready to come out.

I think not telling the truth to the journalist in this instance could be described as unethical but understandable. Trust and respect for the PR person who has lied would be diminished, though a full apology and explanation to the journalist lied to once the truth is revealed would go some way to mitigating that.

We [*PRWeek*] had an instance when we asked two agencies who were rumoured to be merging if they actually were. They flatly denied it. When we a little while later received the press release announcing the merger, I felt furious and it would be naïve to think this didn't affect our relationship with the two PR bosses involved.

Similarly, if a journalist – using legitimate means – gets information showing a high-profile business is about to launch a new kind of business, I think they have a right to be told the truth when they ring to confirm the story. I can understand the PR's temptation to deny the story so their client's competitors don't get an early warning, but if they do, they cannot expect to be fully trusted by journalists in the future. Again one solution might be for the PR person to negotiate and promise the journalist special access and exclusive interviews if they hold off revealing the news until the planned launch date.

I know some PRs will say that you can't trust journalists, but this is seldom true. Most journalists I know have been trained in both the law and ethics of their profession and do care and want to be reasonable and think about unwarranted damage to people and organisations.

There are of course times when a journalist will use 'unethical' means to achieve what they would argue is a greater ethical good. For example, pretending to be someone they are not in order to get a corrupt official or business person to say something they would never knowingly say to a journalist. The justification here for the journalist's deception always has to be that what is revealed is genuinely in the public interest ... and not just something the public are interested in.

Where things become a little more problematic for PR people is when dealing with influencers who have no codes or training and are not always transparent about their commercial relationships. Most behave well and take their role seriously, but I foresee that regulators like the ASA (the Advertising Standards Authority) are going to have to spend more time and energy on the monitoring of influencer behaviour and on the penalties for serious breaches of the codes by influencers and PRs.

Finally, there is the whole issue of who it is ethical to work for. The argument that everyone deserves the same right to PR representation as they do to legal representation seems more difficult to defend in a post Bell Pottinger world (see pp. 72–77). Someone without legal representation may lose their liberty. Someone without PR representation may lose their reputation. Serious, but not nearly as serious as losing your liberty. Though there is some evidence that you are more likely to be wrongly convicted if you have a poor PR image with judges and juries.

It is certainly the case that any PR who represents a person or organisation who has a poor image, or is seen as unethical or even criminal, faces the risk of having their own image seriously damaged, particularly if the client is subsequently proved to have acted wrongly or criminally. The ethical tests for the PR person faced with the opportunity of representing an unliked and mistrusted person or organisation are, first, do I believe what they are telling me?, and, second, are they asking me to cover up or minimise wrongdoing, or simply asking me to explain the positive elements of their activities?

Some of these ethical conundrums can be summed up with the question, 'Is it ethical to do PR for a road safety campaign, that will undoubtedly save lives, when the client is a government who doesn't respect human rights?' I think many PR firms would probably take on the work. After all, lots of PR firms are active in China, despite its poor record on human rights and no real democracy. Applying ethical principles in the real world can be a difficult subject!

This reality means that no one – including journalists – expects PR people to tell the full truth about the organisations they serve. Nor can PR people always avoid uttering an untruth by saying 'no comment'. Such a refusal is now generally seen by the media and public as saying you are not denying the story – which you probably would if it were totally untrue. In the real world, disputes and problems will frequently be glossed over or even denied. Colleagues have to pretend to like and respect each other even if they do not, disagreements at senior level are denied and new product plans kept secret – and PR people have to participate in such 'white lies' and evasions. PR people who sought to tell the full truth in such circumstances would soon find themselves without a job. Indeed, politicians and others who admit the full truth to journalists are often seen as more naïve than praiseworthy by the media. It is worth noting that although journalists often rail against PR people for lying, in reality, their own position is more nuanced. Sometimes the end justifies the means. For example, as mentioned in Box 6.3, major news stories are often the result of journalists operating undercover and adopting a false identity. In such cases journalists are, by definition, lying, but excuse themselves by claiming that it is only in such ways that they can secure information which the public deserves – or would like – to know. This is a utilitarian defence – that the ends justify the otherwise unacceptable means: Immanuel Kant (see pp. 8–9) would not approve!

As journalists are well aware, the organisations which PR people serve are paying for the service, so no one should be surprised that the PR person accentuates the positive and minimises the organisation's negative aspects when portraying it to journalists and others. A truly faithful representation would have to include detailing all an organisation's faults. After all, when you go for a job interview, the prospective employer does not expect you to lie, but nor do they expect you to volunteer a complete list of all your shortcomings! See Box 6.4.

Box 6.4 Francis Ingham on PR Ethics and the Media

According to Francis Ingham, Director General of the PRCA:

I have said in lectures for Simon Goldsworthy at Westminster and Richmond Universities that there are black-and-white issues but those are the minority of issues. Most things are grey. And the code of conduct that our members abide by is there to help them navigate their way through the grey waters of choices to be made. So we have in our code both the duty of truth and the duty of confidentiality. And if, for example, you are working for a client whom you know to be having mental health issues and you are asked by a tabloid newspaper to comment on those issues, or you are working for somebody who is gay but has chosen not to make that public, you have both those duties of confidentiality and truth to bear in mind when you respond. And the crucial point about effective PR professionals is that they can weigh those competing imperatives up and come to the right decision.

Q: What would you say if someone is asked about their relationship with a colleague and they lie about it?

I think that would depend upon the nature of that relationship. Whether they were in a position of power over that person. What the rules of their employer were and if there was a broader public interest in that area. And, again, that's why we give guidance to members so they can navigate those difficult choices.

Some have argued that when people say they have full confidence in a colleague, that's almost invariably a lie. Well, that has become a euphemism for they're going to be sacked, hasn't it? But that's more a matter of language than of morality.

A senior PR industry insider's view:

PR people are professional liars. And that's what they're paid for. They're paid to find a way with words that keeps you just on the right side of legality and improves your reputation or helps it not be destroyed. And you pay them quite a lot of money for it. It is no coincidence that the highest-paid people in PR are in the financial services sector where consummate lying is a work of art and a highly-rewarded one.

Francis Ingham responds to this:

Well, it's a complete parody and pastiche of our industry and it plays to stereotypes that never were true, even if they were popular. Our industry has truth and regard to the public interest at its very heart. It's embedded in our code of conduct. Everybody knows we enforce our code of conduct with rigour and without fear or favour. And I really wish that these people who run our industry down would just accept what they know to be true, namely, that they themselves are lying about this. Our industry conveys truth and serves a public good.

A similar point applies to the popular concept of 'transparency'. This term, with its positive overtones, is much talked about, but often in a rather unthinking way. There is some information which every organisation has to reveal, and even more that it is hard to conceal – so it may be better to reveal it yourself in a controlled way rather than allow it to emerge in a way and at a time which are not of your own choosing. However, we know of no organisation which allows itself to be fully transparent, for example, by disclosing full records of all its internal discussions (as opposed to carefully drafted minutes of formal meetings).

When not telling the truth, many of us – quite sincerely – say that it was simply a 'white lie' (Box 6.5), 'a little fib', perhaps 'being economical with the truth', or even 'being kind' (only a brutal parent would never lie to their child!). People, including journalists, accept that everyone does this to some extent. The real ethical test is whether your 'little white lie' would be described much less kindly by others and seen as an 'outright and damaging lie'.

Box 6.5 A Little White Lie?

One of the authors handled the launch of one of the UK's largest online banks. Pre-launch secrecy was vital as the new bank wanted to maximise its competitive advantage by maintaining control over the timing of the announcement. However, as is often the case, a journalist heard rumours about the preparations and rang up to enquire.

Telling the truth would have meant losing control over the announcement before the bank was ready, leaving competitors with a free hand. Obfuscation and refusal to comment were not an option: the journalist already had the germ of a story and if it was not denied, it would probably be published in some form. The option chosen was to tell a 'little white lie'. The journalist was told that the new facilities were simply a new back office for the bank's existing branch network: untrue, but effective and, it could be argued, harmless as no member of the public or shareholder had been disadvantaged or wronged.

Exercise

If possible, divide yourselves into two groups. One group should construct and write up the most persuasive argument they can for the legal obligation to carry national identity cards. The other group should meanwhile construct and write up the best argument they can against mandatory national identity cards. Each group should then examine the others' case using the truth model in Figure 6.1 for examples of exaggeration or understating the 'truth'.

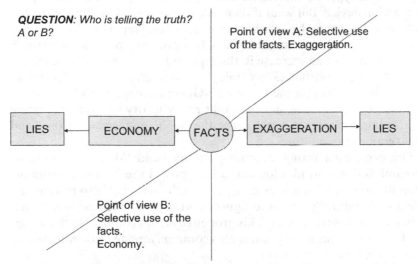

QUESTION: Who is telling the truth?
A or B?

Point of view A: Selective use
of the facts. Exaggeration.

LIES ← ECONOMY ← FACTS → EXAGGERATION → LIES

Point of view B:
Selective use of the
facts.
Economy.

The reaction to a lie is determined by its intent, level of factual inaccuracy and risk
for the recipient of the information.

Figure 6.1 The Truth Model.
Source: Trevor Morris, 2006.

PR's Role in Promoting Good News

PR's role in proactively promoting products, ideas, policies and brand
awareness is generally less controversial than its role in suppressing or
minimising bad news (see below) but it is nonetheless not without its
own ethical issues. Promotion blurs into hype, and that easily becomes a
realm where exaggeration takes hold.

For example, most proactive PR stories are backed up with *evidence* or
facts and figures of the 'one in three women suffer from oily skin ...' or
'over half of small businesses have insufficient savings ...' variety. Sometimes this data is based on detailed research designed originally and primarily to provide useful business and market intelligence. Its use for a PR
story is secondary. But there is also the sort of research commissioned
by PR people specifically to secure media coverage. In both types of research, but particularly the latter, there is a danger that, either by ignoring inconvenient findings or asking questions that tend to solicit 'useful
responses', a partial truth is revealed or even a false impression given. So,
for example, research into national crime figures may show an increase in

a particular type of crime that is likely to stimulate people to buy a crime prevention device. But what if there is another way of looking at the figures that shows that the way the police record and report such crimes has greatly improved, meaning that there has probably been no increase in actual crime, just an increase in the reported crime? Would it be ethical under these circumstances to employ a 'rise in crime' angle? One might argue it is the job of the media, or an NGO or a competitor's PR team, to put the alternative case, but does that really justify knowingly creating a false impression that might cause the public unnecessary worry and unwarranted expenditure?

One cynical marketing communicator once said: 'My attitude towards research is like a drunk's towards a lamppost. I use it more for support than illumination.' Statistics may be factually true, but also misleading. We are all naturally drawn to figures that support our case and turn a blind eye to those that don't. This propensity is not confined to those simply hoping to make money, but is also common among those who believe their cause is noble and good.

Then there is the use of *experts* to back up and add credibility to a story. This occurs where a scientist, psychologist or some kind of expert backs up the story and sometimes even directly endorses the product, service or cause involved. It might be argued that this is fair enough if the endorsement is sincere. But what if it is not freely given but paid for? Should not that be clearly stated? Such endorsements are of course also common in advertising – but there we all know the expert will normally have been paid, even if it is not stated.

Another area of concern can be the *case study* – the example that brings the evidence in a story alive. A fake case study is when a PR practitioner gets a friend or even a member of staff to pretend to be a user of a product, or the sufferer of a problem that the PR's client's product can solve. There was a notable case a few years ago in the UK when it was revealed that the person in a media story said to be suffering from a perspiration problem was in fact an employee, with no perspiration problem, working for the PR firm promoting an anti-perspiration product.[7] The firm, Fuel PR, was shamed and sanctioned by the PRCA, but it would be naïve to think that, under pressure to find a case study that will say exactly what they want and in the way they want it, other practitioners have not been tempted to take the same route, particularly in owned media where there is no journalist who might check the veracity of what is said.

It is noteworthy just how many case studies, particularly related to family and lifestyle issues, are about people who work in 'media' or 'PR' or 'communications'. While the stories may be completely genuine, they just happen to also be colleagues, friends or relations of the PR practitioner behind the story, something which also makes life easier for the hard-pressed journalist.

We asked a senior PR industry insider about this, citing the above example of Fuel PR:

> Oh, let's be clear, the kind of thing that Fuel PR was expelled by the PRCA for is entirely commonplace. Just grabbing some random person, whether employed by you or not, to say they're a concerned citizen or they're a consumer or anything like that, it happens all the time. The only thing that Fuel PR did wrong was to be found out.

There are potential ethical issues around *the image* supporting the story. For example, politicians love to be seen in photographs surrounded by an adoring throng – even when the throng is in reality a few friends, family and supporters herded together by the communications team and photographed to look like a crowd. Or protest groups who claim the numbers attending a march were vastly in excess of the numbers reported elsewhere and support their claims with carefully angled shots designed to make the crowd look as large as possible.

Concerns are also sometimes raised by the images used to promote products such as fashion, beauty and food. The media inevitably tend to reflect the public's desire to see attractive images and to be allowed to aspire to a kind of perfection. But is it ethical to only use models with 'perfect' figures, or to photoshop pictures of people and places to look better than they really are?

It seems hard to reconcile the claims that media images are responsible both for a rise in obesity and a rise in eating disorders like anorexia. But the evidence certainly seems to show both conditions are on the increase, even if the link to PR and media images is unproven.

In many of the above cases – particularly in the consumer field – the journalist or blogger is complicit. They want a good story backed up with some facts, an expert opinion, an emotionally engaging case study and an attractive or interesting image – and they want to obtain it all quickly and easily. Most are fully aware of the tricks of the PR trade and don't ask too many detailed questions. Indeed, many use these tricks themselves when writing their own stories. Their justification is that it is harmless and every story needs to be well told. It can also be argued that when it comes to more serious or controversial issues, it is the job of the journalist or blogger to probe and question the evidence provided, the experts used, the case studies offered and the images employed. But does the fact that a journalist has a responsibility for truth and accuracy absolve the PR practitioner of their responsibility?

Crisis Management and PR's Role in Suppressing Bad News

So much for proactive or positive PR. Anyone with a serious PR role will, at least occasionally, be called upon to suppress or at least reduce the impact of bad news. This is never easy. Bad news is good news for a journalist.

One technique that is used by politicians, governments and companies is *timing*. When an organisation is obliged for legal or other reasons to announce something which does not reflect well on it, they will often wait until there is a glut of news – whether it is one event that is dominating the headlines or a series of big stories. Sometimes such stories can be anticipated, but at other times the opportunity arises on the spur of the moment, as an unforeseen event or disaster unfolds. If the media are pre-occupied with such stories, and consider them more important than your announcement, then yours will receive less coverage than would otherwise be the case, or even no coverage at all.

Another technique is to leave your announcement until it is as close as possible to the major news channels' deadlines. With rolling 24/7 broadcast and online news this technique is less effective than it used to be, but still has some value as there are still key moments for news production and most journalists continue to be slaves to deadlines – the exact times when they have to submit their stories for publication or broadcast. It is hard to overestimate the importance of deadlines. Once a deadline is missed, the news is of less use to the journalist concerned and so the times have to be factored into a PR person's calculations. Obviously, journalists would like to receive news well before their deadlines in order to give them time to prepare their stories and, in the case of TV, get some footage – 'news is where the cameras are'. In these circumstances, it can sometimes be beneficial to make your announcement right up against the deadline. This reflects the fact that the news media have to cover really major developments as soon as they occur – even to the point of newspapers publishing extra editions and broadcasters breaking into programmes. If your story is big enough – and that means really big for the medium concerned – they will have to cover it in this way, and largely on your own terms, as they will have little time to seek alternative information or views. Rolling news may be changing the game but key news programmes at set times still reach a large share of viewers, while newspaper front pages continue to play an important role in setting the news agenda.

Whether or not this manipulation of the news agenda is seen as unethical rather depends on your view of the ethics of the news itself. If you work for a charity, company or government that might be disproportionately hurt by a major story that leads the news, then you are likely to think it ethical to try and avoid it. If, on the other hand, you are a member of the public who has been hurt by a government failing and is keen to see the report revealing the government's shortcomings given maximum prominence, you may feel the technique unethical and even offensive.

Dealing with Hostile Stories

This is best undertaken as soon as possible, ideally before the story actually appears in the media. Usually a combination of the tactics below is employed:

- Complain to the media. PR people can complain about a story – ideally before it even appears – to the journalist concerned, but can also go over the journalist's head and protest to editors and senior management, or even the proprietor of the media organisation. This can certainly place the journalist in an uncomfortable position, and many media organisations will hesitate if they face a barrage of high-level complaints.

  This can be quite a brutal process, involving harsh language and (usually perfectly legal) threats – such as the withdrawal of future co-operation. How ethical this is will be a matter of judgement, and it has to be remembered that journalists themselves can be quite ruthless in gathering stories and can give as good as they get.

- Such complaints can be backed up with threats of legal action, typically for defamation or breach of privacy. Even if they think they might win, media organisations fear the risk, costs and waste of time involved in long-drawn-out legal proceedings. Rival media organisations may also be deterred from running the story if they are told about the threat of legal action. Other threats can include appealing to any relevant media regulatory bodies and the possible withdrawal of advertising – although 'reputable' media will always claim that advertising revenue doesn't influence editorial policy.

  In ethical terms, this can be viewed in a similar light to the previous point. It can be hard to determine how legitimate such threats are – they can made by people who know full well that they will never be acted upon and/or have no foundation, but nonetheless may scare the relevant news media.

- If bad news is anticipated, expectations can be managed by off-the-record briefings and leaks which give the media advance notice of what is happening. If the bad news is already known, it is no longer really news: the sting is removed. Everyone – including journalists – immediately puts a news story into the context of what they already know and expect. Indeed, PR people working for highly successful organisations have to be particularly careful because expectations are so high. If a company which was expected to make enormous profits made a very small profit, it would be reported more negatively than an announcement by a company which was expected to make very large losses and in fact only made a small loss.

These tactics could be viewed as underhand. They certainly illustrate why it is difficult for PR people to be fully transparent in their work.

- If the PR person is in a powerful enough position, they can create and offer alternative news – decoy stories which serve to distract the media from the 'bad news' story. Politicians have been known to dish the dirt on rivals or even colleagues in return for a journalist dropping a damaging story about them.
- If the story does appear, PR people can ensure that it is rebutted as quickly as possible. Challenging the facts in a story is made easier by the speed with which journalists work. News stories habitually contain inaccuracies or errors, or rely on sources which might change their stories. Even if the central thrust of the story is correct, by undermining elements of it, the PR person can weaken its overall credibility.

Other tried-and-tested ways of undermining problem stories include the following:

- Swiftly acknowledging and, where appropriate, apologising for faults or errors, and thereby achieving 'closure'. Although this may seem a hard thing to do, once this is done, the story often peters out, unless there are fresh ingredients, or the problem is too big for a simple apology to suffice. This technique can be combined with the following approaches.
- Attacking or discrediting the source of the story. Personalities are key ingredients in any news story and if they lack credibility or appear ridiculous, anything they say is undermined. Sometimes the PR can supply an alternative source with equal or greater credibility who can contradict or undermine the negative story.
- Making the problem historic. If an organisation faces criticism, they make it clear that the criticisms relate to the past and that things have now changed for the better.
- Pushing the problem away. Typically, this involves setting up a review or inquiry, or commissioning a report. This is readily portrayed as a sensible and responsible course of action, but media coverage will normally die down while the review is undertaken. The delay can be used to prepare properly and the organisation can legitimately refuse to comment further while the outcome of the review or report is pending. Governments tend to be keen on this tactic. By the time the report comes out, the story has usually lost its edge.

- Accentuating the positive. Even in the most critical reports there are often positive aspects. Part of a PR's job is to find the positives and give them plenty of emphasis. They also make sure that anyone from the organisation who is likely to speak to the media is fully briefed on whatever is positive. Even if they have to acknowledge or apologise for problems, they can spend much longer talking about good news and what went right.
- 'Starving' the media. To keep going, news stories need fresh fuel. If the organisation which is at the centre of the storm, having made a statement, refuses to be drawn further and turns down interview bids, the news often dies down (provided of course there are no further revelations from elsewhere).
- Exploiting journalistic and media rivalries. Media outlets (and individual journalists) have a vested interest in undermining – where possible – their rivals' stories.

All these points carry two important health warnings. First, they depend on the amount of power the PR team has and is seen to have – including their ability to control the news emerging from the organisation (not always something that can be guaranteed when things go wrong and people within the organisation are focused on their personal standing and future prospects). Adopting a tough stance with journalists and media organisations may be necessary, but inevitably stores up resentments which can come back to haunt PRs when they and their organisation are vulnerable. Second, PRs will ultimately be judged on whether their approach was a legitimate, 'ethical' one which was in the interests of the organisation and did not endanger or disadvantage the public; or whether their approach was 'unethical' and simply designed to protect an organisation that was seriously at fault and had avoided taking responsibility and proper remedial action for the alleged crisis or problem.

In these circumstances, being effective is difficult. Being effective and ethical is even harder. Such techniques take us into Machiavellian territory (see p. 10) – they sound ruthless, but they are founded on realism, not least the knowledge that they can be effective, and are part of what is expected of senior PR practitioners.

Successful crisis management is hard to detect; in its ideal form, it leaves no traces. The crucial activity is seldom public or documented, and journalists are reluctant witnesses while PR people's self-interest has to be weighed up in considering their own claims about what they have achieved. Maybe nothing at all appears in the media, or, more likely, there is negative coverage and criticism (Box 6.6) – but perhaps this is more muted, less prominent or more balanced than it would have been otherwise. All this is next to impossible to prove. Perhaps the best evidence of its effectiveness is that almost everyone who needs it and can afford it pays handsomely for the service.

Exercise

Examine closely some 'bad news' stories in the media. What evidence can you find of PR being used to play down the stories, and how effective do you think it was?

Box 6.6 PR and Dieselgate

> Someday, Volkswagen's emissions cheating scandal will be studied in crisis communications textbooks. And not in a good way.[8]

In September 2015, 'Dieselgate', the Volkswagen (VW) emissions scandal, erupted as the US Environmental Protection Agency found that the VW Group was violating the Clean Air Act and that their cars were much more polluting in real conditions than in official laboratory tests. Up to 11 million cars worldwide were affected. VW's share price plummeted.

VW already retained Edelman for consumer PR, but had traditionally relied on in-house PR. Facing a massive scandal, it brought in three more PR companies – Hering Schuppener in Germany, Finsbury in Britain, and Kekst in the USA. As one commentator put it, the company moved from reputational constipation to reputational dysentery.[9] It established an in-house 'newsroom' (as it had done before when the company faced negative coverage about the use of prostitutes by executives).

PR people often take centre stage in crises, but their own ethical responsibility is limited. It is unlikely that PR people were aware of the problem in advance. VW itself blamed engineers and technicians, and it's unreasonable to think that PR practitioners could cross-check or even understand technical information of this kind. So PR came late to the scene. But it is also difficult for PR people to plan for major crises of this kind which often arise from unethical or illegal behaviour on the part of other people within the organisations they serve: suggesting that senior people could be guilty of such things could be unpalatable. In practice, PR is often ill-prepared and has to pick up the pieces, becoming the ethical fall guy for others.

Gauging the role of PR as the crisis unfolded is hard because PR agencies are not necessarily transparent. As Hering Schuppener put it: 'We have never and will never comment on any client work that we might or might not be doing.' However, the troubled company they were working for had at least admitted its misdeeds and was seeking to make amends. By April 2016, VW sales returned to normal in Europe – and in Britain sales were unaffected – but was this due to skilful and effective PR, or to shortening media attention spans, scandal fatigue and the shift to social media as a source of information and comment?

Do Social Media Pose Different Ethical Issues?

Social media are meant to be non-corporate, authentic and genuine. Meant to be. But are they? Facebook, Instagram and Twitter, unlike conventional media, do not have journalists or editors that a PR person has to persuade to cover their story. Anything goes, provided it passes the social media's rules on sex, violence and terror. Nor do PR people always fully reveal themselves on social media – although, according to most PR codes, they should (Box 6.7). The requirement to be transparent remains hard to enforce, given the enormous volume of social media activity: just look at how Facebook, despite its enormous resources, struggles to monitor content.

Box 6.7 The UK Government's Office for Security and Counter-Terrorism (OSCT) Raises an Ethical Issue

In 2019, it was revealed by the Middle East Eye news organisation that a social network called 'This is Woke', aimed at young British Muslims, was actually created on behalf of the OSCT as part of the British Government's 'Prevent' counter-radicalisation initiative aimed at tackling Islamist extremism.

This is Woke described itself as a 'diverse social news platform' that engages 'in critical discussions around Muslim identity, tradition and reform'. But the OSCT wouldn't talk to the website Middle East Eye about the project, claiming that to do so would 'prejudice the national security of the UK'.

According to Middle East Eye, some people featured in the videos on the Woke pages did not know it was part of the British Government's Prevent programme.

However, the Home Office, the British Government department responsible for domestic security, said the following: 'We are committed to using all of the tools available to counter the threat from terrorism. The Prevent programme continues to play a vital role in this fight against radicalisation and has had a significant impact in stopping people being drawn in to terrorism.'

Few would argue with the desire to counter terrorism and fight against radicalisation, but is it ethical to be less than fully transparent about who is behind social media posts? The British Government, like many other governments, has been quick to criticise political interference via anonymous social media campaigns. Interestingly, one of the comments under *The Times* story took the view that the end justifies the means, describing the Woke project as 'sensible', but criticising the security services saying they 'should do better job at hiding links to the government'. What do you think?[10]

The Rise of Influencers

Celebrities on Twitter are supposed to use '#ad' when they have been sponsored – though the use of the hash tag is far from universal. The waters get muddier when there has not been a direct financial payment, but the blogger or influencer has been given valuable free products.

As traditional media weaken, for the reasons described earlier in this chapter, online influencers are on the rise. Most journalists have been trained, are members of a professional body, such as the UK's National Union of Journalists (NUJ), and, working within structured organisations, are subject to the professional scrutiny of their editor and other colleagues. In many cases they are subject to regulation as well, for example, most print publications in the UK are members of the Independent Press Standards Organisation, and broadcasters such as the BBC are regulated by Ofcom, a statutory body. Moreover, their media employers have money, so are worth taking to court. While there are examples of appalling behaviour by journalists, it is fair to say that most journalists, most of the time, adhere to certain ethical standards and codes of practice. Simply knowing this is likely to help deter PRs with poor ethics from behaving badly, and while PRs do the best job they can for their paymasters, they normally expect the journalist to display reasonable scepticism: it's a grown-up relationship. But what happens when a PR deals with a blogger or influencer who has received no training, is bound by no code, has no editor, is subject to no form of regulation and is not worth suing, as they don't have much money? Is the temptation there for the PR person's standards to slip, believing that the consequences of being found out are less severe, or that the blogger or influencer is easier to corrupt?

Many bloggers and influencers receive all kinds of free products from PRs (see fashion and travel in Chapter 7). This may not be a direct payment so it doesn't have to be declared, but it is clearly an inducement or 'payment in kind'. So isn't there a danger that PR and blogger are effectively misleading the public?

Exercise

Should bloggers and influencers have a code of conduct and what would it say? Discuss.

Fake Fans and Support

There is always a temptation for PRs to initiate support for their own campaigns by getting friends and family to comment on, like, share and hashtag them. Some of these friends and family may be genuine enthusiasts for whatever they are liking and sharing, but some probably aren't. A big firm with a lot of staff, or a campaigning group with lots of social media savvy members, can quite easily make it appear there is a big groundswell of support for their campaign. Is this ethical?

The practice of fake reviews is also at best ethically dubious – ranging from asking a friend to paying someone to do it. Amazon and Tripadvisor are particular targets for this sort of practice, but it is now also seen on social media, where it may be harder to spot. And what of the firms who take on interns with the promise of useful work experience and then just get them to sit at a desk on social media accounts 'liking', sharing and following things? Surely this is unethical on at least two counts (see pp. 185–188 on internships)?

Most PR people would probably say they agree that it is unethical to buy followers on Twitter and yet there are lots of well-followed accounts that seem to have minimal or no interaction with their followers. Perhaps those followers don't actually exist? Shouldn't an ethical PR person at least be questioning accounts that have large but inactive followings? The trouble is that getting their organisation or client mentioned on a Twitter, Facebook or YouTube account with a lot of followers looks good for the PR people when it comes to campaign evaluation and satisfying those who pay them.

Anecdotally, and rather depressingly, there is a lot of evidence of PR people quite simply inflating their success figures by using some or all of the tactics above and at the same time ignoring evidence on how long people actually watched their 'brilliant two-minute viral video', or actually looked at the page or piece for which they have proudly provided the content.

Presenting media evaluation figures in the best possible light has always been a feature of the PR world, but with conventional media the opportunities to exaggerate are more limited and false claims are easier to expose than is often the case with social media.

Social media hosts themselves can fall into this trap. At one point, Facebook claimed to reach more members of a particular demographic than were actually alive. It told its advertisers that it could reach no fewer than 41 million of a core target group of 18–24-year-olds in the United States. However, Pivotal Research Group pointed out in a note to customers that there are only 31 million 18–24-year-olds in the USA, according to the official census data.[11]

Beyond the world of inflated social media reach figures and the world of spurious grassroots campaigns, there is another grey area for ethics. Wikipedia as a not-for-profit – and therefore independent – online encyclopedia of knowledge has become a powerful and important go-to source for journalists, academics, researchers, students and NGOs. Produced and edited by user editors who often work in the world of research and higher education, it is arguable that it inevitably, albeit unintentionally or unconsciously, leans politically a little to the left. Of course, when it gets its facts wrong, it should be corrected. The difficulty comes when organisations or individuals feel that Wikipedia has made selective use of the facts, including leaving out important information. They may also take issue with the tone of some of the Wikipedia copy. It is at this point that some PR practitioners, acting on behalf of their clients, have altered Wikipedia entries without declaring who is behind the alteration, beyond a hard-to-trace personal name. This takes us back to the issue of honesty and transparency. It is not the altering of the Wikipedia entry that is potentially unethical, but the lack of transparency about who is behind it.

The Wikipedia Community informally call the worst forms of this 'Vandalising'. They also call it *'Conflict-of-interest (COI)'* editing. This, they say, occurs when 'editors' use Wikipedia:

[to] advance the interests of their external roles or relationships. The type of COI editing of most concern on Wikipedia is paid editing for public relations purposes. Several Wikipedia policies and guidelines exist to combat conflict of interest editing, including Wikipedia: Conflict of interest and Wikipedia: Paid-contribution disclosure.[12]

Offenders whose activities have been revealed in the media have included US congressional staff editing articles about Members of Congress, Microsoft, the now defunct PR firm Bell Pottinger (see pp. 72–77), British MPs, the CIA, BP, Sony and the Vatican!

Meanwhile some of the rich and powerful have turned to lawyers to try to force Google to remove past stories that embarrass them while at the same time hiring PRs to manufacture activity that will bring more recent good news to the top of the search engine and de-optimise or push the older, less favorable news down to the second or third page of search results. Your view on whether this is ethical may well depend on what you think of the organisation or individual in question. Search engine optimisation, ensuring that positive search returns appear high on the first page, is a growing area of activity and income for the PR industry – one that inevitably tends to favour the rich and powerful who can afford the fees. Is it right that the reverse of this, the attempt to sweep bad news under the carpet, can be attempted and that Google can be manipulated in this way?

Owned Media

Finally, we need to look at organisations' 'owned media', such as their websites, Facebook pages, Twitter feeds or Instagram accounts, where the PR does not have to operate through a third party such as a journalist or blogger, but can speak directly to its audience. This is clearly a very powerful thing to be able to do, and works particularly well for businesses and organisations that have followers and fans in areas such as fashion, sport, music and some kinds of quasi-political causes. (Meanwhile in the case of many large, important but not fundamentally interesting organisations, such as financial services or utility companies, most people only ever go to their owned media to complain and grumble.)

Most of the ethical issues inherent in owned media are the same as we have looked at above for conventional and social media – selective use of facts, fake case studies and fake fans. But there are two additional areas of concern with 'owned' media. The first is how people's data is used and how privacy is respected. There are now increasingly stringent data protection rules in most parts of the world, with fines for breaches of the rules often in the millions of dollars or euros. PR people are seldom data-literate, nor are they accustomed to dealing with data protection laws and therein lies a danger – they may, through ignorance or misunderstanding, cause or allow a data breach. When it comes to owned media, data isn't just for the geeks but for PR people. Indeed, the ethics of data protection practice are now, unlike so many other areas of PR, embedded in the law. PR people need to know what the law is.

The other area of ethical concern with 'owned media' is the potential lack of accountability (Box 6.8). Fans and supporters are usually well informed on their areas of interest and should be able to spot and expose any shortfalls in honesty or transparency. But fans and supporters are also loyal and often emotional in their attachment, which leaves them potentially open to exploitation by unscrupulous communicators. It is worth noting that in the UK claims made online in owned media are viewed as advertising by the regulatory body, the Advertising Standards Authority (ASA), which considers the truth and honesty of advertisements as well as their decency. Advertising people are used to this kind of regulation, whereas PR people, who were accustomed to operating through third parties, are having to adapt themselves to its requirements.

Box 6.8 Jim Hawker, CEO of Three Pipe, on Ethical Issues Facing the Industry

Jim Hawker, CEO and co-founder of Three Pipe, a top UK social media and digital agency which describes itself as 'here to help brands and organisations to build creative strategies to overcome algorithms' on the ethical issues facing the industry.

There is a battle going on between engagement and the vanity of big numbers. This has arisen because it is starting to get quite expensive for brands to run social media channels. And as the costs increase – social media is increasingly a paid rather than earned channel – so too does the pressure to provide hard data on the ROI (return on investment). This has driven some brands and PR firms to pursue and even buy followers at the expense of real engagement that influences behaviour. Even the move away from brand-owned social media towards working with influencers that directly engage with a brand's audience isn't without its ethical issues as more and more stories emerge of influencers buying followers or charging their followers to participate in sometimes dubious schemes.

With so much competition for social media attention, there is also a tendency for some brands and influencers to do anything to create a storm regardless of whether that storm is actually adding anything to the social good. At least with conventional media there were journalists acting as gatekeepers for truth and responsibility. That safety valve can be lacking with owned social media. But having said that, there is an increasing amount of regulation not just in areas such as healthcare and finance, but even in areas like food, so it is not all bad news. One would also hope that people generally – using the power of social media – will act as guardians of privacy and ethical behaviour, though the facts don't always support this view. For example, some consumers have left Facebook in protest at their perceived failure to control fake news and hate speech, only to join Instagram or WhatsApp, which are both owned by Facebook. Moreover, despite all the furore about Facebook, its share price has remained largely unaffected.

What is going to be really interesting is the impact of the new kid on the block TikTok (www.tiktok.com/en-uk/), the Chinese-backed social media platform. TikTok has grown phenomenally quickly, but presents some interesting issues, not least for national security, with American think tank Peterson Institute for International Economics describing TikTok as a 'Huawei-sized problem' that poses a national security threat to the West. The Chinese also have a different ethical take on censorship and some of the social issues that are commonly aired on social media. Big brands will not be able to avoid TikTok if it continues to grow, but nor will the big brands be able to dodge some of the ethical issues that will arise.

Some critics refer to SEO (Search Engine Optimisation) as though it is sinister and manipulative, but it isn't (or shouldn't be) about changing the story or spin but understanding how Google works and how to present your story in the best way – rather like presenting your CV in the best way and to the right people.

In broad terms, I believe that the ethical issues facing PR in social media are the same issues that have always faced PR ... transparency, honesty and accuracy.[13]

Acknowledgements

Questions and exercises: with thanks to the PRCA and Claire Walker.

Summary

PR's role in media relations now extends beyond its traditional stronghold and unique selling proposition: 'earned' media, the media coverage it influences through working with journalists. In addition to promoting good news, PR includes a more furtive and controversial role in playing down bad news. PR is also involved in producing 'owned' media; organisations' own media outlets, including their websites and social media; and, increasingly, in social and other forms of digital media, it is responsible for 'shared' and 'paid' media. All of this presents PR with new ethical challenges.

Questions

1. During a media interview your CEO accidentally gives an inaccurate figure about your company's capability, making the company sound better than it is. It was not intended to mislead, but the fact is now part of the published story. What do you do?
2. Your boss asks you to get as many people together as possible, including friends and family, to appear at a photoshoot to launch your new product. Is this acceptable?
3. Your privately-owned client asks you to inflate the value of a contract win by half a million pounds (adding about 30 per cent to the overall value) to make it sound bigger and better. There is little if any danger of anyone calling this out. Should you do your boss's bidding?
4. Your boss has suggested that a couple of announcements that are potentially damaging should be slipped out on a busy news day. What do you do?
5. A senior member of the PR industry has been exposed in the media for editing research figures in a way that gives the impression that their product is more effective than it is. Should they be reprimanded or expelled from the relevant industry association?
6. A major part of your campaign's success is based on data from influencers' sites which you are dubious about. What do you tell your client?
7. Should every PR-initiated piece of social media activity carry a '#client' or even '#PR'? What do you think?

Notes

1 See www.holmesreport.com/long-reads/article/global-pr-industry-now-worth-$15bn-as-growth-rebounds-to-7-in-2016
2 See www.theguardian.com/media/greenslade/2016/jun/10/survey-finds-that-prs-outnumber-journalists-by-large-margin; www.bls.gov/oes/#data
3 See www.prca.org.uk/about-us/pr-standards/media-spamming-charter
4 See www.nytimes.com/editorial-standards/ethical-journalism.html#
5 See www.bbc.co.uk/editorialguidelines/guidelines/editorial-standards#introduction
6 For example, www.nuj.org.uk/about/nuj-code/
7 See www.prweek.com/article/1368002/sweaty-gate-agency-fuel-pr-expelled-prca
8 See www.nytimes.com/2016/02/28/business/international/vws-crisis-strategy-forward-reverse-u-turn.html
9 See www.standard.co.uk/business/gideon-spanier-the-vw-emissions-scandal-is-a-case-study-in-how-not-to-manage-a-reputation-crisis-a2958236.html
10 See www.bbc.co.uk/news/technology-49368872
11 See www.theregister.co.uk/2017/09/06/facebook_claims_more_users_than_exist/
12 See https://en.wikipedia.org/wiki/Conflict-of-interest_editing_on_Wikipedia
13 See www.threepipe.co.uk/

Chapter 7

Lobbying and Ethical Outrage

Lobbying is seldom out of the news – and not in a good way. In the UK, the USA, Australia, Canada and most of Europe, the media and activist groups make much of what they see as the undue influence of corporations, the rich and the powerful on governments. Nonetheless, lobbying, which seeks to influence the actions of international, national and local governments and regulatory bodies, is also seen as an essential part of any democracy and is protected – as well as regulated – by the law.

In this chapter we look at:

- What is 'lobbying' – also sometimes called 'public affairs' or 'advocacy'?
- Why lobbying causes so much controversy and, occasionally, scandal.
- How the industry codes of practice – and the law – try to ensure ethical practice and limit abuse.
- What the ethical issues and dilemmas are when practising lobbying in the real world.

Are PR, Lobbying and Advocacy the Same Thing?

People who work in lobbying or public affairs avoid describing themselves as working in PR believing, perhaps erroneously, that lobbying has a better reputation and is more sophisticated than PR with its associations with fashion, celebrity and consumer goods. Certainly, it is true that most people who work in PR are not 'lobbyists' but almost anyone working in PR will at some point over the course of their career work with lobbyists and directly or indirectly support lobbying campaigns. What is also true is that lobbying usually sits within the corporate affairs department in big organisations, along with general PR, and answers to the head of Corporate Relations. Within the large PR consultancy groups, lobbying or public affairs may be a separate division but there is usually a great deal of cross-team working with their corporate, consumer and

financial PR teams – which these groups tell their clients is a major benefit of working with them. Similarly, trade bodies and trade media almost
always include public affairs as part of what they cover, albeit a specialist
part.

Almost anyone working in PR needs to understand what lobbying is
and why it raises so many difficult ethical issues. One of the problems
with this subject area is that practitioners and critics, including the media, use different terms for the same thing. Practitioners in the UK prefer
the terms 'public affairs' or even 'political communications' to the word
'lobbying', feeling it has been devalued by constantly having the word
'scandal' affixed to it.

In the USA, the term 'lobbying' is still widely used, as there 'public
affairs' usually means PR, with a broader range of audience targets than
lobbying. To make things even more complicated, expressions such as
'government affairs', 'government relations' and even 'strategic advice'
are also used by practitioners. And then there is the debate as to whether
non-governmental organisations (NGOs), not-for-profit bodies, such as
charities and campaigning groups, are involved in advocacy or lobbying:
they tend to avoid the latter term.

In America and the UK there are some who argue that advocacy is
the attempt to persuade politicians, officials and the public to support a
cause. This only becomes lobbying when the activity is focused on specific legislation. On this basis, they argue, most activity by NGOs and
non-profits is advocacy, not lobbying.

In practice, this definition makes much of what any lobbyist does 'advocacy'. Most, though not all, lobbying includes an appeal to the public and
politicians through mass media (including social media). If non-profits
want to use the term advocacy – presumably because they think it sounds
more acceptable than lobbying or PR, propaganda or spin – then they
should also call what many businesses and organisations do 'advocacy'.

It's also somewhat disingenuous to say NGOs and non-profits are just
looking for support rather than seeking to influence legislation. Many of
their campaigns are clearly designed to ensure that politicians and government, on the one hand, support certain types of legislation and, on
the other, block or not support other measures that are contrary to the
interests of the NGO. For example, in much of Europe, public antipathy,
and legislative and executive opposition, to GM foods, nuclear power
and, in the UK, fracking, have been driven by NGO campaigns. Indeed,
generally the ultimate expression of an NGO's success is often to stop
or encourage legislation. Changing the law is often easier than changing
behaviour.

There are also some who use the term 'inside lobbying' to refer to direct efforts to influence law and rule-making by talking to legislators
and their teams. 'Outside lobbying' is then used to describe the more

conventional PR and communication attempts to win public support for an issue, albeit in the expectation that public support will translate into pressure on politicians and policy-makers.

Barry Hessenius, in his book, *Hardball Lobbying for Nonprofits: Real Advocacy for Nonprofits in the New Century*[1] refers to 'Advocacy Lobbying'. This is potentially a useful term as it captures the entirety of the persuasive process, but it is not a term that has gained much traction.

It is notable that governments, including those of the UK, the USA, Australia and Canada, use the term lobbying when drafting laws to promote transparency and stop corruption or unfair practices.

So, for the purpose of brevity, we are also going to call the practice *lobbying*. Unsurprisingly, the people employing or undertaking the actual lobbying will continue to prefer terms such as campaigning, communication, public affairs or 'strategic advice'. And, ironically, the people continuing to use terms of abuse to disparage lobbying and lobbyists will continue to be, in many cases, simply the communicators or lobbyists on the other side of the argument!

What Is Lobbying?

Lobbying includes any activity designed to influence the actions of those who exercise the powers of government and those who make laws. This includes not just national legislatures – parliaments, assemblies and congresses, but also central government ministries and a growing number of regulatory bodies. It also includes regional and even local tiers of government as well as international organisations operating globally, ranging from the United Nations (UN), the International Monetary Fund (IMF), the World Health Organization (WHO), and the World Trade Organization (WTO), through to pan-regional organisations, such as the Association of Southeast Asian nations (ASEAN), the United States–Mexico–Canada Agreement (USMCA), the European Union (EU) and the African Union (AU).

Who Lobbies?

When most people think of lobbying, not least its critics, they think of business, in particular big business: giant corporations seeking to influence and manipulate governments. And naturally businesses are major users of lobbying.

But lobbying is also employed extensively by NGOs, not-for-profits and charities as they campaign for or against legislation and policies that they believe may help or hinder the achievement of their goals. Greenpeace, Amnesty International, and the World Wildlife Fund (WWF) are just a few of the many examples of global NGOs that lobby, even if they prefer to call their work 'advocacy' or campaigning.

There are also many trade and professional associations which lobby on behalf of their members, both big and small. These range from national associations for specialist trades, professions and areas of employment, such as plumbers, nurses, doctors and lawyers through to international associations representing, for example, the mining industry. There are also groups representing different ethnicities, gender orientations, age groups, religions and geographic regions, who seek to lobby government.

Even state and regional governments lobby their own central or federal governments which in turn sometimes use lobbying to try to influence other national governments or international bodies. This activity usually comes under the banner of 'diplomacy', but is in effect a form of lobbying.

Most lobbying is undertaken in-house, by organisations' own employees, or by trade and professional associations: see Box 7.1. Lobbying is also offered by a range of suppliers. PR consultancies (all major PR firms offer the service), specialist lobbying firms and public affair consultancies, and, especially in the USA, law firms all represent a myriad range of organisations from the very big to quite small businesses as well as wealthy individuals. Indeed, the PR industry itself lobbies, often, perhaps a little ironically, to try to influence the nature and execution of government legislation to control lobbying. To declare an interest, both authors are Fellows of the Public Relations and Communications Association, one of the main functions of which is to lobby on behalf of its members in all parts of the PR industry in a range of different countries.

Why Lobby?

Governments, legislatures and regulators have enormous power. The laws they pass and the statutory instruments and executive powers they exercise can have a huge impact on businesses, charities and activists and professional groups. For example, governments can decide whether or not fracking is to be allowed and under what conditions. They can demand that social media businesses remove 'controversial' content, determine that qualified lawyers are no longer needed to undertake certain kinds of legal work, or require charities to put in place legally binding safeguarding measures to protect the people they help.

Moreover governments spend vast amounts of money that charities and businesses want to come their way – in contracts, grants, or aid. Then there is the issue of tax. No group, be it a business or a charity, wants to pay more tax!

In other words, there is an almost infinite number of reasons why a vast array of organisations would want to lobby. The problem lies most often not in the fact of lobbying itself, but on whose behalf and with what goal the lobbying is undertaken, as well as the methods used. One group's vital economic interest can be another's environmental nightmare. The question raised is not about the ethics of lobbying per se but the ethics of the lobbyist's goal.

> Every citizen is a special interest ... Blacks, consumers, teachers, pro-choicers, gun control advocates, handicapped people, aliens, exporters and salesmen – are all special interest ... There is not an American today who is not represented (whether he or she knows it or not) by at least a dozen special interest groups ... one person's special interest is another person's despotism.[3]

But before we delve deeper into the ethical debate, we need to look at what lobbyists actually do.

What Do Lobbyists Do?

There are three main areas of lobbying activity:

1. *Monitoring.* Organisations need to know – ideally, well in advance – what government is planning to do in terms of forthcoming legislation or regulation. Even if there is no realistic hope of stopping a planned change, with enough notice, an organisation may be able to at least influence the proposal and better prepare themselves for it. Thus, many organisations pay lobbyists to monitor formally and informally a wide variety of branches of government from parliamentary committees through to regulatory bodies. Monitoring via publicly available, if sometimes obscure, sources in itself is not so controversial, although because it requires expertise and resources, it arguably favours the already strong against the weak. However, when the monitoring is more informal – hints, tips, inside information – real ethical issues arise. How was the information gained? Has money or preferential access played a part? If a lobbyist only ever tells their boss or client what they could have found out for themselves if they had the time, the lobbyist will soon be seen to be less important, which is why they talk up their contacts, inside track and specialist knowledge.
2. *Opposing or amending.* Once a government initiative is underway, there will often be a flurry of lobbyists trying to amend or even stop it ... as well as competing lobbyists working for those supporting the initiative. Research papers are prepared, detailed briefings given, meetings arranged with ministers, regulators or civil servants to try to ensure the views and interests of the lobbying organisation are heard. It is at this stage that the ethical issues come even more

clearly to the fore and where the industry codes of conduct and government legislation to control lobbying come to bear. Has there been full transparency about who has been meeting whom? Are the claims made truthful? Have any special favours that might influence the outcome been granted? Added to this there maybe have been a media relations campaign designed subtly or sometimes not so subtly to apply pressure to the government and the politicians involved. Politicians have to get re-elected. A media campaign that is critical of them and the government may be very unwelcome.

3. *Proposing.* A classic activity for charities and NGOs is to propose or even demand action. This will include all the techniques used to oppose or amend legislation, but added to them there will often be marches, protests, and stunts – some of the latter may even break the law. This of course raises another ethical issue. Is it ethical to break the law in order to change a law or to seek a new law?

The following is a brief and hopefully balanced summary of the arguments surrounding lobbying. It is worth recalling that, as mentioned earlier, it is often the case that the critics of lobbying are in fact lobbyists themselves, albeit for the other side of the argument.

What Is the Case Against Lobbying?

- *It privileges the rich and powerful.* Hiring a lobbyist – as an in-house employee or via a consultancy – costs money. 'Business always has more money than other groups or interests. The rich and powerful are better represented'... or so goes the argument.
- *It is secretive and hard to monitor.* Despite all the laws and codes, much happens behind closed doors, in private 'corridor conversations', or informal meetings at social events. The fear is that only those in the know, or with money and influence, are able to operate the hidden levers of power. This fear is further exacerbated when politicians and civil servants and government staffers are seen leaving public sector jobs by the 'revolving door' to become very well-paid lobbyists. This is what some Americans call 'going downtown'. See Box 7.1.
- *It is open to corruption.* Politicians need money to campaign to stay in power, and donors may well expect favourable treatment in return. In the USA, in the 2016 presidential elections, Hillary Clinton spent $768m and Trump $398m.[4] In some countries the disparity between certain politician's lifestyles and their salaries also raises suspicions about the influence of 'money'.

Box 7.1 Lobbyists in Australia

An exhaustive analysis of the backgrounds of 483 registered lobby-ists has revealed that more than half were previously working inside government, the bureaucracy or party organisations. One-quarter have worked inside the offices of ministers or backbenchers.[2]

What Is the Case for Lobbying?

- *It's a vital part of democracy.* A healthy democracy needs to hear all sides of any argument and listen to as many voices as possible if it is to avoid the tyranny of the majority or the powerful. Groups repre-senting minorities, faith communities, key social concerns, employ-ees (with trade unions lobbying on their behalf), professions, small and big employers – all need to have access to government. Without it, there could be unfairness and social unrest. All voices should be heard. In the USA, the courts have ruled that lobbying is one of the freedoms protected by the First Amendment of the Constitution.
- *It provides information and expertise.* Effective and fair legislation and regulation need to be informed by expert information and views. Without it, laws that impact on the physical and economic well-being of citizens could be dangerously flawed. Governments do not have the resources to do this on their own. Lobbying, it is argued, leads to better law-making.
- *It is regulated and controlled.* There are laws and codes that ensure the right to lobby is not abused or exploited by any particular group. Wrongdoing is rare and punished.

Ethical Codes and the Law on Lobbying

How do the professional codes – and the law – try to ensure there is a level and ethical playing field? PR's professional codes and the law have much to say on the subject – perhaps unsurprisingly as it is by far the most hotly debated area of public relations activity, touching as it does on how ultimate political power is exercised. Most modern democracies use a mixture of law and professional codes and self-regulation to try and ensure that lobbying is fair and ethical. If we included here all the codes and laws, even for just one country, we would use up perhaps half of the words available to us in book. So to avoid this we have endeavoured to highlight the main features that occur in nearly all codes, taking for ex-ample the UK, the USA and Australia.[5]

There are four main areas of focus:

1. Relationships with politicians, civil servants and government representatives, past and present.
2. Transparency about clients and who is actually paying for any activity.
3. Transparency about the actual lobbying activity, for example, any meetings, hospitality or significant conversations with politicians or government representatives.
4. Truthfulness, honesty and accuracy of any statements or information provided, where the issues are similar to those examined in Chapters 4 and 6.

Relationships with Politicians and Officials

Most codes, and this is often backed up by the law, forbid the giving of gifts (in the USA anything over $5 is prohibited!), entertainment or hospitality above what is now usually a very modest level. Direct bribery is of course covered by the law and no practitioner would claim such behaviour is acceptable or ethical. But in recent years the codes and the law have tried to draw a clearer line around entertainment and what may look to some like undue influence or even bribery. A lobbyist may claim that inviting a politician to enjoy hospitality at a major sporting event is just a good way of getting to know or keeping in touch with key political players. But that is not necessarily what it looks like to people on the outside, or people on the other side of a lobbying argument who may not have the money to fund such lavish entertainment: how do they get to know or stay in touch with the right people?

? *Q: What do you think is an acceptable level of entertainment? How much should a lobbyist be allowed to spend entertaining someone?*

In one sense, the tightening of the law has made lobbyists' lives easier. Even if they think the rules are too harsh or restrictive, lobbyists now at least know exactly what is and isn't acceptable.

So far, so straightforward. But things start to get complicated when love, families and friendship are involved. Many people in the world of politics, government, media, lobbying, PR and business know each other. Networks that might have started at school or university become 'useful' in the workplace. Many will send their children to the same schools and find themselves at private dinner parties, family BBQs, even weddings and holidays where they mix with friends, family and acquaintances whose professional lives overlap with their own.

? *Q: Is it realistic to expect people in these circumstances never to talk about work or never to give anything away about their views on a subject that* *might be much discussed in the media and society at large? What would constitute unethical behaviour in these circumstances? What ethical guidelines would you suggest to manage the situation?*

Employing or paying politicians and officials is outlawed or discouraged in many jurisdictions. In the USA and the UK there are now laws and rules preventing politicians and officials from taking up a lobbying position, or being paid by a lobbyist, for at least a year after leaving government, reflecting the desire to avoid the media and public anger that is provoked by the 'revolving door'. Employing or helping the friends and families of politicians is less well covered in most countries and it would be difficult to know where to draw the line – although it's also clear that, for example, offering a good job to a family member or the lover of a politician could be a significant inducement. It is also hard to police tempting hints of future employment for politicians who are stepping down, or officials who are retiring.

These problems are compounded by the fact that many lobbyists are politically active. They are aspiring, or former, politicians and find knowing how the political system works and some of its key players is useful in their working lives – although the UK codes say they should keep their lobbying separate from any personal political work they do as a party supporter, or even as a candidate. In the USA, it is a little different as some lobbyists even assist politicians with fundraisers, campaign finances and setting up PACs (Political Action Committees).

? *Q: You are a lobbyist. There is a politician who can help your client's case. You know this politician is retiring in a year. Would it be ethical to suggest to them that your client would be happy to employ them once they had been out of office for the legally enforceable year? See Box 7.2.*

Box 7.2 Facebook Poaches Second Official to Deal with New Laws

In April 2020, at the height of the COVID-19 crisis, *The Times* newspaper in London reported on the move to Facebook of a media policy expert from the UK Government Department for Culture, Media and Sport. The move meant she would be working with a former Ofcom board member (Ofcom is the UK's regulator for broadcasting and telecommunications) whose move to Facebook had also been reported by *The Times*.

In a leader piece on the same day *The Times* decried 'The revolving door' and said regulations were too lax, noting that the moves were not so much 'poacher turned gamekeeper', but gamekeeper turned poacher.[6]

The following day in a letter published by *The Times* newspaper, a former corporate affairs director of Sainsbury's and AOL

> wrote in support of *The Times* leader, saying of his experience of
> lobbying, 'I quickly concluded that most of the civil servants with
> whom I have dealt have half an ear on the issue you are presenting
> to them and two ears on the value that you may (or may not) add to
> furthering their career.'[7]

Transparency about clients and staff

This aspect of the codes is generally seen as focused on lobbyists working
for consultancies with a myriad of clients rather than lobbyists employed
full-time by a single organisation. Given that one of the big concerns about
lobbying is that it is seen as secretive and privileges those with money and
good contacts, it would seem sensible to force lobbyists to say who their
clients are. Surely we should know if big oil or pharmaceutical companies
or indeed Russian oligarchs or the sovereign funds of non-democratic
countries are using lobbyists and what for? Few would argue against such
codes and laws. But even here there can be complications.

In any political or economic situation there are inevitably times when
negotiations are needed to change a position. Lobbying is essentially a
form of negotiation about changing, stopping or initiating new laws or
regulations. But it is often difficult to progress negotiations if they have
to be conducted in the full glare of publicity. The Australian Government's lobbying regulations go some way to recognising this dilemma:

> A lobbyist is not required to list a body corporate as a client on the
> Register if disclosure of the lobbyist's relationship with the body cor-
> porate *might result in speculation about a pending transaction involving
> the body corporate and that transaction has not previously been disclosed*
> by the body corporate in accordance with its continuous disclosure
> obligations under Chapter 6CA of the Corporations Act 2001.[8]

? *Q: You have been approached by a biotech firm that wants you to provide
monitoring and tracking services to see what is being said about genetic
engineering in the health sector. The firm are worried that the competition,
as well as critical NGOs, will realise they are considering new product development in the field and so has asked you not to reveal their main trading
name, but to declare them in the lobbying register under the name of one
of their lesser-known affiliate companies. They argue this is justified by the
right to consider new products and ideas in private without having to reveal
their hand. Would you agree to do as they ask?*

Q: You run a lobbying firm. You have been approached by a potential client whose scientific research includes animal testing, undertaken within the law. The company has faced protests, including activists demonstrating at the homes of company employees. The activist organisation has suggested on social media that they will extend the protests to any of the company's contractors. Your employees are anxious. Should you have the right to keep the client's identity secret?

As with the listing of clients, the listing of staff (and other paid advisors) is, superficially at least, fairly uncontentious. Where the rules get stretched is when firms are slow to list new team members and do not necessarily give the full details of the new person's working, and perhaps political, life, or indeed their private social connections. What if they are the partner of a prominent politician, but do not share a surname? A name in itself may not be very revealing.

Transparency about Actual Lobbying Activity

Most PR codes relating to lobbying – and increasingly legislation – demand that there is transparency about the content and intent of any meetings, hospitality or significant conversations between a lobbyist and a politician or government representative, such as a civil servant. Apart from the enormous amount of bureaucracy created by recording all these interactions (much of this bureaucracy also falls on politicians and their staff), there are still difficulties in making this work in a way acceptable to all.

The first problem involves defining lobbying and who is a lobbyist. For example, some in the charity and NGO sector claim to be practising advocacy and simply trying to get the public and media to support causes which are in turn picked up by politicians. They say this is distinct from lobbying which, they argue, focuses on specific legislation (see p. 136).

Critics of the NGO view say their ultimate goal is to initiate or change legislation in line with their interests and beliefs (for example, protecting the environment or promoting human rights, but also for much more contentious causes, such as restricting or banning abortion), and that they are therefore lobbyists and should be subject to the same rules as businesses, trade associations and other organisations that lobby.

The NGO argument is that they are acting for the good of society while businesses and other groups that lobby, such as employment groups including teachers, the police or landlords, are working not for the common good but for the often selfish sectional interests they represent. Inevitably these arguments can become circular. Without businesses there would be no jobs and no taxes which would clearly be bad for society, and, in any case, who is to say that one NGO's view of the good of society is the right one? In practice, many NGOs disagree and compete with each other on how best to help society. For example, is protecting the natural landscape a more important societal good than building sufficient housing in desirable locations for a rapidly growing population?

? *Q: Should Greenpeace be subject to the same rules and regulations on lobbying as BP?*

To complicate matters still further, in America it is not uncommon for law firms to help organisations which seek to change the law, but many lawyers reject being called lobbyists and claim the protection of client confidentiality, or describe themselves as offering 'strategic counsel'.

The second problem with the notion of transparency is defining exactly 'how much transparency'. For example, is it really reasonable to expect 'lobbyists' and every politician to reveal everything that was mentioned, particularly in the early stages of a discussion? Most people would find it hard to run their business or working lives if they had to record every meeting and conversation and indicate what they were about. How would it work for job promotions, new projects, closures, disciplinary issues and helping employees with mental health problems? Moreover, formal minutes of meetings can often be deceptive. We've probably all attended meetings where people have asked for things to be left unminuted, or where the minutes are sanitised. Often what's really important takes place in informal conversations before or after the meeting proper – or informally at separate occasions, such as social events. Indeed, attempts to police official meetings can backfire, by making informal conversations where people feel free to speak their mind more important than ever.

People have a tendency to be very keen on other people being transparent, but find 'good' reasons why it doesn't quite apply to them. One of the authors was told – at some length – by a tech entrepreneur how they were passionate about transparency, but when asked how much he earned, he replied it was private!

? *Q: You bump into an important politician in a corporate hospitality box at a major football match. You didn't know the politician was going to be there and you didn't pay for the hospitality as you were a guest. You have a short but very useful conversation with the politician on a key issue relating to your work as a lobbyist. Do you need to record this meeting and its contents?*

Box 7.3 shows that it is sometimes difficult to identify who is a lobbyist.

Box 7.3 A Lobbying Scandal, but No Lobbyist?

Michael Cohen, President Donald Trump's former personal law-yer, was paid $600,000 by AT&T in 2017 to help them understand how the then new administration would react to its proposed merger with Time Warner.[9] Meanwhile the pharmaceutical giant Novartis said it paid Cohen $1.2 million for help with navigating the Affordable Care Act. These two giant businesses weren't the only ones paying the now disbarred Cohen. What perhaps made Cohen so attractive was that he did not have to disclose his work for them under the 1995 Lobbying Disclosure Act as he wasn't a registered lobbyist.

How was this possible? Well, one threshold is that, under US rules, to be classified as a lobbyist, work involving contacting gov-ernment officials must take up at least 20 per cent of the overall work that the person does for the client. Another possible reason is that Cohen described his work as 'strategic advice' rather than lobbying. As AT&T distanced themselves from Cohen, they said, 'Our contract with Cohen was expressly limited to providing con-sultancy and advisory services and did not permit him to lobby on our behalf without first notifying us.'

As it happens, neither AT&T nor Novartis were short of offi-cial lobbyists to help them. In 2017 alone, 112 individual lobbyists from 34 different firms, including AT&T's in-house team, reported lobbying to advance the telecom giant's policy goals.[10] Another 85 lobbyists representing 15 different firms disclosed that they had lobbied on behalf of Novartis.[11]

How Lobbyists Try to Influence Government

We have looked at the key aspects of lobbying, the key criticisms of it and the key elements of the ethical codes. We now want to examine lobbying in practice – through the lens of two of its biggest critics.

In 2014, an article was published in the *Guardian* – a respected left-of-centre national UK newspaper which is widely read online around the world – with the eye-catching headline 'The truth about lobbying:10 ways big business controls government'. The article was written by Tamasin Cave and Andy Rowell from Spinwatch, an organisation which monitors the PR industry. They were promoting their book, *A Quiet Word: Lobby-ing, Crony Capitalism and Broken Politics in Britain*.[12] The headline and the title of the book are indicative of what quite a lot of people think and feel about lobbying, namely, that it is bad and it is all about big business.

In this section we look at these '10 ways' in which big business is said to control government and examine the ethical issues they raise and how these techniques are also used by sectoral interest groups, NGOs, professional and charity lobbyists. We have put in brackets our own more neutral terms for some of the 10 actions.

1. Control the Ground ('Frame the Debate')
    Businesses usually, but by no means always, try to place the debate on the territory which is strongest for them. Conventionally this will be creating and maintaining employment and economic growth. Inevitably environmental groups tend to avoid economic arguments, preferring to focus on social and environmental concerns. In debates on nuclear power, the companies backing it will emphasise its cleanness and lack of environmental impact, which in turn forces most of the environmental groups – and the renewable energy industry – to reframe their arguments around the real and perceived dangers of nuclear power and the need to focus all investment in renewables which, they argue, is where the future must lie. Trying to frame the debate or control the ground does not in itself seem to us to be unethical, regardless of which side you are on – though you may have a personal moral view on where the debate should be grounded.

? *Q: Is it ethical to frame the debate in environmental terms when the sponsor of the lobbying's primary motivation is profit? (For example, wind farm developers lobbying for government grants.)*

2. Spin the Media ('Use the Most Persuasive Messages')
    This is in essence a sub-set of 'Control the Ground' and involves creating messages that play well with the media. Cave and Rowell cite the example of the campaign to win the go-ahead for High Speed Railway (HS2) in the UK on a route that is proposed to run from London to the less affluent Midlands and North. After a shaky start to the campaign, the lobbyists changed the message from a rather tactical one about faster journey times to a message that portrays those against the new line as wealthy people trying to protect their property values against the benefits which would be gained from creating jobs and economic growth in less affluent areas of the UK. Meanwhile those opposed warn of the destruction of ancient woodlands and areas of great natural beauty. Both sets of messages are quite persuasive ... which is probably why the debate dates back a decade and building still hasn't started.

? *Q: Is either side acting unethically?*

3. Engineer a Following ('Identify Allies and Build Support')
    Any organisation lobbying for something benefits from being able to show as broad a range of supporters as possible. The higher the

number of supporters who are likely to vote, the better. Businesses lobbying for property or infrastructure projects will look for support from 'small businesses' (always seen as more human, even noble, than 'big business'), from local governments in search of growth and employment and from community groups which want jobs and investment to offset social decline. The same campaign may attract opposition from environmental groups which in turn may call on the support of walkers and bird watchers or sports groups who don't want to lose recreational space.

4. Buying in Credibility ('Secure Expert Third Party Support')

Many groups that lobby are not generally popular or much trusted by the general public so they look for third party endorsement. This is particularly true for business. As Cave and Rowell note in their book, the tobacco industry in the UK campaigned against plain packaging by calling on the support of small shops that sell tobacco, arguing that their economic viability – and even the viability of local communities – would be undermined if sales were lost to smuggling. They also recruited former police officers to talk about the link between plain packaging and contraband. Meanwhile, in another policy arena, teachers' groups calling for more money look for endorsement from parents' groups worried about educational standards, from police groups concerned about truants causing trouble, and from businesses wanting new recruits with better skills.

Letters to newspapers from groups of 'distinguished' economists, scientists and celebrities are a common feature of lobbying. All are a way of lobbyists saying: 'You don't need to take it from us. Listen to what experts or others are saying'.

Some of these links and claims may be weak and many cancel each other out, but they are a standard part of lobbying. Naked appeals to sectional interest ... we want more money ... we want to pay less tax ... we want to make more profits ... are not very persuasive. The broader and more expert and relevant the support base, the better the case.

?   *Q: Is it ethical to pay, or in other ways advantage, groups whose support may be beneficial to your campaign? For example, giving money to a residents group, or free editorial and publicity support to local businesses?*

5. Sponsor a Think Tank ('Demonstrate Intellectual Credibility')

Any organisation lobbying for something will tend to face the accusation of 'Well, you would say that, wouldn't you?'. To overcome this, lobbyists like to invoke the support of intellectually credible groups, such as think tanks. In reality, few of these think tanks are wholly unbiased, with some being pro free market and others being more inclined to support government intervention. In the UK, the tobacco industry has historically drawn on support from the neo-liberal think tank, the Institute of Economic Affairs (IEA), to justify opposition to the plain packaging of cigarettes. Similarly the Institute of Public Policy Research, which grew out of the left-of-centre British Labour Party, has produced research supportive of a variety of causes around 'affordable housing', a subject close to the heart of traditionally Labour-supporting sectional interests such as teachers, nurses and other public sector groups. None of these think tanks would survive for long if they just slavishly said what the vested interest wanted, but there are sometimes question marks over whether funding or help has influenced their reports objectivity. Ethical questions inevitably arise.

6. Consult your Critics ('Consult Interested Parties')

It is common practice for businesses and local governments to consult the local community when planning major developments. This often entails public meetings, exhibitions, roadshows and a variety of forms of research. Even national governments will do this when considering a major change or development. The ethical issue arising here is, are those doing the consulting really listening or are they just going through the motions? Is it really a form of window dressing? Big blocks of flats and landfill sites still seem to end up getting approval despite extensive consultation and widespread local antipathy.

A common justification – though seldom stated – is for the business or government body supporting the change to say the consultation is to help 'refine' the project, not 'define' it.

? Q: What are the ethical issues of holding a consultation exercise for a major
• building development? Can, or should, the degree of influence the consultation will have be spelt out to those being consulted?

7. Neutralise the Opposition ('Tackle Opposing Arguments')

There is almost always an opposing view to the one any lobbyist is proposing. It makes sense therefore to find out who your opponents are, what they are saying and what their weak points are. Think about who lobbies for and against legalising cannabis, or pro and anti-abortion, or for and against fracking. Where the ethical issues arise is about how far is going too far. Criticising the opposition with general and often grossly simplistic accusations such as 'they only care about profits', 'they are in the pockets of big business' versus 'they are virtue signalling middle-class elites' or 'left-wing agitators' isn't particularly appetising, but in age of aggressive mainstream and social media and short attention spans, this sort of behaviour is only likely to increase.

Where the edgier ethical issues come into play is when research tips over into spying or hacking, or when name calling degenerates into denigration and false but hard-to-refute accusations.

? *Q: You believe passionately in the cause you are lobbying for. You are told that 15 years ago the spokesperson for the opposing lobby was convicted of sexual assault. Would you bring this information into play?*

Q: You are offered, via an intermediary who wants to be paid, hard but confidential evidence about historic unethical behaviour by the opposing lobby. The intermediary will not say how the information was secured, but says it was secured legally. Would you use it?

Q: Is trying to improve your Google ranking with a flurry of positive activity a sensible way of redressing an imbalance or a cynical attempt to manipulate people via the search engine?

8. Control the Web ('Manage the Internet')
   Google rankings are very important. Most people only look at the first page of search results. So when an organisation is getting a lot of negative coverage and negative rankings, there is sometimes a move to offset this by launching a flurry of activity, including blogs, media releases and other content with links to positive news, in order to help re-address what they see as an imbalance. This kind of response used to be primarily confined to businesses having some kind of reputational crisis. However, in recent years, charities and NGOs have started to have sizeable reputational crises which some have responded to by pointing out all the 'good work' they do as a corrective to the negativity overwhelming them. Certainly, activists know only too well that a high Google ranking for the issue they are promoting is a good sign and likely to attract more support and more money.
   Companies and lobbyists – and the Vatican! – have also been accused of trying to manipulate their Wikipedia profiles. Their defence is that they are only correcting factual inaccuracies – though sometimes it seems one person's fact is another person's opinion as companies and activists battle it out (see pp. 130–131).
9. Open the Door
   This doesn't involve the offer of cash or valuable inducements to a politician – both of which are illegal in most modern democracies – but offers of work for the politician's friends and others. As with some of the other criticisms of lobbying, this sort of activity was seen as something done by businesses, but there is now a rapid transfer of political insiders and friends to (often well-paid) NGO and charity careers.

? *Q: You have the opportunity of employing the former colleague and lover of a senior and important politician. They may not be the best qualified candidate, but they are clearly potentially valuable. Do you hire them?*

10. Employ Former Politicians and Senior Civil Servants ('Hire Experience and Knowledge')

Most politicians and senior civil servants are debarred from moving straight into a job where their recent experience will have real, direct value and have to wait a year or more, or apply for special clearance from a government committee. And yet many businesses – particularly in areas such as defence and health – where the government is not only a huge spender, but tightly defines policy, employ many senior former politicians and civil servants (and in the case of defence industries, former officers from the armed forces) and indeed often proclaim it as one of their strengths. This sort of thing is not new, but there is a perception that it is, despite legislation, getting more common.

In summary, the '10 ways big business controls government' is just a list, albeit quite a good list, of how lobbyists – including those acting not just for businesses, but for professions, faith communities, charities, and NGOs – try to win the day with legislators. Almost all of these techniques can come close to the ethical edge. And almost all lobbyists sometimes justify going over that edge in the utilitarian belief that their cause is just and that 'I know the difference between right and wrong, thank you very much.'

? *Q: Lobbying scandals persist, despite trade bodies' ethical codes and the law. What, if anything, do you think can be done to improve ethical standards and reduce the number of so-called scandals?*

Box 7.4 and Box 7.5 illustrate two different views of lobbying.

Box 7.4 'Undermining Our Democracy'

Mining is an enormous and very important industry in Australia generating jobs and money. It is also, of course, controversial, given its environmental impact. In the 2019 Australian election, many observers say it was the Liberal Party's support for a major expansion in mining that helped it defy expectations and beat its great rival Labor to win the election.

The Australian Institute (TAI), describes itself as a wholly independent public policy think tank with a particular concern about the consequences of environmental neglect. In 2017, TAI published a report into the ownership and influence of mining companies in Australia. They announced the publication of the report with a very hard-hitting headline: 'Undermining our democracy: Foreign corporate influence through the Australian mining lobby'.

The report said that the total revenue of mining lobby groups over the preceding 10 years had been $541,275,884 and that mining companies are dominated by foreign interests and foreign companies. The report concludes by saying 'the mining industry is dominated by foreign companies who are spending hundreds of millions of dollars to influence our political process', arguing that the sovereignty of Australia should be protected from outside influence and that only Australians should have the power to influence elections.

What is interesting is that the TIA's attack on the mining companies isn't about any specific wrongdoing, but about what they see as the disproportionate wielding of influence and power by the mining companies.

What do you think? Is foreign ownership of such an important industry fundamentally unethical? And is it ethical or fair if the mining industry has far more to spend on lobbying than environmental groups and policy think tanks like TAI? What if anything should be done?[13] (See also pp. 96–97.)

Box 7.5 Lobbying and the Problem of Fluid Frontiers

Ian Wright, CBE, is the CEO of the Food and Drink Federation (FDF), which describes itself as the voice of UK food and drink manufacturing. Prior to his role at FDF, Ian was Corporate Relations Director of global drinks giant Diageo. Here he talks about lobbying issues now and in the future.

It is essential that there are strong codes and proper sanctions to protect the public from the impact of improper lobbying, which is why there is now in place much of value both legally and in terms of codes of practice.

However, the codes and laws are never perfect, as the nature of lobbying is ever changing and the difficulties of defining precisely what lobbying is are hard to resolve. This, coupled with the difficulty of balancing the need for transparency with the right to some commercial confidentiality and the sheer impracticality of being transparent about everything an organisation does, means that the codes are inevitably work in progress.

For example, when it comes to definitions, is 'advocacy' part of lobbying or something separate? Can reactively responding to government questions and calls for advice be seen as something different from proactively lobbying the government? How much of your time has to be spent lobbying for you to be considered an actual lobbyist? Are NGOs engaged in lobbying?

On this last question it is certainly my view that NGOs should be subject to the same legal and ethical codes as other corporate bodies. If NGOs are not trying to influence government to be supportive of their goals, it is hard to imagine what it is they are doing.

As is the case for businesses and trade bodies, NGOs' purpose and backing should be as transparent as possible. But how far can any organisation be transparent? A trade body should have a visible list of the organisations that are its members. But should it also have to provide details of all the shareholders of each member? Should NGOs have to provide the names of its supporters? How does this sit with privacy and confidentiality?

Similarly, it seems eminently reasonable to say all organisations that lobby should be clear about their primary objectives, but most would find it unreasonable and unworkable to have to fully explain their case and tactics in advance of conducting a lobbying campaign.

Perhaps a way to overcome this problem of transparency is to have sanctions that can be applied retrospectively if it is shown, to the satisfaction of a court, that the outcome of any given lobbying campaign has been detrimental to the reasonable interests of the public or other groups or interests.

One of the most effective sanctions against improper lobbying is reputational damage which, much aided by social media, can hit customer confidence and organisational income. Until recently, reputational sanctions seemed to only apply to business, but the Oxfam and Save the Children scandals appear to have marked a shift in public and media opinion with charities and NGOs increasingly being held to account. This seems to me to be a good thing. Bad behaviour and immorality are not the exclusive preserve of the business world.

Another area of change is the role of 'influencers'. Often, unlike journalists who have editors, owners and professional codes to moderate their behaviour, influencers are effectively freelances who can, like a hired gun, be used by any group who can pay for their support. Who can hold these influencers to account?

The best hope in terms of controlling the worst excesses of influencers in the future may lie with the social media companies like YouTube, Facebook, Twitter and Instagram – though putting more power in the hands of these giants will not be something everyone welcomes.

Finally, there is the issue of lobbyists and politicians looking like a cosy club of people who all know and help each other. It is certainly true that, during the course of varied and successful careers, the breadth of connections that senior players in the world of NGOs, the public sector, government and business have is often far wider than it used to be when people stuck with one industry and sometimes one firm all of their working lives. Overall, this connectivity is probably a good thing – it is certainly an inevitable one – provided that the resultant activity is as transparent as it reasonably can be.

Summary

Lobbying (although often it goes by different aliases) plays a huge and vital role in the life of modern democracies. It is used by not-for-profit as well as commercial organisations and is particularly prevalent in contested and controversial policy arenas. However, the way in which it is undertaken – full transparency is next to impossible – together with its influence on important policy decisions which affect us all – means that it will always be viewed with more than a little suspicion. It remains perhaps the most hotly contested ethical battleground in the PR world.

Notes

1 Hessenius, Barry, *Hardball Lobbying for Nonprofits: Real Advocacy for Nonprofits in the New Century* (Basingstoke: Palgrave Macmillan, 2014).
2 See www.theguardian.com/australia-news/2018/sep/17/australias-lax-lobbying-regime-the-domain-of-party-powerbrokers
3 deKieffer, Donald E., *The Citizen's Guide to Lobbying Congress* (Chicago: Chicago Review Press, 2007).
4 See www.investopedia.com/insights/cost-of-becoming-president/
5 See www.prca.org.uk/sites/default/files/Public%20Affairs%20Code%20PDF. pdf (PRCA code); www.congress.gov/bill/110th-congress/senate-bill/1 (The Honest Leadership and Open Governments Act /USA); https://lobbyists. ag.gov.au/about/code (Australian codes).

6 See www.thetimes.co.uk/article/facebook-poaches-tony-close-from-ofcom-mdrkv7t2w;
www.thetimes.co.uk/article/facebook-poaches-second-official-to-deal-with-new-laws-8skg5d9n5; www.thetimes.co.uk/article/the-times-view-on-public-servants-who-move-to-the-private-sector-revolving-door-ckt27k750;
www.thetimes.co.uk/article/times-letters-how-to-prepare-better-for-the-next-calamity-50rs3mh79
7 *The Times*, 30 April and 1 May 2020.
8 Emphasis added. See www.ag.gov.au/Integrity/lobbyists/Pages/Lobbying-Code-of-Conduct.aspx
9 See www.cnbc.com/2018/05/11/michael-cohen-scandal-lobbying-in-the-trump-age.html
10 See www.opensecrets.org/federal-lobbying/clients/lobbyists?cycle=2017& id=d000000076
11 See www.opensecrets.org/federal-lobbying/clients/lobbyists?cycle=2017&id= D000022163
12 Cave, Tamasin and Rowell, Andy, *A Quiet Word: Lobbying, Crony Capitalism and Broken Politics in Britain* (London: Bodley Head, 2014).
13 See www.tai.org.au/sites/default/files/P307%20Foreign%20influence%20on %20Australian%20mining_0.pdf; www.thetimes.co.uk/past-six-days/2020-04-30/news/facebook-poaches-second-official-to-deal-with-new-laws-8skg5d9n5; www.thetimes.co.uk/past-six-days/2020-04-30/news/facebook-poaches-second-official-to-deal-with-new-laws-8skg5d9n5

Chapter 8

PR Specialisms and Their Ethical Dilemmas

One of the things that makes PR such an interesting area of study and employment is how it interacts with every aspect of life – business, politics and wider society. PR is used by almost every sort of person and organisation that engages with public life, from celebrities and beauty brands, to religious groups, trade bodies and trade unions, through to governments, global corporations and NGOs.

While there are ethical issues that are common to all aspects of PR, there are also issues and, in some instances codes, that are specific to particular PR specialisms.

In this chapter we look at:

- The ethical pitfalls of political PR, which is often characterised as manipulative and even dishonest.
- The issues surrounding government PR and the use of taxpayers' money.
- Internal communications, and how the need for organisational loyalty can clash with freedom of expression.
- Corporate social responsibility (CSR): the need to be seen to be doing good without being seen as cynical.
- Why healthcare has its own ethical code and what the issues are.
- Financial PR, an area of public relations where money matters and companies and even economies can fail if people behave badly.
- Celebrity PR, where privacy and personal ethics battle with both the public interest and what's of interest to the public.
- Fashion and travel PR: where 'freebies rule, OK?' and there are issues around body dysmorphia and the future of the planet.

Political PR

Political PR, meaning *activity undertaken by politicians as they compete for political power and seek to win elections,* is arguably the most discussed and controversial area of PR. It is distinct from government PR which aims to provide citizens with information on their rights, responsibilities and how they should behave and is covered in the next section of this chapter. (Lobbying or public affairs, also sometimes called political PR, is covered in Chapter 7.)

The politicians who govern us have always embraced the arts of communication. PR skills loom large in a politician's armoury. Even dictatorships care about public opinion, but in democracies it is the lifeblood of politics, just as financial realities and the iron laws of supply and demand constitute the foundation for business activity.

Political PR is yet another area which dodges using the term 'public relations' to describe itself. Politicians' sensitivity to public opinion has meant that in many countries they seek to distance themselves from the term, as it has acquired negative overtones, often preferring words such as 'information' or the hard-to-disapprove-of 'communications'. This has not stopped outsiders and the media continuing to use the PR label, often in a negative way, to describe political communication.

Today, in the Anglo-Saxon world and even beyond, probably the most common term used by outsiders to describe political PR is *spin* – its exponents are called *spin doctors*. As a pejorative term for political communication, spin originated in the United States but came into vogue in the United Kingdom in the 1990s. It became firmly associated with New Labour under its then leader Tony Blair. Blair and his team placed particular emphasis on improving media management as they sought to make their party – which had languished in opposition for many years – electable again. The continued use of the term indicates that it still captures an important perception about contemporary political communication, although the currency of the word may be ebbing a little as 'spin doctors' learn to take a less prominent role and other terms, such as 'fake news', have come into vogue.

'Spin' conveys, more powerfully than the term PR itself, a sense of manipulation and even sinister menace. It is firmly associated with the exercise of power. Spin implies that the information communicated is carefully selected and delivered in such a way that it is to the advantage of the sender of the message (and, at least as importantly, to the disadvantage of opponents). Since so much is at stake, the methods used can be ruthless: telling the truth may not be a priority.

When you look at some of the portrayals of political PR in popular culture, spin doctors are almost invariably shown to be clever, manipulative, not to be trusted and sometimes a little mad. (For example, BBC's *The Thick of It*, or the Anglo-American movie spin off *In the Loop*. *Brexit: The Uncivil War*, the Channel 4 TV drama, based on the campaign in the UK to win the Brexit referendum, depicts the use of spin in a real-life campaign.)

Given the importance and controversy surrounding political PR, you might imagine that there is a strong code of ethics to which practitioners have to adhere. But you would be wrong. There are no codes for 'political PR' and of course most practitioners do not even describe themselves as PR practitioners. In the UK, even the limited amount of political advertising that is allowed is not subject to the remit of the Advertising Standards Authority, the body that applies standards of truthfulness, honesty and decency to all other areas of advertising. Political communication is seen as something apart from other forms of PR communication.

> Lastly, see that your whole canvas (election campaign) is a fine show, brilliant, resplendent, and popular, with the utmost display and prestige: and also if it can be managed at all, that there should be scandalous talk, in character, about the crimes, lusts and briberies of your competitors.
>
> (Quintus Cicero, *Handbook for Electioneering*, 63 BC)

Why is this? Well, in some crucial ways, politics is different from promoting, for example, a new broadband service. Politics tend to be much more negative and personality-driven than traditional organisational or brand PR (only rarely do we know the names of the chief executives of the countless organisations which supply our day-to-day needs, but we all know quite a lot, for good and ill, about our heads of government, so politicians' characters really matter). Commercial PR realises that negative campaigns raise awareness of rival companies, making potential customers more likely to consider alternative options. Moreover, such campaigns, which can degenerate into mudslinging, can seem undignified and distasteful, reflecting badly on those who conduct them. In politics, the stakes are different, for the winner often takes all (or at least hopes to do so). Political attacks, however nasty they may seem, can be memorable and effective – more so than simply being positive about one's own policies. As a result, negative campaigning carries on with few holds barred. Furthermore, in many democratic elections there are only two realistic contenders for the top job. Since both are high-profile, the danger of publicising a rival can be largely set to one side. And in their anxiety to win power through the ballot box, the other pitfalls of negative campaigning are overlooked.[1]

> I'm not an old, experienced hand at politics. But I am now seasoned enough to have learned that the hardest thing about any political campaign is how to win without proving that you are unworthy of winning.
>
> (American politician, Adlai Stevenson, 1956)

But this negative and often very personal campaigning raises important ethical issues. What is the effect of this on the public image of politicians, political life as a whole, and people's faith in politics, which in many countries is now at an all-time low? In 2019, less than half (48 per cent) of respondents to the Edelman Trust Barometer said they trusted government.[2] How would we change our view of a business sector if its leaders publicly tore into each other in the way we have come to expect of politicians?

So the question arises, can negative campaigning and personal attacks be justified? What if the drive to win debases our politics?

? *Q: When, if ever, is it acceptable to reveal details of the private life of an opposing politician? Remember this has to apply to all politicians, not just those you dislike.*

Q: What should be the balance in a political party's communication between the positive communication of their policies and negative attacks on their main opponents? 50:50, 25:75, 75:25 or some other ratio?

Q: Research seems to show your party is unlikely to win unless you attack the opposition and its leaders. The public finds policy details boring. Does the importance of winning outweigh the possible damage to overall public confidence in politics?

In addition to negative and personality-focused communication there is another ethical issue confronting political communicators. Governments are meant to rule for everyone in the country concerned, but they are unlikely to win the election and become the government in the first place if they try to appeal to everyone rather than targeting the people who are most likely to vote and in the areas where the votes matter the most. The brutal realities of political campaigning mean that the target audiences which matter comprise those people who: (1) are most likely to vote – this is invariably middle-aged and older people rather than young people; (2) might vote for the party concerned, but have not yet finally decided (committed voters are unlikely to be swayed); and (3) vote where their votes count (this will depend on the electoral system, but piling up surplus majorities in particular areas achieves nothing – as Hillary Clinton found when she won the popular vote but lost the US presidential election to Donald Trump in 2016). Indeed, if people are likely to vote for a rival party, the (usually unmentioned) logic is that is better to discourage them from voting at all. In politics, market share is king: there is no point winning a record vote if your opponent does even better, and a victory on a low turn-out is still a victory.

? *Q: Is it ethical to target your PR messages in such a way that ignores key groups within the population? Does the political end justify the PR means (a utilitarian approach)?*

There is a question – a very difficult one – that everyone involved in political PR should perhaps ask themselves 'Am I doing this because it is good for the country, or am I doing this because it is good for the party and the party is good for the country?'

Government PR

Government (as opposed to party political) communication, at least in the UK and other countries who follow the UK model, is in the hands of permanent civil servants who serve governments of any complexion and operate in a non-partisan way according to strict guidelines. Such, at least, is the theory. But as we see below, government communication can be subject to party political pressure.

Democratic governments have a split agenda. On the one hand, they have responsibilities to all citizens (and beyond that to the international community), but, on the other hand, they are controlled by political parties which never forget that they are forever campaigning for re-election. This difference has considerable implications for communication. This tension between government responsibility (providing essential advice and information to all who need it) and political marketing (showing how good you are in the hope of being re-elected) is at the heart of much of the controversy about government communication.

Government (as opposed to political) communication is typically about rights and entitlements, duties and behaviour, matters which affect all citizens regardless of their political allegiances, but messages about such issues are often sensitive and it is tempting for politicians to talk up good news and play down the bad. The audiences selected should reflect non-partisan priorities, not electoral considerations. This has formed part of the backdrop to the high-profile communications during the COVID-19 pandemic, where around the world government medical and scientific experts have appeared alongside elected politicians. In theory, politically neutral public officials should ensure that the system is not abused, but it is striking that the UK expenditure on (supposedly politically neutral) government advertising rises just before elections! It is also notable that in countries like the UK the rules restrict advertising and communication by government in the weeks running up to an election ... a clear acknowledgement of something that is usually denied, namely, that government communications have a potential impact on political outcomes.

The Code of the National Association of Government Communicators (they never have PR in their job title) UK has 16 points.[3] All the points seem fair and reasonable at first glance, but the difficulties arise in their interpretation in the real world where political bosses want to be successful and need to be seen to be successful. As is so often the case with codes, there are points calling both for transparency and also confidentiality. These two points can often be hard to reconcile.

Similarly, the UK Government Communication Service has clear rules on propriety, by which they mean, 'presenting the policies and programmes of the government of the day properly and effectively'. To achieve this, they say government communications should be the following:

- relevant to government responsibilities;
- objective and explanatory, not biased or polemical;
- not be – and not liable to being misrepresented as – party political;
- conducted in an economic and appropriate way, and should be able to justify the costs as expenditure of public funds.[4]

While it is true to say that generally government communications are less controversial and seen as more ethical than political communications, that doesn't mean there are no issues.

For example:

1. Is it really possible to select facts to make a communication case without showing some bias? One fact may be true, a selection of facts is often better described as an opinion. And the choice of wording can also leave people open to accusations of bias.
2. Are campaigns being focused on areas of policy in which the government is having some success rather than in areas that are causing more difficulty? (A bit like a CV that focuses, inevitably, on your strong points rather than your weaknesses.)
3. Are campaigns being focused on policy areas which will appeal most to the government party's supporters?
4. Are campaigns being focused on geographical areas which are electorally important to the government party?
5. Do more money and effort seem to go into telling people to pay their taxes than into telling them what their entitlement to benefits are?

? *Q: Take a look at some communication campaigns by your government. Do they pass the above tests?*

There are also some situations where the style of the communication can be ethically controversial. For example, in the UK, the government, or public bodies, often produce communications in the language of particular immigrant communities. This at first glance seems inclusive and reasonable, but it has been argued that this disincentivises immigrant communities – and particularly women at home – from learning English and thereby being able to participate fully in civil society.

Exercises

1. Should a government PR use links to styles of music that sometimes encourages misogyny and violence in a bid to communicate with difficult-to-reach young males? Does the desired end justify the means?
2. Imagine you are a communicator for a government department. The minister has called for a campaign to promote agricultural subsidies. It makes sense to target the campaign on agricultural areas. But it is also true that the minister's political party draws much of its support from such areas. What do you do? How would you justify your decision and what issues might this present?
3. The mayor of your city has asked for a campaign designed to ask the public to help reduce pollution. The wording they want includes reference to how much has already been achieved in this field by the mayor. Coincidentally, the mayor is standing for re-election in 6 months' time. What do you do?
4. The Department of Health has asked you to work on a campaign encouraging people to take more exercise. Meanwhile the Treasury has recently sold off hundreds of public recreation areas to property developers. What do you do?

Most government communicators in democracies pride themselves on their impartiality and codes of conduct – and generally rightly so – but that doesn't mean that they don't have to be alert to a range of ethical conundrums. The goal of most government or public sector communication is – at least in theory – social good rather than direct and specific business benefits as even messages aimed at business should not favour particular firms. This can sound attractive but also carries its own responsibilities, as we shall see when we look at the ethical issues for NGOs.

The Third Sector and PR

Most people associate PR with the world of business or politics. However, they are less familiar with its – wholesale – use by the third sector, i.e., not-for-profit organisations, non-governmental organisations (NGOs, also known as activists), charities, campaigning organisations, think tanks and religious bodies – everything from the local church, or dogs' home, through to Greenpeace, Oxfam and Amnesty International. The

'PR practitioners' in the campaigning and charity sector are often known as 'activists'. This is partly because the third sector is another realm – like government – which carefully avoids the term 'PR' to describe what it does. It means that many outsiders who criticise PR completely overlook the activities of such organisations – particularly when they themselves work for them.

These organisations deploy an enormous amount of PR muscle power – even if they call it campaigning or something else – and are heavily engaged in media relations and lobbying. Unlike commercial organisations which have to devote most of their time to producing goods or delivering services, campaigning NGOs can often concentrate all their energies on PR, including high-profile publicity stunts of a kind of which commercial PR people can only dream. The business model of a campaigning organisation is, after all, simply to raise money and secure support in order to campaign to secure its goals. So, for example, Greenpeace offers no services – other than, some would say, a good conscience to their donors and supporters – but spends all its energies trying to get other organisations, such as governments, to behave differently.

Some NGOs focus on offering real services, such as kenneling for abandoned dogs or feeding disaster victims, and largely avoid political campaigning. Some, such as Oxfam, not only provide services on the ground – such as help to victims of famine – but also campaign for political and social change.

An advantage of working in the not-for-profit sector is that you can take bigger risks – even break the law. The media and indeed much of the public tend to be tolerant of the behaviour of NGOs, even when they do not entirely share their views. This is not really surprising. Business organisations are about making money. Public sector organisations are about exercising power or telling us what to do. The not-for-profit sector seems – uniquely – to be about idealism and doing good. Consequently, when Extinction Rebellion obstructs traffic to protest against climate change, or Greenpeace trespass on a private farm to oppose genetically modified (GM) food trials, they achieve a great deal of generally favourable media coverage and often only a gentle ticking-off from the authorities and none from the PR bodies whose codes they are breaching. A commercial or public sector organisation breaking the law to secure publicity would not only provoke massive negative media coverage but would face the full weight of the law and the sanctions of the PR industry.

So, what are the ethical issues raised by 'do-gooding' bodies breaking not only ethical codes but the law to achieve their goals? Does the utilitarian 'ends justify the means' argument stand up to scrutiny, particularly if a majority of the population doesn't agree with some or all of the 'ends'?

Exercises

1. The NGO you are working for believes that company Z is not abiding by national and global codes on the sourcing of rare metals needed to make mobile phones. They have asked a hacker to get inside Z's computer system to find evidence that can then be given to the media. What do you do?
2. The boss of your charity is an inspirational leader and has indirectly helped save the lives of thousands of refugees. He is also prone to making inappropriate remarks to female staff at social events. A journalist you know asks you if you have ever seen any evidence of this. You have. What do you do?
3. A wealthy but controversial supporter of your NGO agrees to pay the airfare and hotel costs for a group of journalists to visit a country where you believe serious human rights abuses are taking place. The supporter insists on remaining anonymous. The BBC has reported that the trip was paid for out of general donations. Do you correct their error?

As the world saw a few years ago with the Oxfam and Save the Children scandals (see p. 95), the fact that people say they want to do good, or believe they are doing good, does not mean they are good. Nor does it mean that NGOs' law-breaking *means* are justified by the *ends* they seek. There are egos, self-delusion, politics, envy and greed in all walks of life – including the not-for-profit sector.

Internal Communications

All organisations, of whatever kind, have their own forms of communication – between management and staff (vertical communication) and among colleagues (horizontal communication). Internal communications refers to the planned, deliberate and centrally directed vertical and horizontal communication within an organisation.

Internal communications play an important and often healthy and proper part in organisational life, but, like all forms of communication, are, on their own, morally neutral. In so far as people pay them any attention (they seldom receive much scrutiny), their views on internal communications will vary, depending on what they think of the organisation concerned, the issues at stake, the methods used and the validity of any concerns of the employees.

But, of all the main branches of the contemporary public relations industry, internal communications are the one that best realises the propagandists' dream of full control (see pp. 25–29). This makes it all the more surprising that critics of PR, who often liken the whole industry to propaganda, hardly ever talk about internal communications. Unlike media relations work, where the PR practitioner seeks to influence – but never fully controls – media coverage, here PR people exercise full control over their own, managed media. There is no journalist or blogger acting as a filter. Their messages can be promoted at will, while staff seeking to put across alternative messages find internal media closed to them. Thus, internal communicators enjoy a monopoly of communication, the ideal of propagandists. Employees can only escape the monopoly by leaving their jobs.

Censorship

This monopoly also depends on an organisation's ability to censor rival forms of communication. Unlike other PR people, internal communicators enjoy the ability to apply real, formal sanctions to anyone who contradicts the organisation's view of their world. It is accepted – so much so that it usually passes without comment or consideration – that we relinquish many of our rights of free speech when we take up employment. The organisations which employ us are, with hardly any true exceptions, not worker democracies but autocracies or oligarchies run by people who are usually accountable to others – shareholders, voters, or members and funders in the case of not-for-profit entities.

Employees are obliged to receive the ideas and information communicated by their employers, and at the same time they forfeit the right to speak out, although special allowance is sometimes made for 'whistleblowers' in the case of serious abuses. Bringing one's employer into disrepute is a commonly accepted basis for dismissal, while breaching confidences and speaking to the media without permission often constitute disciplinary offences. The employer's monopoly of formal internal media channels leaves only informal options fully open to employees. Typically, these comprise private emails and text messages, word-of-mouth exchanges – for example, conversations around the water cooler or photocopier – or alternative forms of written media, such as graffiti. Organisations can and do monitor online comments by members of staff, so the advent of social media has not really changed the principles outlined above – indeed, it has in some ways made it easier to police staff behavior through email alerts, careful searches and follow-up action. Social media leave a trail. People have been fired for criticising or mocking their employer on what they thought were private Facebook pages or Twitter messages.

In some cases highly dangerous or even life-threatening practices in organisations as diverse as businesses, hospitals and charities have not been exposed because employees were too frightened to speak out, or those who have spoken out have been punished and even fired for breaching their employment contracts.

This degree of control has been sharpened by the near collapse of alternative channels of communication, most notably those provided by trade unions, coupled in some cases by the increased job insecurity associated with the 'gig economy'. Of course, astute internal communications experts realise that making their control too obvious is counterproductive. Sometimes limited dissent is allowed – staff comments are sought – but this process is often tokenistic and carefully circumscribed. In 2018, Google staff across the globe felt obliged to walk out in protest at the company's treatment of sexual harassment.[5] This was followed in 2019 by allegations that a woman who had spoken out about the treatment of women was dismissed unfairly.

Beyond paid employment, internal communications affect us: in educational institutions, for example, students as well as staff are subject to their influence as are volunteers within NGOs and charities – indeed, NGOs have to place particular emphasis on internal communications with their volunteers to keep them in line, as they are unpaid. For most people living in liberal democracies, these internal communications regimes are the closest they ever come to experiencing the powerful, closed propaganda systems associated with communism, fascism or novels such as *1984*.

Of course, for people who don't like what is being communicated or feel unable to speak out, there is always the option of leaving their job – but that is often easier said than done, and indeed other employers are likely to have similar internal communications regimes. All of this means that those PR people who practise 'internal communications' have a particularly heavy ethical responsibility.

Exercises

1. There are complaints on informal staff channels about staff shortages and the danger this poses. One member of staff in particular seems to be behind the complaints. The Head of Human Resources has denied there is any risk and proposes making the use of any unofficial work-related social media groups such as WhatsApp a dismissible offence. What do you do?
2. You have been asked to write some copy for the company about 'our exciting new change management plans'. You have been told not to mention that the plans will involve some job losses as this could lower morale and affect sales. What do you do?
3. All your organisation's staff photos feature people from minority ethnic groups and people with visible physical disabilities. The reality is that the organisation performs poorly on diversity of employment despite taking steps to improve. Is this ethical?

Corporate Social Responsibility (CSR)

Corporate social responsibility (CSR) refers to the popular idea in affluent democracies that businesses should not just make a profit, but should also make a positive difference to society. PR people claim to play a key role in CSR. In the USA, it is a core part of PR briefs and nearly all major PR consultancies now claim to offer CSR as an essential and integrated part of their service. The idea is not new. Well-run businesses which are concerned about their reputation have always responded to public, government and NGO pressure to improve the quality of life both through their own business practices and by helping and supporting charities. The public's and the media's reactions to such initiatives have always been rather ambiguous.

This cynicism about PR goes back a long way. In 1938, in the comic film *Four's a Crowd,* Errol Flynn plays the Hollywood's first self-styled PR man. When challenged about what precisely his job entails, he replies:

> It's simple. Most of my clients have more money than reputation. I sell them fine reputations through their donations to charity. So they'll die with easy consciences and the public hailing them as great benefactors. They like to die that way...[6]

Or, as Jack Lemmon's PR man in the 1962 film, *Days of Wine and Roses,* puts it as he seeks to impress his stern, sceptical father-in-law:

> I suppose you might say my job is sort of to help my client to create a public image... well, for example, let's say my client, Corporation X, does some good, something that could be of benefit to the public... well, my job is to see that the public knows it.[7]

These may seem to be cynical portrayals but they have become commonplace. How often have you heard something done by a business or celebrity described in a derogatory way as 'just PR'?

These early popular media portrayals of PR show that CSR in some form has been with us a long time and the same is true of criticism of CSR. CSR poses three dilemmas for PR.

First, how to balance businesses' financial duties with social and environmental responsibilities. Publicly owned companies – generally the biggest and most influential businesses – have a legal, fiduciary duty to shareholders (which, it should be stressed, include pension funds and millions of ordinary people through their savings) not to waste money and to make a profit. It is claimed that companies with good CSR tend to perform better than average. However, there are also plenty of examples of large companies which are – rightly or wrongly – seen as not caring much about CSR but which still do very well. For example, it is unlikely that Ryanair, Walmart, Primark, Facebook or Amazon would come top of a poll measuring public perceptions of CSR activity. Oddly enough, champions of CSR usually prefer to dwell on other examples, including many much smaller companies.

So can the benefits to shareholders of CSR be measured? How can the hard cost be measured against what often seem to be soft benefits? The answer is that it is difficult. At the heart of this dilemma is how you balance what can be competing business and social imperatives. For example, the need to sell a lot of beer set against the need to be seen to be encouraging responsible drinking. The need to compete with low prices and the need to pay workers competitively – if you increase pay too much, jobs may be lost. The desire to be green versus the need to use power – and should that be nuclear- or wind-powered? And what about coal power that creates a lot of jobs in comparison to nuclear and renewables? Should businesses minimise their tax bills even if outsiders claim they are acting irresponsibly by doing so? These are tricky and complicated moral issues.

Second, doing good vs. looking good. PR is seen as glamorous and, sometimes, powerful by the outside world – but not wholly trustworthy (look at how it is portrayed in popular culture on TV and film – see pp. 23–25). Unsurprisingly, PR practitioners, particularly those involved in the PR trade bodies, are generally keen to emphasise PR's involvement with CSR. Knowing that PR does not always have a positive reputation, they like to use CSR to try to give the industry an image of morality and social responsibility. But in so doing they can generate public cynicism about CSR – 'if PR people control CSR, it must all just be PR spin and window dressing', or so it might be thought. Sadly, this can undermine the credibility of some genuinely positive moves by businesses.

In 2007 and 2008, the UK banking giant Royal Bank of Scotland (RBS) was a leading proponent of corporate responsibility, annually producing glossy 50-page reports on its CSR performance and winning CSR industry awards. By 2009, RBS, following the banking crisis, had had to be rescued by the British government, thereby spending billions of pounds of taxpayers' money which might otherwise have been spent on schools, hospitals and those in need.

What PR's most active proponents of CSR never explain is why PR is specially qualified to wield a moral compass or why PR practitioners are particularly well placed to advise on what is responsible (as opposed to what is popular, or how things will play with the media, arenas where they have some expertise). Can PR people really claim to be experts in rival methods of power generation or be able to resolve arguments about carbon offsetting, arenas where many technical experts disagree? Finally, they fail to explain properly how PR can reconcile some of the dilemmas and contradictions inherent in a business trying both to make money and do good.

To gain widespread acceptance over a period of time, a corporation's policies must seem to be in the public interest. Whether they are or not is often a matter of considerable debate. At its worst, CSR can look like cynical 'virtue signalling'. At its best it can do much good.

Third, PR professionalism versus personal politics. Is a PR person's first duty to serve the client, assuming that what they are asked to do is legal, rather than to promote their personal view of what is responsible? Many PR people involved in CSR use terms such as a 'softer form of capitalism' and 'reinvigorating ethics'. Both statements are loaded with value judgements. What are their qualifications to assess what is 'responsible' or say what is ethical? Some stakeholders might oppose supporting a gay charity while others want to combat AIDS; some would like to support a church or mosque while others believe in a totally secular society. Some abhor alcohol, others do not. The list is almost endless.

Thus, the focus some PR people put on CSR raises awkward questions which they often seek to dodge. Are PR people working in CSR really more moral or ethical than others? Or are they just more opinionated? If they really are more moral, should they be in politics, religion or the public sector rather than in PR? Is there a danger that their passion could undermine their objectivity and duty to give the best advice?

In reality, PR people working in CSR seldom advise their paymasters to do something they think is 'responsible' or 'ethical' but which is unfashionable and unpopular – and which will lose money. They would not be long in a job if they did. Instead they have to walk the tightrope of dilemmas and contradictions at the heart of doing business in a pluralistic society.

In summary, as society continues to progress along broadly liberal lines, business, as ever, will play a key, if controversial, role. PR will be at the forefront of communicating what are at times contradictory goals.

? *Q: How far is it ethical for a business legally to minimise the amount it pays in tax?*

Q: Is it ethical for makers of high calorie drinks to sponsor grassroots sporting activity?

Q: Is a western company funding a campaign to tackle 'period poverty' in the Third World no more than a liberal cultural imperialist?

Q: Would 'Corporate Social Popularity' be a more accurate title for the practice of corporate social responsibility?

Healthcare PR

Healthcare PR is defined by the PRCA as 'any Public Relations and Communications that engages the public with health and well-being or seeks to serve the health and well-being of people'.[8] Like financial PR, which we cover next, healthcare PR is unusual in being extensively regulated by non-PR bodies. For example, in the UK, PRCA members agree to ensure that 'they are familiar with, and do not breach, relevant national regulations and relevant codes of professional conduct' such as the Association of British Pharmaceutical Industry (ABPI) code[9] and the Proprietary Association of Great Britain (PAGB), which is the UK trade association which represents the manufacturers of branded over-the-counter medicines, self-care medical devices and food supplements.[10] Every developed country will have its codes. A good place to look for European healthcare codes is the European Federation of Pharmaceutical Industries Associations (EFPIA).[11]

All these codes not only reflect and support the law, but in some cases go beyond the law. They are also extensive and detailed. For example, the ABPI code runs to 41 pages and 29 clauses and even specifies the maximum that should be spent on a meal for entertainment (at the time of writing £75.00 plus tax and tips: clause 22.2). While the detail can seem overwhelming, the broad principles are clear – though always of course open to interpretation.

On page 4 of the code in an overview of principles, point 6 states: 'Information about prescription only medicines made available to the public must be factual, balanced, not misleading and must not encourage prescription of a specific prescription only medicine.' Point 9 states: 'Transparency is an important means of building and maintaining confidence in the pharmaceutical industry.'

Point 10 states:

> Companies must ensure that their materials are appropriate, factual, fair, balanced, up-to-date, not misleading and capable of substantiation and that all other activities are appropriate and reasonable. Promotion must be within the terms of the marketing authorisation and not be disguised.

Unlike in most areas of PR, poor ethical practice in healthcare could, at its most extreme, be a matter of life or death, so these codes are important and yet there are still ethical issues and difficult decisions to be made.

A quick glance at the site of an organisation like drugwatch,[12] or even Wikipedia,[13] will show you just how controversial healthcare issues can be, despite all the codes and regulations. Perhaps this is not surprising. Healthcare companies, particularly those manufacturing pharmaceuticals, can make enormous profits, but the cost of developing new products can be enormous too. The stakes are high in terms of money and careers. Outright financial criminality is fairly rare, but people are tempted to push rules and regulations to the limits or to turn a blind eye to data that doesn't support the case being made, or indicates side effects and problems that might undermine confidence in a product.

Of course, many of the criminal and unethical acts that have occurred in healthcare are not the fault of PR people. Indeed, people working in healthcare PR are usually not specialist research scientists or clinicians and are therefore dependent on others for truthful and accurate information. Nonetheless, they have a duty to be on their guard, particularly as they are often the first people to hear of criticism or problems via the media, bloggers, patient groups and NGOs. Trigger warnings of problems might include: sudden and large increases in price; an increase in usage not backed by any new scientific evidence; allegations of side effects; and claims of addiction. All of these may be easily explained and justified, but all are worth looking at. A good PR person should at least be asking questions of senior management when such things occur.

A rapidly growing area of healthcare relates to mental health. Mental health awareness has increased dramatically over recent years with celebrities and even the British royal family speaking out about it. Undoubtedly, drugs can play an important role in managing and even curing some problems, but what if people become overly reliant on them or expect too much of them? Do natural remedies such as taking more exercise and walking in the countryside get passed over or forgotten? Prevention may be better than a cure, but the financial rewards accrue to those who develop cures. Is there a danger that doctors and pharmaceutical companies are medicalising, for profit or status, what may just be the sorrows and ups and downs of everyday life?

A specific area that has caused considerable controversy is 'disease awareness programmes'. Some critics see these as a back-door way for companies to bypass the regulations and promote their drugs without actually even naming them. Patient groups keen to promote their cause are also in need of resources to help them communicate – resources that pharmaceutical companies with related drugs may be happy to provide.

This is also associated with the topic of 'well-being', where the ethical waters can become particularly murky. Well-being is something everyone is likely to aspire to, despite it being a rather nebulous concept, with the science behind it being unclear or invisible. One of the best known and controversial examples is 'vaginal steaming' as promoted by Gwyneth Paltrow's Goop brand.[14]

Another example is vitamin supplements. These are hugely popular, but the scientific support for their efficacy is, at best, shaky. Some PR people working on promoting such products will argue that, even if they don't work, they do no harm and may have a placebo effect that makes people feel better. But the counter-argument is that some people believe, or assume, that taking supplements means they don't need to worry about including vitamins in their everyday diet and, as a result, damage their health.

Similarly, there are a range of alternative therapies that lack conventional scientific or medical proof, but are nonetheless popular, such as reflexology and aromatherapy, while the claims for homeopathy are highly contentious. Proponents point to thousands, even millions, of happy users. Critics say that most, if not all, of the benefit comes not from the therapy, but from the patient having someone to talk to and taking the time to relax them – unlike the general practitioner who can often give no more than ten minutes to each patient. The outcome of the therapy may be good, even if the science isn't. Does that matter?

When people are sick or unhappy they are particularly vulnerable and suggestible. This leaves a particularly heavy responsibility on the shoulders of those who try to promote any kind of cure or treatment.

?• *Q: Is it ethical to promote products or therapies that have a placebo effect but the benefits of which are not medically proven?*

Q: If it is, what would you include in a PR and communication code of conduct for such products and therapies?

Q: Is it acceptable for healthcare PR people to use friends and family as case studies?

Q: Does the end (making people well) justify the means (scaring people)?

Financial PR

As with so much in public relations, there is no clear agreement on what constitutes financial PR. For the purposes of this book, however, we are distinguishing between financial services PR and financial or 'City' PR. Financial services PR is about promoting financial services and products to businesses or consumers. This may include savings, investments, loans, current accounts, pensions, and so on. This is sometimes called retail finance.

But financial PR, also sometimes called City PR in the UK, taking its name from London's financial district, and, in the USA, called Investor Relations, is distinct from PR for financial services. It employs the most highly paid consultants in the business and can be hugely important, contributing to the making and breaking of companies. It is also one of the most secretive and least-known PR specialisms. Financial PR derives its importance from the decisive role a company's reputation plays in determining its share price. Media reports can quickly push the price up or down, with all-important consequences for the careers of senior executives and the fate of corporations, however large or seemingly invulnerable. It comes to the fore at times of change or crisis, such as mergers, acquisitions, and corporate opportunities and difficulties. Typically, the target audiences for financial PR are limited: they are the small number of financial analysts and others in the fund management and corporate finance fields who determine whether large volumes of a company's shares are to be bought or sold. Media relations work is focused on specialist business media such as the *Financial Times* and the *Wall Street Journal*, as well as business journalists in other media.

Financial PR shares many features with healthcare. It is highly regulated. This reflects the fact that, while not quite a matter of life or death, unethical behaviour can result in financial disaster for private individuals and businesses. Truth, accuracy and transparency are vital. And, as with healthcare, in addition to the codes of the industry bodies such as the PRCA and CIPR, there are non-PR bodies who control and regulate what is done. These include:

- the FSA or Financial Services Authority in the UK;
- the SEC or Securities and Exchange Commission in the USA;
- the CESR or Commission of European Securities Regulators;
- not forgetting, the IMF (International Monetary Fund), the EU, the World Bank, and so on.

Notably none of these bodies was able to prevent the financial collapse of 2008.

The most obvious form of unethical PR behavior is insider trading – using confidential information to enrich yourself on the stock market by buying or selling shares (usually using a friend or relation) in advance of important public announcements. Insider trading is now illegal in most countries and so is no longer a purely 'ethical' issue.

But there are other ethical issues to worry about. Hostile takeovers of companies are a rare example of an area of commercial PR which can become personal and negative, as companies and their leaders seek to disparage each other. More generally, and to a much greater extent than most other forms of PR, financial PR is about playing down, within legal limits, news which companies do not wish to emerge.

It is not unknown for damaging details of senior executives' private lives to be revealed during contested mergers and acquisitions. The information seldom appears in official form but nonetheless somehow emerges into the public domain. Are infidelities, drug taking or dodgy associates really relevant to someone's ability to run a business? Doesn't even the richest, and perhaps obnoxious, tycoon have the right to some privacy? Does the fact that the media will publish the story and the public will find it interesting justify telling the story as being in the public interest?

Similarly, while it is often illegal to withhold key financial information or information that may impact on the financial well-being of an organisation, there are some grey areas. As we all do with our CVs, PR people will promote all the positives and ignore the negatives. We have never seen a CV that boasts of innumeracy, or an inability to be punctual, but nor have we seen many business documents that willingly admit to weaknesses and flaws, despite the potential importance of such information to shareholders and employees.

The question to ask yourself in these situations is 'would I have been angry and disadvantaged if this had been done to *me*?' If the answer is yes, then, at best, you are not earning a reputation for being trustworthy and ethical. At worst, you will be seen as cynical and ruthless – though clearly for some people such a reputation has done them no harm, at least in the short term.

Exercises

1. Following the death of your grandmother, you inherit some money. Your client, whose shares are quoted on the stock market, is about to launch a new product that seems sure to do well. Do you buy shares in the company?
2. Your client is fighting a hostile takeover bid from a Japanese company. An unofficial history of the company reveals that it used slave labour during the Second World War. Do you make use of this information?
3. Your client's shares are at an all-time high with investors both big and small keen to get a piece of the action. However, you know that there is a real chance that in the next few months the client might well lose one of its own biggest clients which would undoubtedly lead to a fall in the share price. What is the proper thing to do?

Celebrity PR

Celebrities play a central role in contemporary culture and a large and seemingly growing proportion of media content is devoted to their activities. The lion's share of this is supplied by the PR industry. Celebrity PR crosses over into other areas of PR partly because the original reason for a celebrity's fame often involves another sector covered by specialist PR – for example, fashion, music, entertainment, sport and food. In addition, one of the most typical ways by which PR people seek to secure publicity for products (or indeed NGOs or even political parties) is to win, or pay for, celebrity endorsement.

Most people in PR are accustomed to dealing with clients which are, in the main, structured, disciplined organisations which attempt to behave in logical and fairly predictable ways. Celebrities are individuals who have often achieved fame or even notoriety precisely because of their idiosyncratic behaviour and turbulent lives. If a new product causes problems, it can be altered or dropped, but the scope for repackaging an individual personality is much more limited. Similarly, if an employee of a corporate client steps out of line and speaks to the media, they can be disciplined or sacked, but if a member of a celebrity's family causes problems, they cannot readily be dealt with in the same way: you can't fire a relation! All of this means that celebrity PR and the handling of the personalities it entails often require a different approach and can pose some interesting ethical issues.

A particular issue is privacy. Most celebrities have got where they are at least in part by courting the media, usually with the help of PR. The media, therefore, and not surprisingly, find it a little hypocritical when celebrities and their PRs try to invoke their right to privacy when it suits them. But don't celebrities have some rights to privacy despite their taste for media coverage?

For example, at the time of writing, no professional football/soccer player has ever come out as gay while still playing at a top level of the game. But what if a PR knows their client, a top male footballer, is gay? Maybe his friends and even some of his team mates know, but his religious and very conservative parents do not. A journalist, who has previously profiled the footballer in a positive way in a fashion magazine – a profile that resulted in a profitable sponsorship deal with a top brand – gets in touch seeking confirmation that the client is gay and says it would be brilliant if they came out as the first top flight gay professional footballer. The PR knows the journalist will run the story if confirmed, even if asked not to. They also know the client would be devastated if they confirmed the story. On the other hand, refusal to comment will be taken as confirmation that the story is true. What should they do? Should they just deny it? The client has a right to privacy and has done and said nothing hypocritical to deserve being outed against their will. Moreover, the lie hurts no one. Should the PR take it a stage further and arrange for the client to be seen out and about with a female model? Should they resign, ceasing to work for the footballer? Or should they beg the client to come out, saying it would be great for them, football and society? For most people these are not easy questions to answer (see pp. 113–114, for one possible answer to this kind of dilemma).

Would the same rights to privacy apply in the following case, one where PR people might be involved on both sides? Imagine a celebrity has sold the publicity rights to their wedding. As part of the deal, they have spoken publicly about their total devotion to their new partner. But another celebrity comes forward with details of an affair with the first celebrity, a relationship which has continued after the wedding. How much right does the newly married celebrity have to privacy? Does the fact that she or he has been hypocritical and has been paid for a false story change the equation?

Or let us imagine the client is a 'wannabe' celebrity whose main claim to fame is a recent relationship with an existing high-profile married celebrity. They have some intimate photographs and some salacious anecdotes about the relationship. Do you approach a friendly media contact and give them the story, or even negotiate a fee for it? Is that ethical? After all, the celebrity concerned really isn't a very nice person.

One of the authors knows a PR who represented a celebrity who, having lied once about her age in an interview, decided she had to stick to her new (younger) age. The PR when speaking to the media had to stick to it too. Should the PR have resigned? Or is it just too inconsequential to worry about?

Some argue that, in a fundamental way, celebrity PR is ethically compromised, but practitioners may respond that so are the media and society that lap up the stories. Why blame the PR?

? *Q: How much right to privacy does a publicity-hungry celebrity have?*

Q: Are 'little white lies' acceptable in defence of someone's privacy – and how does one decide what's 'little' and 'white'?

Q: Should celebrities get involved in causes they don't really believe in to make themselves look good?

Q: Does celebrity PR debase PR?

Fashion and Travel PR

There was a time when fashion and travel PR were seen as the easy and intellectually undemanding wings of PR, but no more. Take fashion PR, as an example. Fashion is blamed by some for destroying the environment, causing body dysmorphia, including anorexia and bulimia, exploiting child and female labour and perpetrating a variety of forms of cultural exploitation and appropriation. The PR guns of the NGOs are increasingly training their weapons on fashion (see pp. 104–105).

Travel PR faces many of the same sorts of problems as fashion PR, even as the industry seeks to survive the body-blows inflicted by COVID-19. Environmental challenges, 'long-haul short breaks' and flight-shaming. For the overwhelming majority of people, long-haul travel is only possible if they fly – and any significant lowering of the environmental impact of such flights is not something that will happen soon. Unlike with fashion, there is no ready solution – either you fly and damage the environment or you don't, and most people want to keep flying. The destruction by visitors of the very environment they were persuaded to come and visit through the effects of mass tourism is also a live issue, as are endless accusations of cultural imperialism and appropriation.

Fashion and travel PRs not only need to be available to advise their clients and employers on these issues, but must also decide where their own ethical lines are drawn. Of course, for both fashion and tourism, many of these aren't just PR but are industry and societal ethical issues, but does that absolve the PR practitioner of responsibility for any of the ills, real or imagined, caused by what they promote?

And, finally, let us look at bribery! Most countries have laws to counter bribery. In the UK, the Bribery Act 2010 makes it a criminal offence to seek to influence people's behaviour improperly by offering them financial advantages. Other countries, including Australia and the USA, have similar laws, as we saw when we looked at lobbying (see Chapter 7). Clearly, no one wants to see politicians or civil servants being influenced in this way. But such laws are also relevant to fashion and tourism PR people, as they are frequently involved in arranging hospitality and providing gifts or valuable services of different kinds in the course of their work. The consequence of them over-stepping the mark may be less serious than when a politician is unduly influenced, but there could still be a potentially corrupting influence on social values. For example, lifestyle PR people often provide journalists with beauty products or treatments, and travel PR practitioners provide journalists with holidays. In both cases the gifts are provided in the hope of favorable media coverage, although the arrangement is not a formal one (see Box 8.1).

Box 8.1 PRWeek Agony Uncle, April 2014

Q: I work in fashion PR. My boss gets me to 'lend' valuable items to fashion journalists, obviously in the hope of favourable coverage. How does this sit with the industry's codes of ethics? Is it okay?

It sits uncomfortably with the codes of ethics. These say you shouldn't make payments or gifts in return for coverage. And, in fairness, direct payment or big gifts are very rare – though not in all cultures and countries. What is much more common is the sort of thing you describe, where there is no direct link between the gift or never to be returned 'loan', but there is a clear hope of some future benefit.

If you were working for a big corporate or government department, the idea of any gifts or loans beyond hospitality would be unthinkable – though even what is an appropriate level of hospitality is open to debate. But consumer markets such as fashion, travel and motoring have always been seen as slightly different. Journalists need to experience products to review them. Moreover, giving or loaning a journalist a product is no guarantee of good coverage, or so the argument goes. And given the parlous financial state of most media, the likelihood of publishers and production houses paying for everything they feature is diminishing rather than growing.

It is not something that, if I were you, I would resign over – but I'd love to know what readers think.

Clearly, PR people need to consider what is not just legal, but what is proper and reasonable, for example, it is unlikely that providing a modestly valued goody bag to journalists attending an event would be deemed improper. Providing journalists or bloggers with all-expenses-paid holidays to an exotic destination also may not be illegal, but is it ethical if the reader is not made fully aware of it – or is that really more of an ethical problem for the journalist?

? *Q: Should PR lead or follow society when looking at social and environmental impacts such as fast fashion?*

Q: Is there a maximum value level which gifts to journalists should not exceed and, if so, what is it?

Q: Should all media clearly say whether products or services they show or write about were paid for, temporarily loaned or received for free? If yes, should this apply to everything or only things over a certain value?

Summary

Most specialist areas of PR have broadly similar ethical issues. How do you balance the often competing interests and values of customers, client, society with your own interests? How do you weigh up the demands for transparency and confidentiality and for privacy and full disclosure? But, as we have seen, as well as these common issues there are issues that are unique to each specialism and these often feature in specialist codes of conduct. There are seldom easy answers, not least because there is seldom full agreement on how to balance the competing demands of politics, society and the economy.

Notes

1 See Chapter 6, of McNair, Brian, *An Introduction to Political Communication* (London: Routledge, 2017) for a thoughtful analysis of the use of 'Negatives' in political communication.
2 See www.edelman.com/trust-barometer
3 See https://nagc.com/code-of-ethics/
4 See https://gcs.civilservice.gov.uk/guidance/propriety/
5 See www.bbc.co.uk/news/technology-46054202
6 *Four's a Crowd* (Warner Brothers, 1938, dir. Michael Curtiz, 91 min.).
7 *Days of Wine and Roses* (Warner Brothers, 1962, dir. Blake Edwards, 113 min.).
8 See www.prca.org.uk/sites/default/files/downloads/PRCA%20Codes%20 of%20Conduct%20-%2028th%20Feb%202019.pdf
9 See www.pmcpa.org.uk/thecode/Pages/default.aspx
10 See www.pagb.co.uk/codes-guidance/
11 See www.efpia.eu/relationships-codes/
12 See www.drugwatch.com/manufacturers/
13 See https://en.wikipedia.org/wiki/List_of_largest_pharmaceutical_settlements
14 See www.businessinsider.com/gwyneth-paltrow-didnt-want-goop-articles-fact-checked-monetize-eyeballs-2018-7?r=US&IR=T

Chapter 9

PR Business and Management Ethics

We have looked so far at the ethical issues surrounding the practice of PR in all its guises, but what about life in a PR department within an organisation, or in a PR consultancy? How are such issues handled? There is little point – and a lot of hypocrisy – in proclaiming you are an ethical PR practitioner if you are also a bad employer, don't pay interns, pay suppliers late, and overcharge or exaggerate your abilities and successes.

In this chapter we look at:

- *People*: recruitment, retention and staff welfare and what organisations might need to do in this area to be judged as ethical;
- *Practice*: how consultancies and departments need clear guidelines and values on what is and isn't acceptable if they are to be credible in their claims they are ethical;
- *Profits*: money matters. How promptly suppliers are paid, how transparent charging is and whether tax is avoided all raise ethical issues.

In Box 9.1, a leading PR practitioner discusses ethical concerns within a global PR group.

Box 9.1 Interview with David Gallagher, President Growth and Development, International, Omnicom Public Relations Group

Managing Ethical Concerns Within a Global PR Group

David Gallagher was formerly Chief Executive for the European Region of Ketchum, one of Omnicom's global PR networks (others he now supports at the group level include Fleishman Hillard, Porter Novelli and Portland, and he is directly responsible for Omnicom PR Group agencies in France, Italy, the Netherlands, Portugal and Spain). Omnicom Group, currently the world's largest

marketing communications group, also comprises many advertising and other marketing services brands. Gallagher started his
PR career in the USA, but has been based in the UK for 20 years,
making him probably the most senior practitioner with extensive
experience of both of the world's largest PR markets. He has served
as chairman of several national and international trade bodies, including the British-based Public Relations and Communications
Association (PRCA). In 2020 he became the first chairman of the
PRCA's Ethics Council.

*Q: How are ethics governed within the Omnicom Public Rela-
tions Group (OPRG)?*

OPRG agencies promote ethical business conduct through
training, client stewardship reviews, careful consideration of
prospective assignments, clear codes of conduct, and processes
for confidential complaints. All employees receive training in
general business ethics as part of their introduction to all parts
of the Omnicom Group and throughout their careers. This
takes the form of a range of regularly updated online modules,
which staff are required to complete, and concern such matters
as maintaining propriety in dealings with clients, appropriate
hospitality, protecting confidentiality and proprietary information, among others, but are not focused on PR or communications as such. These are addressed with standards and training
developed by individual Omnicom PR companies for their specific areas of business, and include guidance on matters such
as transparency, documentation, journalistic standards, social
media and influencers, as well as information related to client
industry codes and regulations, including healthcare, financial
and government communications guidelines and rules.

Today most OPRG companies now have their own ethics
(or similar) committees to review ongoing work and to assess
client briefs and requests, and potentially unresolved matters
could be referred to the corporate group level.

Gallagher describes how he helped established a business stewardship committee and framework at Ketchum about ten years
ago to consider ethical, legal or practical questions arising from
new business opportunities, and to review independently ongoing
work. Prior to that, such matters were generally left to the agency
executive committee, which included the chief executive and the

chairman, and other business unit heads. Establishing a separate stewardship committee which did not include those people meant that ethical or other concerns would be considered independently of the business issues. He states:

> Generally Omnicom's PR companies are also governed by the relevant PR codes of ethics wherever they are based. For example, in the UK, its PR agencies are members of the PRCA, the main national PR body, and the equivalent applies in other countries. Employees may also choose to be individual members of PR bodies, and can opt out of working for particular clients in particular fields if they have personal or other objections.

Q: Who will Omnicom's PR companies work for?

In general, new opportunities (or new assignments from existing clients) are examined through multiple lenses, and these include the nature of the client or its industry, the nature of the brief or the assignment, social or cultural perspectives (some of which change over time), and pragmatic business considerations, including views from employees, shareholders and other clients. Ethics plays a role in all cases, but as 'good ethics' can be subjective, other factors must also be considered.

Clearly, requests for services that contravene our own codes of conduct, that of our industry bodies, or the laws and regulations of the markets in which we operate, are rejected out of hand.

There are few, if any companies or industries 'banned' outright, but several have been rejected by many of the agencies for reasons that may touch on ethical considerations, but largely centre on business pragmatism. The tobacco industry, including vaping and e-cigarette products, is off-limits for most of our agencies that also have ongoing partnerships with health-related organisations. Some agencies in the group have taken similar decisions on opportunities from clients in the gambling and weapons industries, but again on consideration of practical concerns from employees and other clients.

Many of our agencies enjoy long and productive relationships with government clients, supporting projects (e.g., health promotion, nutrition awareness, public safety, enrolment, etc.) with domestic markets and, in some cases, from a government to international audiences. The latter case in particular illustrates the need to monitor public/social sentiments as relationships between governments can shift quickly.

In one example, Gallagher describes how during his time at Ketchum, the agency worked for the Russian government, helping it to prepare the G7 Summit in St Petersburg. Most of the work was of a technical nature, assisting the government with media credentialling, interview management and general press office support. However, the company was criticised publicly following the Russian war with Georgia, and other clients became concerned – as did staff, and this was one issue leading to the establishment of Ketchum's stewardship committee and ultimately a decision to end the assignment with the Kremlin. Ketchum and other agencies in the group still support international and domestic clients within Russia, but none works for Russian state interests. He states:

Other opportunities are reviewed on a case-by-case basis, and some have been rejected as too sensitive or risky, usually in volatile parts of the world, but – like all the major marketing services groups – Omnicom PR agencies are involved in China, where, in common with others, it sees enormous potential – and increasing sensitivity.

Q: What do you see happening in the future?

In a hyperconnected world, it has become much harder to keep secrets. Work for questionable clients will be exposed, and the danger of upsetting existing clients, with their own concerns, has become more important. The workforce also has its own ethical concerns. With a growing number of areas of contention – for example, mounting anxiety about carbon emissions, something which affects all kinds of sectors, PR people will confront more and more questions which are difficult to answer.

The growing focus on ethics is common to all the countries with which Gallagher has dealings, and he sees little difference between the USA and the UK in this respect, even if attitudes towards particular issues (e.g. abortion) may vary. He states:

Conversely, the old industry bugbear of conflict of interest has become less important. Within large agencies, separate teams can potentially work in isolation for competing clients, using scparate servers, confidentiality agreements and with full transparency to all parties.

Overall, ethical concerns are viewed seriously but pragmatically. Morality plays its part – but so do business requirements. Pressure to generate income in the short term has to be reconciled with serving clients' longer-term interests. It remains difficult to work for an unpopular client, even if they are – and you believe they are (or may be) – in the right. If other clients deem it unacceptable – and/or it upsets the workforce – then that may be the determining factor.

The PR industry is just now waking up to the risks associated with 'fake news' – including age-old propaganda along with cutting-edge 'deep-fake' content technology, automated social media swarms – and it's increasingly difficult to separate the legitimate from the bad actors in the creation, dissemination and amplification of news and information. Many agencies will understandably look to convert the fears these dangers evoke into risk-mitigation packages they can sell to clients, but the real need is for multidisciplinary collaboration across communications, design, technology, journalism, psychology and others to identify the best opportunities for preventing the spread of fake news.

People

How often have we read of major organisations which proclaim they are ethical and driven by the desire to do good, but turn out to be poor employers when it comes to diversity, equality of opportunity, or protection from bullying and harassment? Ironically, perhaps some of the most high profile cases have involved charities such as Amnesty International, Save the Children and Oxfam. Is it that they believe that because their cause is ethical everything they do must be ethical? Or is that they believe the ends justifies the means? Or is it that they just didn't bother to think about the day-to-day ethics of employment?

Internships

For many readers of this book, their first experience of PR was, or will be, as an intern. So we will start this journey through the business and management ethics of PR with *internships* (Box 9.2). Increasingly, people wanting to work in PR have to have done one, if not two, internships before they are considered for a full-time role. In itself, it is quite reasonable that firms want people who have some knowledge and work experience of PR. An internship is also a useful way for the internee and the host to see how they get on and for the internee to find out if they actually like working in PR. So far, so uncontroversial. Where the problem arises is with money. There is now a widely held view in the industry that interns should be paid – but it is more widely held than it is practised. Working for free or 'expenses only' might not be unreasonable for a one-week internship, but when internships start to run to several months – and sometimes even longer – many young people lack the savings or financial support to be able to take up the opportunities, particularly if they are hoping to work and live in an expensive city such as London, Sydney or New York, where many of the most sought-after internships are located. Inevitably, this means that many internships are effectively 'inherited' by the friends and family of people in the host organisation, thereby ensuring that the PR intake remains predominantly white, well-educated and reasonably affluent. Is this an ethical issue? It certainly seems to be hypocritical and unethical to proclaim your belief in diversity and then actively and knowingly pursue a policy that militates against it.

Box 9.2 Internships

According to Francis Ingham, Director General of the PRCA:

> Our view is very straightforward: that interns should be treated with respect, given decent work to do that will further their career development and, at a basic minimum, be paid for what they do as the law requires. And the industry, again, has moved on very significantly over the last decade and now that sort of way of treating interns is absolutely the norm and the expectation. And again, that's something that we are proud of having helped advance.

On the other hand, a senior PR industry insider offered the following view:

> The reality is that unpaid internships are still all over the PR industry. They're just hidden as work placements or favours to friends. And it normally is friends. Let's not imagine this old boys' network is gone. It hasn't gone at all. It's still about middle-class people doing favours to middle-class mates. If you look at the PRCA's campaign, for example, when was the

last time they named and shamed or expelled a member for
not paying interns? We all know that these unpaid internships
still exist but nobody talks about them. It's another element,
another example of PR hypocrisy.

The defence of those who do not pay interns is that, first, arranging and
planning internships are often costly, with only limited benefits to the
host organisation; and, second, many areas of the PR business are not
profitable enough to be able to afford to pay interns.

In 2016, a UK charity advertised for 'highly organised and self-
motivated individuals' to join as unpaid interns in a PR and Comms ca-
pacity, working part-time on flexible hours in return for travel expenses
but no other payment. A furore ensued. The Director General of the
PRCA, Francis Ingham – the PRCA were running a campaign to nor-
malise paying interns – described the charity's behaviour as 'shameless
exploitation'. The charity countered that they were operating within the
law, offered a structured mentoring programme and used volunteers in
many other areas of their operations.[1]

The argument that the charity did not use, but others often do, is that
if interns have to be paid, there will be fewer internships available and
young people will lose out on valuable experience. The counter-arguments
to this are, first, that when minimum wage laws were introduced, it was
argued by some that it would lead to a fall in the availability of low-paid
work when the evidence seems to show that it has made no difference to
overall employment levels.[2] Second, well-run businesses should be able
to afford to pay people for their work and using unpaid interns simply
keeps ailing organisations on their feet and constitutes a form of unfair
competition as businesses paying their staff are undercut.

In May 2019, the PR Council in New York adopted a new policy man-
dating that all its member firms pay US interns at least the minimum
wage for their market – the new rule was due to come into effect in January 2020. The only exception is for very short term (of no more than 2–3
weeks) 'externships' consisting only of shadowing. The PR Council made
much of how the new policy would help attract 'more diverse talent'.[3]

In the UK, PR giant Weber Shandwick teamed up with the Media
Trust (a communications charity) and the Taylor Bennett Foundation[4] to
launch an internship programme targeting less-advantaged young people and ethnic minorities in a bid to boost diversity and bring new talent
to the industry. Weber's sister agency Golin pledged to house new interns
rent-free in London for their first month.[5]

What do you think? Should it be illegal not to pay interns in all circumstances and do you think it will ever be illegal (Box 9.3)? Should charities
be exempt from the expectation that interns will be paid?

Box 9.3 *PRWeek* Agony Uncle, July 2019

Q: I recently did an internship at a consultancy where at least 20 per cent of the workforce consisted of interns. We were paid expenses, but nothing else. I didn't like to push the point as the firm was finding money tight having recently lost a big client and I found the internship useful and enjoyable. But is this ethical and is it common?

I very much hope the answer to both questions is NO. Not paying interns is actually bad for the industry as it helps firms that aren't profitable to survive instead of improve. It is also not fair as only people with financial support from their family are likely to be able to afford to take up unpaid internships. The PRCA has run a very good campaign to stop unpaid internships, but clearly there is still work to be done. It is certainly beyond me how some bosses can claim to believe in fairness and diversity and then not pay their interns. A principle isn't a principle until it costs you something ... it is just virtue signalling.

Recruitment

The next stage of the employment process is recruitment. It is against the law to discriminate against people on grounds of race, religion or sexual orientation, but is there a diversity plan that sets targets for the employment of a representative cross-section of the population? And, if there is, then the next question is 'how representative?' Few PR consultancies have a balanced representation of the over-fifties or of men. You might say 'does it matter?' as the over-fifties and men are not generally seen as minorities suffering overt or innate prejudice. But there is also an issue with 'positive discrimination' to ensure a diverse work force. First, 'positive discrimination' must, by definition, be unfair to some individuals and, furthermore, it is argued by some (including those from minority groups), that it is patronising and potentially even harmful to minorities to favour them over others on the basis of their minority status rather than because of their skills and suitability.

But the challenges don't stop with having a *diversity* plan that sets targets and monitors performance on dimensions like race, gender and disability. Is it possible to make the actual recruitment process completely unbiased? There is evidence that in many countries simply having a foreign-sounding name means your CV is less likely to be picked out.[6] Similarly, age can work against you, as can gender. If you really want to avoid this sort of unconscious (and sometimes conscious) bias, should firms be using 'blind' applications where name, age and gender are not asked for? Some of the big management consultancy practices are trying this approach and say they are already finding it is boosting their diversity (Box 9.4). In 2016, the management consultants EY removed university degree classifications from their entry criteria and experienced an increase in candidates from lower socio-economic backgrounds.[7] Other techniques to improve diversity include undertaking outreach programmes in deprived and ethnic minority communities and offering paid apprenticeships which appeal to those who don't want to go to university or can't afford it.

Box 9.4 Diversity

According to Francis Ingham, Director General of the PRCA:

> I think the industry has never been more diverse. Every year the PRCA data says we become more diverse. Now, it's a slow process. But it's definitely getting there. And the industry has a great desire to speed that up. So the PRCA has a school outreach programme to go to schools in disadvantaged areas. It has had a massively positive reaction from the industry. The industry's embracing of the apprenticeship programme; the outreach that's taking place all across the community in terms of disability; the work on mental health. Our industry has never been more committed to becoming more and more diverse in every regard.

? *Q: So, do you think PR departments and agencies have an ethical responsibility for diversity? Are 'blind CVs' the way ahead?*

Recruitment is also a good time to examine your *gender pay gap*. In the UK, it is now a legal obligation for businesses with more than 250 staff to publish the variance in men and women's pay.[8] It is of course illegal, and has been for some time, to pay women and men differently for the same work, but, at the time of writing, women, on average, earn less than men, making this an ethical rather than just a legal issue. Leading the field on the pay gap may not just be good ethics, but an excellent recruitment tool, given the predominance of women in PR.

A senior PR industry insider reflects on working conditions in the industry:

> Well, some would say that they are under an awful lot of pressure and, certainly for the networked agencies, their owners have spent year on year insisting they increase turnover and they increase profitability. And how are they doing that? Well, they're squeezing more and more out of the people who work for them. Hence the repeated reports of mental health illness within the industry. That's people being paid not a lot of money, early, mid-twenties in terms of age, working themselves incredibly hard to make American holding companies even richer.

The response of Francis Ingham, Director General of the PRCA, was:

> The industry has never taken mental health more seriously or work–life balance more seriously than it does today. The agencies I see absolutely accept their broader responsibilities and are making massive efforts to do the right thing, whether that's about diversity, social diversity, school outreach, mental health, mums returning to the industry. And that's something we celebrate.

Retention

Once the recruitment of people is over, there is the ongoing process of *retention* – keeping and developing staff, involving pay and conditions, working hours, training, and mental and physical welfare. Most bosses like to be liked and all need to be seen as a good employer, but in the bid to 'out-benefit' their rivals, there is anecdotal evidence that some PR firms and departments seem to forget that the most important factor in job retention is a satisfying job where people feel *their work is valued*. Free drinks on a Friday and two duvet days a year don't help much if people are unhappy with what they do. Nor does ethical posturing and leaping on to fashionable bandwagons – not unknown in PR consultancies – cut much ice with employees if senior managers are seen as harsh and insensitive taskmasters.

A good starting point perhaps would be for all managers, including senior managers, not just to know the names of the people working for them, but know a little about them and their life outside work. Being asked by the boss how your kids are getting on at school or how the hunt for a new flat is going tends to make people feel good about their employer and their job. Knowing your team a little isn't just kind, it is effective. One of the authors was told early in his career to MBWA – manage by walking about – and found it a sure way to find out what is really going on, who is who and what morale is like. It also helped develop some lifelong friendships.

Another effective but also ethical technique is to listen to staff – not just their gripes – but their ideas on how to solve problems and what needs doing. Too many managers talk over their team and are too didactic in their management. They might have got to where they are by being dynamic and decisive, but as companies and departments grow, managers need to delegate and trust more and that does involve really listening, not just telling.

Senior managers also need to lead from the front. If the boss works very long hours, the staff will inevitably start to imitate that behaviour – or leave. Saying you care about your staff and mental well-being, but then working 12-hour days and weekends isn't really ethical. Similarly, managers need to be careful about what perks they get and how visibly they consume them. Encouraging cycling and fitness at work while being chauffeured in a 6-litre limo is not a good look and could encourage cynicism!

Appraisals

Appraisals are, most people seem to agree, important. And yet people from both sides of the management divide also moan about them. Often this is because proper time is not given to them, with dates and times too often being changed due to 'pressure of work'. And there is the additional problem that many managers have not been given even basic training in how best to conduct an appraisal, with the result that staff often dread them. It is no good for an organisation to say they care about staff development if they don't invest the time and training needed to make appraisals work.

- Make space and time for appraisals … and keep to it.
- Be specific, not general. Saying 'Your work needs to improve' is not helpful as it is too vague. You need to say how to improve and in what way, and offer help if needed.
- Start with the things that need to be fixed – don't end with them, or that is all that will be remembered.
- Talk performance not personality: say 'Try to make sure the people who report to you have a chance to express their views', not: 'You are too overbearing with your team'.
- Use open and clarifying questions like 'How do you think we can improve this?' or 'What do we need to do to help?'
- Use the power of three: three areas for development or three really good things. Too many goals lead to confusion and selective amnesia!
- Finish on a positive.

At first glance, this may not look like an ethical issue but a management check list, but surely it is unethical not to help people realise their potential, particularly if that is what they have been told the organisation believes in.

Training and Benefits

Training within the PR industry has improved enormously in almost every country over the last decade and yet there are still people who have never been on any kind of PR training course. Training is an integral part of any CPD (continuous professional development) programme. It is not against the law to fail to offer training and CPD, but it is certainly poor business practice and, if the organisation has proclaimed its belief in, and support for, its people, it is surely unethical as well as hypocritical. On a positive note, increasingly training for managers includes how to create an inclusive environment free of bullying, harassment and any form of discrimination.

A good range of benefits is now fairly standard in the PR consultancy world, ranging from traditional healthcare and pension benefits through to free massages, duvet days, long service sabbaticals, and therapy and guidance on mental health issues – looking after the mental health of staff is increasingly seen as a must-have rather than a nice-to-have employee service.

What people want and expect an employer to care about and do something about is an ever expanding field and some things that at the time of writing are seen as ethical issues, such as diversity targets and mental health support, may become legal obligations in some countries by the time this book is published, such is the speed of change. Even now, these changes are perhaps only in part about ethics as such: they are also about competing for and retaining labour and maintaining a highly polished corporate reputation in a competitive market.

One area of ethics that probably everyone agrees on is the need to be kind and well mannered – and yet some PR firms and departments fail to reply to applications, leaving the applicants in a state of limbo. Some even fail to reply to unsuccessful interviewees! This is not just unkind, but also poor practice. People tend to remember the organisations that treated them badly. But it works the other way too (Box 9.5).

Box 9.5 A Two-Way Street

Much of the above rightly focuses on what the employer can and should do. However, interns and new recruits to the PR industry have their own responsibilities, and some of these have ethical overtones. Apart from the general issues discussed throughout this book, it is important, particularly at the outset of a career, to establish a reputation for reliability and diligence. Doing what you have committed yourself to doing is a form of honesty; not doing so may well mean letting other people down – something that, if done for no good reason, is fundamentally unethical.

? *Q: A rival PR firm asks you for a reference for a former member of staff. You had to ask her to leave as her work had become very poor. Her marriage had broken down and she had had some mental health issues. She was fundamentally a nice person and you would love to hear that she had found herself a new job. What do you do?*

Practice

PR consultancies and departments need clear values and guidelines on what is and is not acceptable professional practice if they are to be credible in their claims to be ethical. PR consultancies also need to be clear on what sort of organisations they are prepared to work for and those they won't.

In Chapter 5, we examined who you should and shouldn't work for (Box 9.6). As we discussed, one person's high ethical principle can be another's unethical activity. At best, having too many ethical scruples can seriously narrow your job opportunities and, in the case of a PR firm, lead to slow growth or even failure.

Box 9.6 PR Work for a Tobacco Company

According to Francis Ingham, Director General of the PRCA:

> Most of our members would not work for tobacco companies but, in the interest of full transparency, Philip Morris International is a PRCA member. It operates within our code of conduct and is staffed by very ethical and professional people who are transparent in the work that they undertake.

Is it ethically wrong to work for an oil company or coal company if, for the foreseeable future, oil and coal will be needed? Is it wrong to work for a tobacco company if tobacco is still legal (Box 9.7) or a betting company if betting is legal and enjoyed by many people? Are all arms manufacturers bad or are some acceptable and why? It has been said by some that 'a totally ethical PR firm is a small PR firm', and of course anyone can style themselves an 'ethical PR practitioner'. Clearly, some of these issues are a matter of opinion, not fact or law. What is usually undisputed is that PR firms should allow their staff to say no to working on clients they think are ethically wrong – though it is likely that if a member of staff objects to the ethics of too many clients, in due course the management will start to object to them.

Box 9.7 A Principle up in Smoke

One of the authors, when the boss of a PR firm, always refused to take on cigarette business despite being a heavy smoker himself. He knew smoking was unhealthy and highly addictive and didn't want to do anything to promote it.

His firm pitched for a government anti-smoking campaign, but was disqualified because he was a smoker and the client thought it would look bad if it was revealed that a smoker was in charge of the PR. His argument that his smoking made him very well placed to understand what would persuade smokers to give up held no water with the client.

(PS: Some years later he did finally give up smoking!)

As we have mentioned elsewhere (see pp. 103–104), the idea that you need to be passionate about the cause you serve sometimes rears its head. Some clients insist that the PR people who work on their account should be passionate for the product or cause they are promoting, but is this logical, let alone ethical? Imagine you own a vegan food business. Might not a vegetarian PR be more likely to know what might persuade vegetarians to convert to veganism than a passionate and committed vegan? And is it even possible to be passionate about some things? One of the authors was once told by a client that all of his team 'should be passionate about gravy'!

Beyond the issue of whom you should and shouldn't work for is how you actually work and what you're prepared to do. Is the firm or department's business practice ethical? In particular, are they honest, transparent and do they respect confidentiality? Those companies and departments that are members of industry trade bodies and have signed up to their codes on conduct (see Chapter 4) will certainly have agreed to some form of the following:

- *Being clear and transparent* on the sponsor or interest behind any activity you undertake. So, if your group of newsagents and tobacconists opposing new anti-smoking regulations are being funded by a tobacco company, the link should be clear. A group that isn't quite what it seems is often called a 'front group'. This clause would usually also cover fake case studies and packing meetings or public events with people posing as something they are not.
- *Committing to not using false, inaccurate or misleading information.* This a fairly easy commitment to follow if you are talking about outright lies ... saying black is white, that a 100 is a 1000 or something

works that doesn't. It's unethical and if the lie is revealed – as outright lies often are – your credibility will be undermined and even destroyed. You may also, in some instances, be subject to the force of the law. Where it is less clear is when facts are omitted or some facts are privileged over others. Everyone naturally tries to put the best case for their cause and, if they can actually see the weaknesses in their case, they think exposing its weakness is someone else's job. During the Brexit debate in the UK both sides – the leavers and the remainers – accused each other of lying and exaggeration. But as they were talking about a future yet to happen, there could be little certainty or few facts that could not be disputed, so, it could be argued that no one was lying, but nor were they telling a provable truth.

- *Not using bribery, inducements or improper influence.* As we have seen in Chapter 7 on public affairs, bribery is now covered by the law in most countries and is usually fairly easy to define – paying or rewarding an official to get an unfair advantage in violation of the principles of transparency and fair play. However, this area of ethics develops its own shades of grey when we consider hospitality, gifts and 'help' to the friends and family of someone you want to influence. Buying and having a meal with somebody you wish to influence is seen by many as a civilised and sensible way of developing understanding and making a relationship work for both parties. How big does the bill have to be before it becomes potentially corrupting? Similarly, most people want and like to help friends and family with jobs, introductions and useful news and gossip. Indeed, it often makes good business sense because you know their strengths and weaknesses and should be able to trust them. But it can also look like nepotism and unfair advantage. This is also a grey area in terms of media and influencer relations. Is a free holiday for a journalist akin to bribery? Is it still bribery if the journalist says their trip was paid for by the company reviewed? What about motoring PR? Clearly a journalist can't be expected to buy the cars they review, but how long should they be lent a car for, and is it acceptable to pay for the journalist to try the car in some exciting and exotic location? Should you give an expensive road bike to a bicycle blogger? Much of the make-up, food and fashion PR markets are based on giving journalists free samples. But how much is too much is still a question to be answered. Any PR department or PR firm needs to have some guidelines on what it believes is and isn't acceptable.
- *Paying commission.* Under the heading of bribery and inducements we also need to consider the issue of paying commission for new business. In the PR agency world, paying a commission to a person or organisation who introduces a piece of new business is fairly common. In itself this is not unethical. It is quite reasonable to pay

for a service that enables you to secure business you would not have otherwise been aware of, or wouldn't have been considered for. But that is based on the proviso that the person receiving the commission has done nothing improper in making the introduction and helping secure the business. Would it be ethical to pay commission to someone who works for the firm the agency has pitched for? It is unlikely that their employers would approve if they knew that an employee was earning money by tipping off or even helping an outside agency to win the business. Imagine, for example, that your brother-in-law lets you know that the firm he works for is looking for a PR agency and meets you privately to give you tips and advice on how best to pitch for his firm's business. You might feel that this is acceptable if their motivation is just to help a relative and you feel confident that, while you may have got an advantage over your competitors, your brother-in-law's employer has not been cheated in any way as your agency's proposal still had to be good enough to be chosen in preference to the proposals of the other agencies competing for the business. But then your brother-in-law asks for a 10 per cent commission on the value of the business that you have won. Now what do you do? Clearly if you pay your brother-in-law a commission, this will come from the money that his employer is paying you. If the employer found this out, they would certainly sack your brother-in-law for breaching their employment contract with him and dismiss your agency for lack of transparency and honesty. In this instance, the outraged reaction of the employer clearly indicates that they see this behaviour as unethical. As we have discussed earlier, a key way of deciding if something is unethical is to think how you would feel if you were on the receiving end of it.

* *Honouring confidences.* Naturally, no one wants to work with or for people who give away information that might be damaging in financial or reputational terms. But what if the information you have been given illustrates poor, or even illegal, business practice? For example, you are working in a hospital and see internal figures marked 'private and confidential' that show an unexplained increase in mortality rates. When you ask questions about what is being done about it, you are ignored. Don't you then have an ethical duty to tell the outside world, despite the confidentiality agreements you will have no doubt signed when you were employed?

? *Q: A valued business contact asks you to employ their recently graduated son over the summer. You like and trust the contact so you take on the son. From day one, he is late and his work is very poor. He is regularly taking drugs – he jokes about it to one of your team. At the end of the second week, you ask him to leave. What are the ethical issues here? And what do you say to the contact if she calls and asks what happened with her son?*

Q: Your flat mate and good friend works for a company that your PR firm has just pitched for. You signed a Non-Disclosure Agreement (NDA) which included information that the company is shortly going to close the current head office where your friend works. In a few weeks' time your friend is completing the purchase of their own flat near the office, totally unaware of the planned closure. Who is your loyalty to – your long-standing friend or the NDA and your company?

Q: You are interviewing a potential member of staff who currently works for a competitor. They are being very indiscreet about the competitor's figures. This is very useful information, but you find the technicalities a bit hard to follow. Would you slip on the recording device on your phone so you can be sure you've got it right and would you tell the interviewee you had done so? Or would you say nothing, or would you terminate the interview?

Profits

A good test of ethics and morals is money! Some people are inclined to talk in grandiose terms about their ethics when they are unlikely to ever be called upon to test their principles in real life in a way that would cost them money. Bill Bernbach, the great American ad man, famously said, 'a principle is not a principle until it costs you money'. This is particularly true for PR firms which have to make a profit to stay alive, but is also true of PR departments who can win plaudits from senior management if they save money and strike good deals with suppliers.

Late Payment

One of the biggest bugbears of business is late payment which occurs when an organisation does some work, incurring all the attendant costs, including salaries, but the client or customer takes months to pay (Box 9.8). So, in theory, the business is doing all right. It is making money, but in practice it has a serious 'cash flow problem'… there is no money in the bank to pay the bills. Experts even debate if cash flow is more important than actually making a profit.[9] Governments often say they are going to act to prevent late payment which inevitably hits small businesses (which is what most PR firms are) particularly badly. But while governments are generally fairly prompt payers, they seem reluctant to actually outlaw late payment, preferring to leave it to market forces to sort out.

Box 9.8 PRWeek Agony Uncle, June 2016

Q: I am a one-man band owed money by a firm that claims to be ethical. Ironically, they always pay late. What can I do?

Any organisation that says it is ethical but habitually pays late is a liar. Late payment is a vicious circle that starts with big boys bullying smaller boys. Firms that claim to be ethical but don't pay interns are also liars. Sadly, some firms that like to make grandstanding statements on ethics don't practise what they preach. A principle isn't really a principle until it costs you something. Paying promptly and paying interns cost you something. Saying you are ethical costs nothing. What can you do? Unfortunately not much – unless you are prepared for your dislike of late payment to cost you future business from your 'ethical' firm.

As a result of government inaction, business often gets into a negative cycle of late payment ... the big company in search of good cash flow and better profits pays the medium-sized company late and so in turn that company has to pay the small company late. Ideally, everyone should be paid within 30 days, but the reality is often 60 or even 90 days. A not uncommon tactic used by unethical companies wanting to pay late is to blame the system, for example, claiming that payment has been delayed because the invoice didn't have the right purchase number, or there was some minor error in the way the invoice was submitted.

Large companies who use PR to proclaim their commitment to fairness and a vibrant economy undermine these claims to virtue when they pay businesses late – including sometimes the very PR businesses they employ to proclaim their virtue. In turn, the PR businesses moan about the injustice of late payment and how it hurts them while themselves taking months to pay their small suppliers and freelancers.

In the UK, the Federation of Small Businesses estimates late payment costs small and medium-sized enterprises £13 billion a year and results in the closure of about 50,000 companies a year.[10] There may be selfish practical justifications for late payment, but it is hard to see any ethical ones.

Transparency in Charges and Costs

Transparency in charges and costs is a key part of many PR codes of conduct around the world, but, yet again, it is easier to talk the talk than walk the walk. Buying a tangible product is a fairly straightforward process. You examine the quality and suitability and compare it with rival products before making a purchase. It gets much harder when you are buying a service. How can you compare different reflexologists, doctors, accountants or PR people? Even if you had the time to try a range of them, it wouldn't be that easy.

Most PR firms, like accountants and lawyers, have hourly and daily rates, but unlike accountants and lawyers they are not generally able to charge their clients in arrears for the hours actually worked but instead have to estimate (hopefully basing their calculations on timesheets for similar work in the past) how long they think the work they are committing to will take (Box 9.9). The reason for this is that clients are reluctant to give their PR firms a blank or open-ended cheque: they want to know in advance how much money they are committing to so they can plan and budget. In fairness, clients understandably don't much like giving accountants and lawyers a blank cheque either, but, first, there is a long tradition of doing so which is hard to shift – though it is slowly changing – and the use of lawyers or accountants is often a formal requirement in a way that using PR isn't. And, second, accountants and lawyers are closed shop professions who are better able to protect their charging rates as entry is restricted and cutting prices is not only frowned upon but can be sanctioned by their professional bodies. This is not something that, in the authors' view, PR will ever be able to do, despite its professional bodies increasing strength (see pp. 78–85 for a fuller explanation). It is generally only in the fields of crisis and financial PR, where the stakes are very high and the need can be urgent, that PR can charge in arrears for hours worked.

Box 9.9 A PR Joke

PR practitioners often complain about being pressurised into over-servicing their clients, but it's not a one-way street.

> A PR consultant has a fatal heart attack and finds herself at the gates of heaven talking to St Peter.
>
> 'St Peter, there must have been a mistake. I'm only 40. I'm sure I'm not meant to be here yet. I still have important work to do.'
>
> St Peter is sympathetic and goes off to check the records on the celestial computer. A few minutes later he returns looking a little bemused.
>
> 'It's a mistake, isn't it?' says the PR consultant.
>
> 'Well,' says St Peter, 'According to the time you have charged your clients, you are 92 years old.'

All of this means that charging for PR is somewhat haphazard. The extra money a PR firms makes in one job having overestimated the hours needed is then lost in the next job which takes longer than anticipated, often, though not always, through no fault of the PR firm. A fair client understands this and accepts the ups and downs of charging, providing overall they are seeing results and feel they are getting value. Unfair clients, who will never pay for extra hours or work but always want underservicing refunded, tend to end up with their PR agency becoming less and less transparent as it tries try to maintain a reasonable margin on the business. A good negotiation and a good relationship are ones where both sides are happy and both feel it is fair (Box 9.10) ... and, the authors would argue, ethical.

Box 9.10 A Fair Day's Pay for a Fair Day's Work

The PRCA told an independent agency owner to repay £1,500 to a start-up company that made ceiling mirrors for adult bedrooms. The dispute arose over the terms on which they were working together. The PRCA ruled that there had been a misunderstanding, with the agency owner, who was an individual member of the PRCA, regarding the fee as payment for work undertaken while the start-up saw the payment as simply the start of a longer-term partnership. Some months into the relationship the agency said that it would no longer be able to work for the client due to other commitments.

The PRCA's committee ruled that the agency owner was in breach of clause 1.1 of its then new Professional Charter, which requires members to 'deal fairly and honestly' with all parties. It said that setting out a proper contract could have avoided the problem. Refunding the £1,500 was made a condition of continued membership of the PRCA and the agency owner was also required to take a PRCA ethics course. Instead he decided to leave the PRCA.[11]

A disagreement of this kind could, of course occur, in any line of business, but the fact that the agency owner was a member of the PRCA meant that the aggrieved client had some recourse on ethical grounds – otherwise, as would be the case in many business sectors, their only resort would be the courts, where purely legal considerations would apply.

A casual-sounding business relationship of this kind is perhaps particularly common in the PR field, reflecting the fact that PR practitioners often work for and with people they know in a rather relaxed way and are not as insistent on proper contracts as some other kinds of business and professions.

Finally, it is noteworthy that although the agency owner was disciplined, he was able simply to leave the PRCA without it affecting his ability to practise PR – although it might affect the view of future employers and clients, were they to know.

Apart from time, the other area of money where issues can arise is costs and expenses. For example, if an agency commissions and pays research firms or celebrities on behalf of a client which then pays the agency back at a later date. In these circumstances, because the agency has a lot of clients and buys a lot of services, it may well get a discount from the supplier which wouldn't be available if the client bought the services themselves. So, should the agency pass on this discount to the client? Some agencies now pass on all discounts to avoid any accusations of lack of transparency. On the other hand, some agencies take the discount and add a commission or handling charge to all bought-in costs, arguing that they are not a bank and, unless the client pays them immediately (which few do), they will be out of pocket until they are paid. Other PR firms, tiring of the arguments, ask clients to pay suppliers directly. There isn't a right or wrong answer to these issues other than to say that is clearly not very ethical or good business to be unclear on what your policy is. No one likes nasty surprises or uncertainty.

? *Q: Because you pay promptly, a photographer has offered you a discount for all work. Your client does not pay you promptly which causes cash flow problems. Do you pass on the discount to the client? What other options are there?*

Q: You are negotiating a contract for PR with a large company who employs a 'procurement manager'. The previous PR firm, with whom you are friendly, tells you that the procurement manager always tries to knock at least 5 per cent off the price quoted, so advises you simply to add 5 per cent to the price you would have quoted so that the procurement manager can negotiate you down to the price you wanted and expected. Do you follow this advice?

Q: You undertook a hugely successful project for a client … more successful than anyone expected. The primary reason for the success was you had an inspired idea which a TV journalist you know well really liked and used. The problem is that you quoted a low fee for the project as it didn't involve much time. Do you tell the client it took longer than expected (it didn't), ask for a bonus, or accept it as part of the ups and downs of business?

Conflicts of Interest

Conflicts of interest occur when you are representing both sides to a competing argument or are representing directly competing organisations. This is fairly straightforward when there is very direct competition – Pepsi v Coke, for example, but what about representing the phone business of Apple and the PC business of HP? Competing companies, but non-competing business areas. Or representing a company that offers pensions and one that offers savings products? Or Rolls Royce and Skoda?

Clients are strangely inconsistent about conflicts of interest. It was a well-established joke in the agency world that having one client in a particular field was experience, while having two clients represented conflict and three clients expertise. Some business sectors seem very keen to have PR firms with expertise in an area – travel, fashion, sport and music being obvious areas of specialisation – provided that the PR firm doesn't represent an out-and-out competitor. Clients seem to prioritise market knowledge over conflict. But, as we have seen elsewhere, the key issue is transparency.

Taxes

Death and taxes are the only two certainties in life and unsurprisingly most people want to avoid both as much as possible for as long as possible. Avoid being the key word. Tax evasion is a crime. Avoidance involves bending and testing the rules, evasion involves lying and fraud – though there is a disputed area in between the two upon which judges have to rule.

Starbucks found that avoiding – quite legally – taxes in the UK caused them a lot of reputational damage and in the short term at least led to a drop in sales. Paying next to no tax did not sit well in people's minds with Starbucks' claims to be an inclusive and socially aware business. Starbucks changed their tax-paying policy, but nonetheless it created the impression in some consumers' minds that Starbucks is unethical – a tax-dodging, American conglomerate, forcing small retailers out of the high street, as one comedian described it.

The problem with taxes, particularly for large firms, is that, first, as legal entities, they have a duty to maximise shareholder return which would logically suggest they shouldn't pay more taxes than they are legally obliged to. Second, it is fairly easy for large multinational businesses legally to move their money around the world to minimise tax. Stopping this sounds easy in theory, but how to do it without stultifying the free movement of capital that powers the global economy is harder, particularly as politicians are reluctant to put their country at a disadvantage by moving first. At the time of writing, Facebook, Apple and Google are facing criticisms – particularly in Europe – for how they handle their tax affairs. These companies claim their goal is to make the world a better place, but this seems to be undermined by their reluctance to pay the taxes needed to help make the world a better place. Legally they are in the right, but ethically they are in an uncomfortable position. They benefit from the rule of law and a fair and independent judiciary but can seem reluctant to pay the taxes needed to sustain such legal systems.

Tax avoidance is less visible among PR firms – for a start, most aren't publicly owned or traded – but still occurs. One particular area which is growing in ethical complexity for PR firms is the employment of freelancers. Many people prefer the flexibility and potential tax advantages of working freelance, and even those who don't like it prefer freelance work to no work. Similarly, employers like the flexibility and tax savings that using freelancers can bring. But when does using, or being, a freelancer become a tax dodge? Is someone really a freelancer if most of their work comes from one source, and shouldn't they then be entitled to normal employment benefits such as holidays and pension? The COVID-19 crisis has been particularly hard for freelancers who are often one of the first costs to be cut when the going gets tough. The tax authorities in most countries are now acting to clamp down on what they see as an abuse of the freelance system.

? *Q: You represent a luxury housebuilder that operates mainly in the north of the country. One of your other clients who works in retail development has bought a mid-range house builder that operates in the south of the country. At the moment you haven't been asked to work on PR for the newly acquired mid-market company, so do you need to even mention it to your other luxury client? You recently had to let two members of staff go due to your business being slow.*

Q: You work for a major taxi company. You are approached by a leading bicycle manufacturer to work for them. You could really do with the business. Do you need to tell the taxi company?

Box 9.11 and Box 9.12 demonstrate ethics in action in PR work.

Box 9.11 *PRWeek* Agony Uncle, December 2013

Q: We were asked to pitch for an online betting account. I, and many people in the consultancy, dislike betting, but we could have done with the revenue. Should we have gone for it?

Betting is perfectly legal so there is no practical reason why you shouldn't have pitched. But what would have been the impact on you and your team? How would you have felt about yourselves?

Box 9.12 Ethics in Action: Examples from the UK's Chartered Institute of Public Relations

- In 2014, the CIPR retrospectively expelled a member who had failed to pay money due to a former employee at a company which he owned and which had gone into liquidation. It emerged that the individual concerned had owned a number of companies in similar circumstances and others had complained about his behaviour. As the CIPR argued, company law may permit companies to be liquidated, but that does not absolve members of personal responsibility under the CIPR Code for the way in which they run a business or treat employees, suppliers and others. The suggestion that he was a member of the CIPR implied a degree of probity.[12]
- Two former professional qualifications students were expelled from the CIPR for plagiarism. They are not eligible to reapply to join.[13]

Summary

Ethical issues have a significant bearing on human resources in PR. This includes the potential exploitation of unpaid interns, and wider concerns around staff recruitment and retention. There are also concerns about what it is and isn't permissible to do when undertaking PR work. Practitioners have to balance business realities, including the need for PR agencies to make money. and the need for PR departments to justify their existence, against wider ethical concerns.

Notes

1 *PRWeek UK*, 24 October 2016.
2 See www.bloomberg.com/opinion/articles/2019-01-24/u-s-economy-higher-minimum-wages-haven-t-increased-unemployment
3 *PRWeek UK*, 22 May 2019.
4 See www.taylorbennettfoundation.org/
5 *PRWeek UK*, 8 February 2017.
6 See www.bbc.co.uk/news/uk-england-london-38751307
7 See www.prca.org.uk/sites/default/files/PRCA%20Diversity%20and%20Inclusion%20Guidelines%20-%20Web.pdf
8 See www.gov.uk/guidance/gender-pay-gap-reporting-overview
9 See www.investopedia.com/ask/answers/111714/whats-more-important-cashflow-or-profits.asp
10 See https://cpa.co.uk/crack-down-on-the-late-payment-culture/
11 *PRWeek UK*, 12 December 2016.
12 See https://newsroom.cipr.co.uk/cipr-terminates-the-membership-of-colin-higgins/
13 See https://newsroom.cipr.co.uk/cipr-terminates-membership-of--2-former-students/

Chapter 10

The Ethical Future

In this penultimate chapter we will look at what the future might hold for PR in terms of ethical issues. Inevitably, such a chapter can be based only on analysis and speculation. By definition, there is no research or data that can tell us what will happen – only what has happened. Experience of what has gone before is useful as it may have lessons for what might happen in the future, however, it will only help us so far. Situations and events may be broadly similar but values and circumstances change over time. Some things which are seen as perfectly ethical today may not be seen that way in the future.

In this chapter we are going to look at:

- As advertising and PR increasingly overlap in the field of marketing communications, will new ethical pressures arise?
- What are the ethical issues that may be thrown up by changing social, political and economic environments?
- In an increasingly global world, how can PR deal with the different ethical expectations in different societies?
- Should PR lead or reflect changing ethical values?

Box 10.1 and Box 10.2 discuss the future of PR ethics.

Box 10.1 The PRCA Ethics Council

In 2020, the Public Relations and Communications Association, representing over 35,000 practitioners in 66 countries, launched its Ethics Council. David Gallagher, FPRCA, International President of Omnicom Public Relations Group and Ethics Council Chairman commented:

> As a professional community we have spoken for decades about the need to set and maintain higher ethical standards in communications around the world; now the time has come to act, and I cannot imagine a better place to start than with the people on this new council.[1]

Box 10.2 Looking to the Future

According to Francis Ingham, Director General of the PRCA:

> I think public expectations have moved on, and it's simply the case that, before you appoint a PR agency or go to work for a PR agency, you should expect and demand of them the kind of ethical values that have become the norm within the PR world. And the fact is that the people operating outside of those norms get smaller and smaller every year. So it's a great testimony to the industry's desire to embrace self-regulation and to embrace higher standards voluntarily rather than having them forced upon them.
>
> The market I see around the world is, of course, at different stages of development, depending upon where you go. But there are certain common themes. There is the growth of digital. There is the move to more strategic advice. The blending of disciplines. There's an increased emphasis, year on year, on professionalism and ethics and, in the wake of Bell Pottinger (see pp. 72–77), I've given speeches on ethics in places as diverse as Johannesburg and Delhi and Singapore and Dubai and Moscow and Istanbul. And the whole PR world is fully seized of higher public expectations and the need to meet those expectations.
>
> The future of ethics is absolutely at the heart of everything that the industry does. It's front and centre. Never been more vital and gets more and more important with every passing year.

A senior PR industry insider says:

> PR's ability to go under the radar, deliver messages that aren't so blatant as an advert, it's damaging to advertising and it's beneficial to PR. it's part of the reason why PR has grown every year now for 10, 15, 20 years and why advertising is slowly declining. It's not the only reason, but the people who can't advertise any longer are looking for a way to get their message over. And that's by employing PR people.

Do Social Media and the Overlap with Advertising Create New Ethical Issues for the PR Industry?

Digital communication is a commonly used but rather confusing term. It refers to neither an audience nor a particular aspect of PR, but instead to a specific communication channel: 'digital media'. Digital media are a means to an end (conveying messages to selected audiences, albeit with greater scope for interaction with those audiences), not an end in themselves. It is worth bearing in mind that there are hardly any PR consultancies – or indeed advertising agencies – devoted to other media categories, be they TV or print. Perhaps what people really mean by digital media is social media. Certainly, it is social media that are raising some of the most interesting ethical issues for PR.

Seeking to influence content on existing news sites – ranging from www.bbc.co.uk/news to online versions of newspapers such as the *New York Times* or the UK's *MailOnline*, or from the *Huffington Post* to established big name fashion and celebrity blogs – fits in well with the traditional skill set of PR practitioners. These activities are just as much about securing third party endorsement as dealing with journalists working for traditional newspapers, magazines, television and radio – the original rationale for the PR industry. But, as we discussed in Chapter 6, posting directly on social media is rather different – it involves publishing material directly, content which is unmediated and lacks third party endorsement. Journalists no longer act as gatekeepers, referees and factcheckers. PR people are of course deeply involved in such an important and potentially lucrative area of business. However, it is undoubtedly taking PR in a new direction. It is noteworthy that, in the UK, online promotional material is regulated as *advertising*.

The rise of social media and the relative decline of many forms of traditional media have contributed to a greater blurring between advertising and PR (after all, simply posting on social media also doesn't fit the classic definition of advertising as 'paid-for communication'). Both PR and advertising (and many specialist variants) compete enthusiastically for social media business. Meanwhile the increasing struggle for income among media organisations has also meant that they are more eager than ever to accept sponsored content or advertorial which stylistically may be more like PR than advertising, but is, nonetheless, 'bought' rather than 'earned' media.

However, as PR becomes ever more involved in posting on social media and in sponsored content and promotions, its practitioners may be crossing a line in terms of transparency and openness. Is it always clear to the public who has been paid to say what? Has the media owner been paid? Has the influencer or micro-blogger been paid or otherwise rewarded? The more blurred these lines become, the less PR – or any communication on social media – is likely to be trusted.

In the greater scheme of things, it may not matter much to outsiders whether these aspects of marketing communications are called PR, advertising, social marketing or something else – but the lack of transparency about the money and motivation behind what appears on social media not only raises ethical issues but could also undermine the credibility of the PR and communication industry.

We think it likely therefore that the various trade bodies for the competing communication disciplines, as well as the social media owners, will come together to create and enforce some clearer transparency rules. It is noteworthy that the UK's self-regulatory body, the Advertising Standards Authority,[2] took over responsibility for online advertising in 2011 and now most of the complaints they tackle relate to online media. One danger for PR people is that, unlike their advertising counterparts, they are unaccustomed to regulations and are therefore perhaps more likely to fall foul of them in the new environment in which they work, one where journalists no longer take ultimate responsibility for what is published or broadcast. Enhanced self-regulation will probably come into effect not so much for profound ethical reasons but because if they don't, governments – who all at least claim to hate fake news and opaque communication – will take charge themselves.

Box 10.3 offers contrasting views of PR's role in digital media.

Box 10.3 Contrasting Views on the Ethical Implications for PR of the Rise and Rise of Digital Media

According to Francis Ingham, Director General of the PRCA:

> As Director General of the PRCA, I would say that the growth of digital and social media has been entirely positive for our industry. It means there is no place to hide. It's raised expectations. It's made everybody who wishes to be a publisher and a commentator. It's also increased the power of PR but, I would say, increased it for the purpose of good.

A senior PR industry insider says:

> Digital allows people a way around things. We've seen it in the UK general election of 2019. The Conservative Party clearly astroturfing with its Twitter account. The other parties doing, frankly, exactly the same thing. And the very muted comments from the professional bodies criticising this but not really going all in on it. It's just given PR another way to lie.

The Hot External Ethical Issues of the Future

Public relations is on constant guard duty, looking out for whatever issues happen to be of public concern and which impact upon those who pay for its services. Usually these concerns and controversies are reflected in the media. When the attack comes, PR will be in the front line.

It would seem to be almost certain that climate change or 'climate emergency' will continue to grow in importance as an issue, even if attention has been deflected by the COVID-19 pandemic and its repercussions. Already arts institutions are deciding, or being forced by activists to decide, that culture is ethically incompatible with sponsorship from companies such as BP that are involved in non-renewable carbon fuels. Rejecting the generous sponsorship of such companies does of course have ethical consequences. For example, the Royal Shakespeare Company (RSC) in the UK, having consulted a large number of young people, ended its partnership with BP who had supported a £5 ticket scheme for 16–25-year-olds.[3] Arts organisations are seldom flush with cash, particularly in very uncertain economic times. At the time of writing, the RSC had found no alternative funds to fill the gap left by the rejection of BP's sponsorship. So it seems the 'good' of giving young people access to the theatre is trumped by the desire to do everything possible to downgrade support for 'carbon polluters'. This is called an ethical decision by some, and certainly points to a future where working for any organisation involved in non-renewable energy, such as oil and gas, will be described by some as unethical. Will carbon-based businesses be seen, as cigarette companies are today, as legal but ethically undesirable?

Indeed, what will be next in line? Will PR people soon be advising their clients to refuse sponsorships or partnerships with car manufacturers, airlines and meat producers because it is unethical? Or will they be advising their clients to avoid these sectors because involvement with them might cause reputational damage? Perhaps it will be for both reasons.

An organisation or an individual's lowest motive isn't always their only motive. Every year some rich people give enormous sums of money to charity. Do they do this because they believe in the causes or because they want to look good and hope for a reward conferring status, such as public honours, medals or ceremonial positions? Or is it for both reasons?

? *Q: Would it be fair or justified to say working for an oil company is unethical? Discuss. Does your personal use of fossil fuels alter your decision-making process in any way?*

The desire to 'save the planet' is also likely to see increasing pressure to decrease meat consumption. NGOs (see SIGWATCH[4] and Box 10.4 on p. 210) have over the last four or five years been increasingly campaigning against meat, though it is only fairly recently that the issue has become mainstream and started to feature regularly on TV and in conventional news media. So if meat, or at least high levels of consumption of it, is increasingly seen as unethical, will it be considered unethical to work for McDonald's, or any supermarket that continues to promote meat consumption? Does the fact that they simultaneously promote vegetarian products make it any better?

Another major part of the economy that is coming under ethical attack, while also being profoundly affected by technological developments, is the automotive industry. Will promoting 'gas-guzzling' four-wheel-drive vehicles be seen as unethical? At what point might people think it shameful to work for any organisation that is involved in carbon-burning vehicles? Is Uber ethical because it encourages people to forgo car ownership, or is it unethical as it encourages people to make less use of public transport as they opt for the comfort and convenience of a car with a driver?

Or what about overseas travel? Seeing other countries, or so it is claimed, helps broaden the mind, increases tolerance of other countries and ethnicities and enriches life, as well as boosting the economies of the countries concerned. Indeed, the hiatus of the 2020 pandemic quickly sounded loud alarm bells about the impact on the tourist industries upon which so many jobs depend. But travel is also highly polluting. Pricing may be one way to reduce consumption of air travel, but such a move would undoubtedly increase the cost, meaning that travel would probably revert back to being something only available to a rich elite, as in the early decades of the twentieth century. So how to weigh up the almost certain reduction in travel for the less well off with a measurable benefit in terms of reduced carbon emissions?

Nor is it simply about leisure travel. As ever, self-interest plays a part. The authors have taught for many years in universities which – in common with the higher education sector in many countries – are highly dependent on air travel to transport their supply of fee-paying students, not to mention the conference-going and research activities of teaching staff. While many academics have been quick to highlight the dangers of climate change, they have been more reticent about the issue when it really hits home.

? *Q: How can society balance the competing desires of reduced pollution and increased access for all to the benefits of independent travel by plane or car?*

Box 10.4 Five Sustainability Trends for Brands to Watch

Posted on 6 December 6 2019 by INFLUENCE.

Robert Blood, founder of SIGWATCH, the activist group tracking and issues analysis consultancy, has identified five sustainability trends from his firm's activist group campaigning data that businesses will need to take into account to protect their brands in the coming years.

1. *War on plastics and packaging rages on*

We're already seeing intense pressure from activists for commitments to reduce plastic use in general and single-use plastics in particular; campaigning has rocketed six-fold since 2015
and shows little sign of abating.

Who'd have thought that global brands like Coca-Cola,
used to defending the nutritional value of their products,
are now struggling to defend the containers their products
come in? Brands switching to 100% recycled plastic may help
to stave off some of the criticism, but without more supply
to meet demand, new packaging approaches will still be
required.

We can expect to see much more comprehensive waste
collection systems in restaurants and stores, extended to other
forms of packaging to increase recovery rates. Laminated car-
tons will be under renewed scrutiny because of the difficulty
of recycling, with a possible backlash against non-packaging
single-use disposables, even hygiene products, such as wet
wipes and single-use gloves.

2. *Veganism is the new vegetarianism*

Veganism is going mainstream and this time it's for environmental reasons, not animal welfare or personal health. This is
another trend that has been driven largely by environmental
groups. Campaigning against meat eating 'to save the planet'
more than doubled in late 2019 and remains at twice 2017 levels, and five times 2013 levels. As far as activists are concerned,
the push to eat less meat is critical to decarbonising agriculture
and our modern lifestyles, and is just as important as driving
less and ceasing unnecessary flying.

Vegans reject all animal-sourced products, including non-
food products like toiletries. We may well see more vegan sections in shops, as we already see organic sections in food areas,
and more vegetarian and vegan options on menus, promoted
enthusiastically as 'green and clean', while meat moves from
the core of food choices to the fringe.

Brands closely associated with meat like McDonald's and
Burger King have already anticipated this trend by adding
non-meat options to their menus, but most food firms are still
wedded to meat as an essential ingredient. This is not sustain-
able for meeting consumer demand.

3. *Deforestation*

Any product whose ingredients are sourced from commodity or intensive tropical agriculture is being called into question by campaigners. They are alarmed by increasing deforestation and biodiversity loss driven by palm oil plantations in Indonesia, Malaysia and parts of central Africa, and by soy farming and cattle ranching in Brazil, Peru and Argentina. The Amazon fires in 2019 triggered a spike in campaigning: activist activity more than doubled in just three months. Expect 'deforestation-free' products to emerge as a new category for foods and even non-foods like toiletries, with much more prominence than before, and more demand for brands to provide third party proof of thorough audits and certification.

4. *Clean beauty*

We can expect to see the 'clean food' concept applied to personal care as consumers become sensitised by rising levels of environmental and climate anxiety from activists and the media.

This notion of combining ingredient simplicity with green sourcing is already feeding into brands, such as Ren with its 'Clean Screen' sunscreen ('good for the skin, good for the environment'). To exploit the 'clean beauty' trend, brands will need to be able to promise all 'natural', almost certainly organic ingredients plus declarations and transparency on sourcing and promises of no or minimal environmental impact. No animal testing will be a given, and, probably, vegan certification too.

5. *Low carbon*

As climate concern goes mainstream, brands will be under pressure to respond meaningfully, and easyJet with its headline-grabbing tree-planting carbon offset commitment is pointing the way.

Consumer brands are beginning to adopt climate-friendly tags (cf. English Shaving Company's no plastic all-metal razor and the advent of bamboo-handled razors, and Bulldog's 'carbon neutral' moisturiser for men, whose advertising carries the slogan, 'A smaller carbon footprint is the way to go').

Brands will need to make carbon footprint declarations on packs and to look at ways of reducing carbon emissions, covering everything from land use in growing plant ingredients to energy consumption during manufacturing and logistics. Petroleum-based ingredients and materials, including plastics unless recycled, will also be a no-no.

And aside from the environment and the well-being of the planet, what about diversity and social inclusion? Twenty years ago, little was said about these issues. Although in many countries it was already illegal to discriminate on the grounds of race or sex, there was little focus on the percentage of women or ethnic minority candidates who actually made it to senior levels and certainly there was no talk about the need to embrace LGBTQ+ rights, or why it might be good to hire people from economically and socially deprived groups with limited access to internships and work experience. That has now changed. At the time of writing, organisations in many countries are struggling to come to terms with the implications of the Black Lives Matter movement.

Research shows that racial prejudice and homophobia, while still present in society, are much diminished and that most people believe that people should be selected for jobs on merit not social class. So far so good, but as we saw in Chapter 9, being a fair and diverse employer isn't without its ethical pitfalls. Is positive discrimination patronising? Does it simply turn a largely unconscious form of discrimination into a more conscious one? In the UK, a white man who wanted to be policeman won a case for positive discrimination when he was turned down not on ability, but because the police service were trying to fill an ethnic quota target and he didn't fit the criteria.[5]

Q: Is positive discrimination a contradiction in terms?

As we have seen, one of the ways of overcoming unconscious bias or discrimination is to have 'blind job applications' where discriminators like age, ethnicity and sex are not shown. This is as yet not widespread but we predict this is one area of ethics which might become enshrined in law over the next decade.

There is also the minefield of self-assigned gender. This seems fairly uncontroversial until you come to issues such as changing rooms or indeed competitive sport. People don't want or like to be called prejudiced or discriminatory, but, on the other hand, many people are uncomfortable about finding themselves in competitive sports with people inherently much stronger than them, or in a changing room with someone with visibly different sex organs. This is an area of ethics that could reasonably be described as still being the subject of debate.

Another area where it is proving difficult to achieve true ethical agreement is age discrimination. Many people would argue that older workers should relinquish their positions to enable younger people to have a chance to climb the career ladder, but older people have rights and expectations too. In any case, what age is old now? When pensions became commonplace, the expectation and reality were that many people died within a few years of retirement. Retirement was then, in the eyes of many, a blessing that came too late. But now longevity has increased enormously and it is not uncommon for people to live well into their late eighties and early nineties.

? *Q: Should organisations who claim to believe in diversity and fairness have quotas for older staff?*

None of the above issues are totally new, but they are all – be it meat, tech monopolies or social diversity targets – likely to become bigger and, at least for a while, more controversial as society, and within it PR, settles down on its new ethical norms (by which time new issues will have arisen …).

Box 10.5 COVID-19 and PR

It is far too early to judge the full impact of COVID-19 on the kind of issues discussed in this chapter. However, there are some interesting pointers. First, while perhaps no-one would like to admit it, it was noticeable how concerns about environment faded into the background as the storm clouds of the pandemic gathered – a good example of how one concern can trump another. Second, concerns about the plight of the developing world – another big talking point – slipped down the agenda. The bad economic prospects for the relatively strong economies of the developed world seemed likely to translate into horrendous outcomes for much weaker economies as they lost such trading and other opportunities that they had. This likelihood became at best a second-order concern. Finally, in spite of some rather moralistic fighting talk, the PR industry quickly had to face up to plunging levels of business, redundancies and bankruptcies. When the livelihoods of you and your friends and colleagues are on the line, almost any business can seem better than no business.

Ethics and Global Human Rights

It is now axiomatic that we live in a *global economy*. Notwithstanding the fallout from the COVID-19 crisis (Box 10.5), the tensions between the USA and China, and the UK's withdrawal from the EU, this looks likely to continue, albeit with some major jolts on the way. What is not axiomatic is that we live in a *global society*. There are still huge differences in culture and values between East and West, between democracies and countries with other systems of government, and between secular (where religion plays no formal role in how the community is ordered)) and non-secular societies.

The West elevates and celebrates the individual while in the East, in countries such as China, the group or society often takes priority. In the West, we talk a great deal about freedom, but elsewhere this can be seen as an excuse selfishly to undermine society's spirit of cooperation or even to erode fundamental religious values. These views may be strongly at variance with those held in much of the developed world but they are often sincerely held. So how do you reconcile the desire to allow and respect cultural differences with the desire to fight homophobia, sexism and censorship?

The Football World Cup scheduled to take place in Qatar in November/ December 2022 is an interesting case in point. FIFA's justification for Qatar as the location is that the Arab world has largely been excluded from world football events and that it is high time this discrimination ended. The case against Qatar is partly about suggestions of corruption. There are allegations that Qatar won the bid thanks to bribery – otherwise, people say, why have a sporting event in such an extraordinarily hot country? But another, and sometimes linked, issue is that Qatar has a poor record on human rights, particularly against homosexuals – homosexuality is illegal in Qatar and can be severely punished.

While there is a sizeable minority in the West opposed to the legalisation of homosexuality and gay marriage, the prevailing majority ethic is now actively to promote inclusivity. Top-flight professional football has a bit of catching up to do on this front. Homophobic abuse is still occasionally heard on football terraces and thus far there has been no openly gay top-level professional footballer.

? *Q: Should PR people work for companies or organisations that are involved in Qatar 2022?*

Some of the big tech companies such as Google and Facebook have also run up against the desire of less democratic societies to control their citizens, particularly on social media. Should those companies withdraw their services from those countries, thus denying millions of people the pleasure and personal freedom their products and services can bring? Or should they respect the right of each country to set their own rules and ethical parameters – even when those rules are made by unelected or corruptly elected leaders and would not be acceptable in the tech company's country of origin?

As touched on earlier in the book, there is also the issue of how Western brands should deal with popular services – such as the Chinese government-backed social media platform TikTok – emanating from societies that are less liberal and less democratic than those of the West. Some may argue that Western brands should respect people's right to use whatever social media platform they prefer and that, in any case, it is not realistic to boycott an entire society and economy, while others argue that the Chinese government cannot be trusted not to misuse the data they collect and, moreover, are responsible for major human rights abuses (see pp. 91–93).

? *Q: Is it ethical to do PR for Huawei who, it is said, receive funding from the Chinese military?*

Another issue that bubbles under the surface and sometimes breaks cover is the amount of power in the hands of the media and technological giants, such as Facebook, Uber, Airbnb, Google, Amazon and Apple. Without a doubt these organisations have made life easier and more interesting in many ways. They have, however, generated all sorts of social problems which they seem slow to address, ranging from cyber-bullying, data theft, and the provision of fake news, to insecure employment and quasi-commercial monopolies.

We predict that the concentration of power (and private data) in the hands of so few firms will increasingly be seen by politicians and influencers as unethical. Some of the big names may be broken up. And while working with or for these giants may continue to be well paid – at least at the senior level – it may also cease to look 'cool' or be seen to be sign of success and a liberal outlook.

? *Q: Is it ethical or desirable to be so dependent on such powerful organisations that have few, if any, major competitors and are often richer than small countries?*

Should PR Lead or Reflect Changing Ethical Values?

PR is a profoundly social activity. Consequently, a lack of social acceptance – at least in the desired 'opinion-forming' circles – would render PR ineffective. Broadly, PR and its practitioners need to be seen to be in line with the prevailing ethical norms of the liberal elite in the media and on social media, on issues such as race, gender, climate awareness and human rights. Not to be so is likely to invite at best public criticism and at worst a torrent of abuse and name-calling, all of which can be very damaging to an organisation or brand. The fact that these 'prevailing ethical values' may not reflect the views of even half of the population is ignored by those promoting them. Their justification for ignoring the majority is that changing social or ethical values is a good and necessary thing and that the ends justify the means – a classic utilitarian line of argument. Certainly, in the UK, for example, gay marriage was not supported by the majority of the population, but once legalised, acceptance followed quite quickly – even though a significant minority of the population continue to think gay marriage is wrong but find it hard to get their 'illiberal' views heard in the 'liberal' media.

However, PR's proximity to the liberal elite can leave it stranded and out-of-touch in a damaging way – the majority of the PR world looked on helplessly and with great anguish as Donald Trump was elected president, and as the British electorate voted to leave the EU.

As we have seen, values change, so it makes rational sense for PR and its practitioners to try to be seen as up-to-date and reflecting ethical values. But is there an ethical imperative for PR to actually take a lead on ethical issues? No doubt today's cutting-edge ethical issues can and probably will become mainstream. In the 1960s, PR had to adapt and respond to what were seen at the time as dramatic social changes – the Civil Rights movement, the anti-Vietnam War campaign, feminism and the emerging Green Movement, all of which made very effective use of PR techniques themselves – were just some of the radical new manifestations of that generation with which commercial and public sector PR had to contend. They proved to be the precursors of today's environmentalism and the increasing desire among well-educated publics to seek to improve the societies in which they live, a trend which has created new opportunities as well as challenges for PR. As discussed above, today two of the biggest challenges facing many organisations are how they can demonstrate to critical media and publics that they wish to minimise their impact on the environment and respect human diversity.

But organisations and PR people need to be careful. The reality is that PR as a discipline, whether used by a business, NGOs or governments is amoral – neither necessarily good or bad. The morality arises not from the communication itself but the objective of the communication. Ultimately, PR people are paid to help achieve the objectives of those who pay them, not to decide for themselves how to make the world a better place. A false claim to morality is worse than no claim at all: no-one likes hypocrisy. Even honest attempts to assert the ethical high ground can sometimes appear at odds with the reality. Green airlines or animal-friendly meat anybody?

? *Q: Should PR people be leaders rather than just mirror-makers?*

Q: Should PR people be urging their clients and paymasters to take active and vocal positions on the social issues of the day? Some in the PR industry argue we should. What do you think – and, if so, on what basis should they make such decisions?

Box 10.6 discusses the important social influencing process called Nudge theory.

Box 10.6 Nudge Theory: PR and the Ethics of Changing Behaviours

The COVID-19 crisis has brought awareness of 'Nudge theory' to the fore. Governments have grappled with ways to get people to do what they don't naturally want to do, such as keeping their social distance, without causing social unrest and resentment. Legislation and enforcement clearly have a role in ensuring social distance is maintained and infection rates are reduced. But coercion is seldom popular, particularly in the long term, so increasingly governments have looked to persuasion, PR and what are called nudge theories.

Nudge is not really a new idea, just a new word for the science and practice of influencing behaviour. Sometimes a nudge is about language, for example, people are more motivated to take action if the communicator says something is 'costing you money' rather than the less compelling 'you could save money'. Sometimes it is about physical nudges, such as putting an image of a fly in male urinals to encourage accuracy. And sometimes it is about playing on people's desire to belong and be like others – the reuse of towels in hotel rooms is said to increase by around 25 per cent when new arrivals read on the note in their bathroom that most guests choose to reuse their towels.

There are nearly as many definitions of nudge theory as there are uses. The Wikipedia definition, which is as useful as any, is:

> Nudge is a concept in behavioral science, political theory and behavioral economics which proposes positive reinforcement and indirect suggestions as ways to influence the behavior and decision making of groups or individuals. Nudging contrasts with other ways to achieve compliance, such as education, legislation or enforcement.

In essence, nudge theory is about nudging people to do the 'right thing' rather than forcing or demanding that they do. But, as ever, the ethical issues surface when trying to define what is the right thing. Nudging people to take more exercise, maintain social distance and eat more vegetables seems uncontroversial. It is what proponents would describe as 'libertarian paternalism' – influencing positive behaviours without coercion. However, what if nudge is being used to encourage people to consume more chocolate, support a cause you believe is wrong, or buy gas-guzzling cars?

The classic nudge principles were first outlined by Robert Cialdini in his 1984 book *Influence: The Psychology of Persuasion*.[6] Most, though not all, the principles are in common use by PR practitioners:

1. *Reciprocity*. People feel obliged to return favours. Why else would PR people go out of their way to help journalists even when there is no immediate benefit?
2. *Authority*. People look to experts for guidance. From the latest make-up techniques to advice on pensions, PR people use experts to persuade their audiences.
3. *Scarcity*. The less available something is, the more people want it. This is often utilised by PR and marketing people by saying that something is 'available only for a short time' or in a 'limited edition'.
4. *Liking*. Making yourself likeable so people are more likely to say yes to you.
5. *Consistency*. People want to believe they act in a way that is consistent with their values. Political communicators will often say things such as 'all people who believe in democracy will ...' or 'those who really care about the environment', followed by a call to action.
6. *Social proof*. People look to what others like them, or admired celebrities, do to guide their behaviour. One only has to look at the use of celebrities to endorse their messages by brands, charities and political parties.

Other techniques include the 'default option', which involves making the option you are trying to promote the default option or norm. For example, people are more likely to choose a green energy solution if it is the default option rather than just one of several offered. However, this method can also be used to get consumers to accept further marketing approaches when completing a purchase or order – the default option being to receive such messages. Similarly placing fruit by supermarket tills increases sales, but so too does placing confectionary in the same place. Decreasing portion size can be a good way of subtly reducing over-eating. It can also be a subtle way of brands charging consumers the same for less.

So the big ethical issue that the use of nudge by the PR, political and marketing community raises is whether the object or purpose of the nudge is deemed good or bad. There are no easy answers here. Research shows that people found behavioural policies to be more ethical when they are aligned with their political attitudes and less ethical when they are not.[7]

But there are other ethical questions that the use of nudge raises. For example, is it ethical to influence people without them being aware that it is happening? It is often said that PR is more effective than advertising because the target audience is less aware they are being influenced. Do people lose their agency and autonomy if they behave in a particular way without realising why they are doing so? Is nudge just a form of manipulation or social engineering?

Some also question the efficacy of nudge, arguing that it seldom leads to lasting change. Certainly, it is true that communication campaigns using nudge techniques to reduce smoking and drink driving took decades to be effective and required the full backing of the law and, in the case of cigarettes, the tax system. Changing people's behaviour is not easy. The power of nudge, like the power of PR itself, can be overstated both by some of its proponents and opponents.[8]

Using nudge, how would you do the following?:

- increase STI testing take-up;
- reduce phone use in cars;
- reduce food wastage in your canteen.

Summary

Rapid change in the media, as well as in society, political life and the economy generally is having a marked impact on PR. An industry which grew up with traditional media has been adapting to the era of social media where its role overlaps with that of advertising. While PR people are naturally anxious to exploit these opportunities, the nature of the work poses new ethical challenges. PR also has to adjust to other changes, not least the rise of new ethical concerns such as the climate emergency and the impact of globalisation and crises such as COVID-19.

Notes

1 See http://news.prca.org.uk/prca-launches-global-ethics-council/
2 See www.asa.org.uk
3 See www.rsc.org.uk/news/we-are-to-conclude-our-partnership-with-bp
4 SIGWATCH is a global research and strategy consultancy specialising in understanding NGOs (activist groups) and the impact of their campaigns on corporate reputation and social responsibility. See www.sigwatch.com/index.php?id=173
5 See www.bbc.co.uk/news/uk-england-merseyside-47335859
6 Cialdini, R., *Influence: The Psychology of Persuasion* (New York: Harper Business, [1984] 2007, revised edition).
7 Tannenbaum, D., Fox, C. R. and Rogers, T., On the misplaced politics of behavioural policy interventions. *Nature Human Behaviour*, 1 (10 July 2017): 1–7.
8 Some further reading on Nudge theory is given in the Appendix: Ariely (2009), Carnegie (2006), Epley (2015), Goldstein et al. (2017), Martin et al. (2015) and Thaler (2016).

Chapter 11

Conclusion and Our Ethical Checklist

We conclude by arguing that, despite much criticism from others, as well as some of its own people claiming the moral high ground in rather implausible ways, public relations plays a valued role in contemporary life. It is seen as vital by all modern organisations, performing a crucial role in charities' campaigning and in politics, as well as in commercial life. It is also essential to free media, and indeed can be seen as a symptom of the freedom enjoyed in modern democracies. In a world which often seems increasingly fractured, PR has to try to bridge divides. It is a discipline which requires its practitioners to try to understand others – and that is surely not a bad thing. Finally, we offer a checklist designed to help with ethical decision-making.

Outsiders often see public relations as being about power, politics and spin, or launch parties and celebrities. While there are elements of truth in these views – as there are in many stereotypes – the reality is that most people in PR work hard, spend a lot of time in the office planning, preparing and undertaking PR work, and are employed by useful but unglamorous organisations in the public, commercial or not-for-profit sectors. Their work is seldom very controversial and doesn't often hit the headlines. Only a tiny percentage of PR people spend their time working for celebrities or top politicians. And yet it is true to say that a career in PR can be varied, fast-moving, exciting and fulfilling.

That of course does not make PR any more ethical than other occupations – but it does not make it less ethical either. As we have seen, views of the moral standing of PR often depend on a subjective take on whom it is serving. Of course, over and above the cause they are serving, PR people can be unethical in their day-to-day dealings – but so can anyone else, whatever their line of work.

It is useless for PR people to complain about it, but PR's public face will always depend on the mass media – industries which, despite being heavily dependent on PR, resent their reliance. Journalists and critics are swift to pick off the less attractive facets of the PR industry, but the equivalent could be done for any occupation. Champions of journalism often try to distance themselves from the large numbers of their own kind who work for popular newspapers, magazines and news sites majoring on gossip and entertainment, or even those who have been imprisoned for crimes committed in the course of their work (as has happened in the UK, but at the time of writing we are not aware of any UK PR practitioner being imprisoned for a work-related offence). Even the highly positive view of the medical profession in most countries is seldom based on the work of doctors being paid large fees for elective cosmetic surgery. All occupations can be seen as having their high points and their low points – with a lot of much more mundane middle ground in between. PR's misfortune is that the pinnacles of its achievement are rarely acknowledged – the best PR is, after all, famously invisible – while its abuses are cheerfully exposed whenever possible.

PR may, in itself, be morally neutral, but almost everyone uses and values it, whatever they call it. The politician you detest surely uses PR – but so does the person you want to replace them. Critics of PR change their tune without noticing when it is a matter of PR for *their* books, universities or campaigns. Charities, religious organisations and all campaigners are great users of PR, just as much as companies, even though they normally avoid the term. As we have seen, one of the great global issues of our time, climate change and its implications, is being brought to our attention courtesy of some pretty heavyweight, vigorous PR, as are issues relating to race and identity.

What's in a Name?

As this indicates, public relations people continue to be troubled by what to call themselves. Although the term 'PR' was coined as a polite name to describe what they do, replacing tarnished terms such as propaganda, for many the term has itself become shop-soiled and is to be avoided at all costs. Those working in NGOs always say they engage in campaigning, not PR or lobbying, and many of those who work in government or the corporate sector prefer to avoid the term public relations, often basing their job titles around words such as 'communication'.

Nonetheless, it doesn't seem that the term 'public relations' will be disposed of so readily. Despite the angst, all the alternatives lack clarity – communication is a hopelessly vague term – and also lack the brand recognition that PR possesses. It is striking that the huge marketing services conglomerates which straddle the world – companies such as Omnicom, WPP and Publicis – generally choose to keep using the name to distinguish their PR firms from their advertising agencies and other services – for the sound business reason that it is recognisable to their existing and potential clients (and indeed to potential employees).

'Public relations' also has staying power because it is thoroughly insti-
tutionalised. Bodies such as the Public Relations Society of America, the
Chartered Institute of Public Relations, the Public Relations and Communications Association (which only recently changed its title from the
Public Relations Consultants Association, but wisely kept 'public relations' in place) and the International Public Relations Association are
unlikely to abandon calling themselves PR bodies overnight – and the
same goes for the international trade paper, *PRWeek*. Many books (including all of ours), training courses and university degree programmes
also use the name, and there are even PR museums. Nor is it a term that
PR's frenemies in the news media, or indeed the entertainment industry,
are going to give up using any time soon.

In the end, people know that changing the name only changes the
wrapping paper. For an industry that is often criticised for being more
concerned with image than substance this is a self-defeating tactic – it
could even be seen as a piece of unethical spin. If there are issues that PR
people have to confront, then they need to do so in other ways.

PR at the Centre of an Organisation

PR people are among the few people in an organisation – the others are
the chief executive and perhaps the financial director – who are involved
in almost everything of significance that happens to it. Be it a new product
launch, a public affairs campaign to change the law, a financial merger or
takeover, a sudden crisis, personnel changes at the summit of the organisation, or a campaign to win community support... whatever is top of the
agenda, the PR team will be involved. Few other jobs offer such variety.
It may be true that finance rivals communication as the essential life support system of any organisation: after all, money touches on all aspects
of organisational life. However, few who work in finance will have the
breadth of experience and involvement that PR practitioners enjoy.

Indeed, one reason PR people may be coming to the fore at top levels
in modern political and corporate life is that in the increasingly techno-
cratic world of modern politics, government and business life, they are
among the few who span the boundaries of the different specialisations
to which others belong. They may lack specialist knowledge of much of
what the organisations they serve do (as we have mentioned, PR people
are generally not engineers, financial experts or software designers, for
example), but, uniquely, they combine a broad knowledge of the key issues in a wide range of areas with all-important presentational skills,
understanding of the media and, beyond that, a sense of likely public
reactions. In a nutshell, good PR people need to speak 'human'. Bridging
the gulfs between the very different people who inhabit the separate silos

which make up modern organisations is not in itself a moral act, but it is a precondition for greater understanding and hence can pay ethical dividends.

Naturally, there is a price that sometimes has to be paid. As we have discussed elsewhere, PR is not always a well-respected or well-liked industry. Outsiders often see its practitioners as glamorous but manipulative and not always trustworthy. Why is this?

Well, apart from the popular media portrayals of PR on TV and in film as either fluffy or Machiavellian (see pp. 23–25), PR's central position within organisations also places it astride some of the contradictions and dichotomies found in all aspects of life. For example, businesses assert their customers' interests are paramount and then increase prices to please the shareholders who actually own them. They claim they care passionately about the good of society but are happy to see people consume more of their product than is healthy. Government departments promise to spend more on the things we want without increasing taxes. Charities like to say that all their aims are noble but in fact often compete ferociously with rival charities and can be tempted to do what is popular rather than what is right. Organisations do these things not because they are staffed by liars or people of low principle, but because some of these contradictions are all but impossible to resolve satisfactorily, and because they reflect our own dilemmas as voters and consumers. We all want more hospitals without paying more in tax. We think that almost all areas of government expenditure should be priorities. We want low prices but also want ethical sourcing and manufacturing for the products we buy. We want a greener planet but also want energy-consuming cars and overseas holidays. And we would far rather blame governments and large companies for the problems that arise than blame ourselves or our friends and families.

PR, resting as it does at the heart of organisations and all that they do, has to try to communicate what are at times conflicting aims and objectives. Broadly, the more controversial the cause is, the more PR there will be. And because PR has to demonstrate results to its paymasters in a tough, competitive world, its practitioners have to play hard – sometimes too hard – as they try to earn a living. Inevitably, as the messenger and the public voice of the organisation, it may come under attack, not least because there are always groups in society which feel an organisation should not do what it does, or should do it differently. Even bastions of seemingly selfless behaviour and moral rectitude such as churches and hospitals are criticised.

Some in the PR industry hate their public image and the way they are depicted as not entirely trustworthy manipulators. Journalists get annoyed by the fact that in the morning they may be called by a PR person trying to sell them a story about how great their organisation is, but in the afternoon the same PR may become unforthcoming or even obstructive when the journalist is pursuing an angle which is less favourable to the organisation. Our view is that almost all industries have their stereotypes and it is naïve to think PR will be any different, but the very fact that PR comes under attack underlines its importance and centrality. If people like a message, they call it a campaign, if they are weary of it, they call it PR, and if they dislike it, they call it spin or propaganda. The frequent use of all these terms demonstrates how PR is central to the marketplace of ideas upon which any democracy and free economy depend. Ironically, some of the most frequent users of the term 'PR' as a form of abuse are people who themselves are in what are in reality PR roles: they are attacking the PR of those with whom they disagree!

PR at the Centre of Society

If PR is at the centre of organisations, it is also at the centre of society. Politics depends on PR to communicate its policies and promote its personalities. Businesses depend on PR to create a favourable climate for their activities and to help sell their products. NGOs depend on PR to persuade people to act in the ways they want and to raise money for their campaigning. Countries depend on PR to help communicate their values and create a good image, encouraging tourism or promoting investment. Even the media themselves use PR to persuade us to read their words, tune in to their broadcasts and visit them online.

Public relations may not have benefited from some of its false claims to virtue, which are at best naïve and at worst provoke derision. However, PR, in the sense in which we describe it in this book, only thrives in democracies and is, indeed, a symptom of freedom. Dictatorships have little need to refine their skills in media handling, at least within their own borders where they directly control the media. They make use of persuasive techniques but ultimately rely on coercion. Democracy, on the other hand, is about persuasion in a competitive, free marketplace of ideas, and PR plays a key part in the process as its exponents supply the media with a wide range of information and views (see our book, *PR – A Persuasive Industry?*[1] for further discussion of this.)

Nor is PR omnipotent, as some of its critics and proponents like to claim or imply. Big companies, powerful politicians and well-known celebrities, despite their enormous PR resources, can go from hero to zero almost overnight. Many PR campaigns have little or no impact on the behaviour of the people they are trying to reach, and on the other hand some industries, for example, those supplying extreme pornography and illegal drugs, thrive, despite having no organised PR and despite enduring huge volumes of negative media coverage. For almost every PR message, there is a counter-message, either from a competitor or a critic: everyone can use PR, and just about everyone does. The fact that not all PR works is right and proper. Not every point of view, product or cause can win. Maintaining free and independent media is vital, and indeed public relations plays an underappreciated role in sustaining the work of journalists, but without PR how would all the groups in modern society argue, debate, inform and try to persuade each other?

PR jobs are relatively numerous, varied and well-paid because PR is highly valued by all kinds of organisations. And PR has grown apace in almost every country in the world as democracy and free markets have taken hold.

Healing Divisions

It is a commonplace of our times that societies are becoming more divided and more polarised, with increased tension between what are sometimes seen as the liberal elites (often younger, better educated, wealthier and resident in big cities) and much of the rest of the population. This is reflected in a range of countries across the globe – examples of what are seen as populist successes include the election of Donald Trump in the USA, the result of the Brexit referendum in the UK, the election of Jair Bolsonaro in Brazil, the surprise result of the Australian election in 2019, the electoral triumph of Modi and the BJP in India, and perhaps the challenge posed by the National Front and the *gilets jaunes* in France.

Public relations practitioners' lifestyles and aspirations certainly bring most of them closer to the world of the metropolitan elites – but if they are to be good at their job, there is another dimension to their role which is lacking in many other occupations. While it would be a claim too far to say that PR people are more moral than others, they certainly have to be in the business of understanding very different audiences. The essence of their craft is communicating with distinctive groups of people and trying to persuade them to act in particular ways. That involves empathy and the use of emotional intelligence as they reach out to people who live completely different lives to them. Whatever PR people's private views about the audiences they are trying to reach, they have to think about what makes them tick and accept that simply showing contempt for such people will seldom be effective. In a polarised world, where many people are happy simply to hurl abuse, trying to understand others cannot be a bad thing.

And finally, before we finish…our suggested ethical checklist for practitioners (Box 11.1).

Box 11.1 Our Ethical Checklist

1. Is the proposed activity legal? If not (and this applies primarily to those in not-for-profit organisations), how would you justify breaking the law and are you prepared to accept the consequences?

2. Is what is proposed in line with any professional codes to which either you personally or your organisation has signed up? Does it follow the spirit of those codes as well as the letter?

3. How do you personally feel about what is proposed? Even if you wouldn't feel proud (not everything we do can give us a moral high!), would you feel ashamed? Does it pass the 'do as you would be done by' test? Would it at least seem fair, albeit unwelcome, if you were at the receiving end?

4. How do you think your colleagues, and indeed others working in the industry, would view it?

5. What about non-PR people? How would it appear to journalists, or to other people you might work with, or for, now or in the future?

6. Discuss the issue with relevant people, considering both pros and cons.

7. Beyond the workplace, how do you think your friends and family would view what is proposed? Imagine explaining what you might do to a 'civilian'; how would it sound?

8. Add in a little cultural sensitivity. How might what is proposed appear to different audiences – older/younger, poorer/richer, from different backgrounds, or of different ethnicities, or in different countries?

9. Distil the competing arguments. Play devil's advocate. Imagine a tweet or series of tweets, or a news story, stridently attacking what you have done. How does that feel?

10. Look to the future. No-one has a crystal ball, but how might what is proposed look in a year's time – or five years?

Note

1 Morris, T. and Goldsworthy, S., *PR – A Persuasive Industry?* (Basingstoke: Palgrave Macmillan, 2008).

Appendix
Suggestions for Further Reading and Sources of Information, Stimulation and Entertainment

Books are useful, but it's also important to keep up with relevant stories in the media. Online sources such as the free-to-access www.theguardian.com/uk/media are helpful, as is *PRWeek*. URLs, here and in the notes, were accurate at the time of writing.

Books

Ariely, Dan (2009) *Predictably Irrational: The Hidden Forces That Shape Our Decisions*. HarperCollins.

Bell, Tim (2014) *Right or Wrong: The Memoirs of Lord Bell*. Bloomsbury.

Bernays, Edward L. (1928) *Propaganda*. Horace Liveright.

Bivins, Tom (2018) *Moral Distinctions in Advertising, Public Relations, and Journalism*, 3rd edn. Routledge.

Black, Eben (2017) *Lies, Lobbying and Lunch: PR, Public Affairs and Political Engagement: A Guide*. Bite-Sized Business Books.

Blackburn, Simon (2003) *Ethics: A Very Short Introduction*. Oxford University Press.

Boorstin, Daniel J. (1962) *The Image, or What Happened to the American Dream*. Penguin.

Borkowski, Mark (2000) *Improperganda: The Art of the Publicity Stunt*. Vision On.

Burt, Tim (2012) *Dark Art: The Changing Face of Public Relations*. Elliott & Thompson.

Burton, Bob (2007) *Inside Spin: The Dark Underbelly of the PR Industry*. Allen & Unwin.

Campbell, Alastair and Stott, Richard (eds) (2007) *The Blair Years: Extracts from the Alastair Campbell Diaries*. Hutchinson.

Carnegie, Dale (2006) *How to Make Friends and Influence People*. Vermilion.

Cave, Tamasin and Rowell, Andy (2014) *A Quiet Word: Lobbying, Crony Capitalism and Broken Politics in Britain*. Bodley Head.

Clifford, Max and Levin, Angela (2005) *Max Clifford: Read All About It*. Virgin Books.

Coombs, W. Timothy and Holladay, Sherry J. (2014) *It's Not Just PR: Public Relations in Society*. Blackwell.

Cutlip, Scott M. (1994) *The Unseen Power: Public Relations. A History.* Lawrence Erlbaum.

Davies, Nick (2008) *Flat Earth News: An Award-winning Reporter Exposes Falsehood, Distortion and Propaganda in Global Media.* Chatto & Windus.

deKieffer, Donald E. (2007) *The Citizen's Guide to Lobbying Congress.* Chicago Review Press.

Dunn, Jim (2008) *Very Private and Public Relations.* Thorogood.

Epley, Nichols (2015) *Mindwise: How We Understand What Others Think, Believe, Feel, and Want.* Penguin.

Ewen, Stuart (1996) *PR! A Social History of Spin.* Basic Books.

Fawkes, Johanna (2017) *Public Relations Ethics and Professionalism: The Shadow of Excellence.* Routledge.

Fitzpatrick, Kathy and Bronstein, Carolyn (eds) (2006) *Ethics in Public Relations: Responsible Advocacy.* Sage.

Goldstein, Noah, Martin, Steve, and Cialdini, Robert (2017) *YES! 60 Secrets from the Science of Persuasion.* Profile Books.

Grunig, James E. (ed.) (1992) *Excellence in Public Relations and Communication Management.* Lawrence Erlbaum.

Grunig, James E. and Hunt, Todd (1984) *Managing Public Relations.* Rinehart and Winston.

Hargreaves, Ian (2003) *Journalism: Truth or Dare.* Oxford University Press.

Hollingsworth, Mark (1997) *The Ultimate Spin Doctor: Life and Fast Times of Tim Bell.* Coronet.

Jackall, Robert and Hirota, Janice M. (2000) *Image Makers: Advertising, Public Relations, and the Ethos of Advocacy.* University of Chicago Press.

Keeble, Richard (ed.) (2008) *Communication Ethics Now.* Troubador.

Klein, Woody (2008) *All the Presidents' Spokesmen: Spinning the News – White House Press Secretaries from Franklin D. Roosevelt to George W. Bush.* Praeger.

Lippmann, Walter (1922) *Public Opinion.* George Allen & Unwin.

Leigh, Rich (2017) *Myths of PR: All Publicity Is Good Publicity and Other Popular Misconceptions.* Kogan Page.

L'Etang, Jacquie (2004) *Public Relations in Britain: A History of Professional Practice in the 20th Century.* Lawrence Erlbaum Associates.

L'Etang, Jacquie (2007) *Public Relations: Concepts, Practice and Critique.* Sage.

L'Etang, Jacquie, McKie, David, Snow, Nancy and Jordi, Xifra (eds) (2016) *The Routledge Handbook of Critical Public Relations.* Routledge.

Lloyd, John and Toogood, Laura (2015) *Journalism and PR: News Media and Public Relations in the Digital Age.* IB Tauris.

Martin, Steve, Goldstein, Noah, and Cialdini, Robert (2015) *The Small BIG: Small Changes That Spark Big Influence.* Profile Books.

McBride, Damian (2014) *Power Trip: A Decade of Policy, Plots and Spin.* Biteback.

McNair, Brian (2017) *An Introduction to Political Communication.* Routledge.

Miller, Karen S. (1999) *The Voice of Business: Hill & Knowlton and Postwar Public Relations.* University of North Carolina Press.

Moloney, Kevin (2019) *Rethinking Public Relations: Persuasion, Democracy and Society.* Routledge.

Morris, Trevor and Goldsworthy, Simon (2008a) *PR – A Persuasive Industry? Spin, Public Relations, and the Shaping of the Modern Media.* Palgrave Macmillan.

Morris, Trevor and Goldsworthy, Simon (2008b) *Public Relations for Asia.* Palgrave Macmillan.

Morris, Trevor and Goldsworthy, Simon (2008c) *Public Relations for the New Europe.* Palgrave Macmillan.

Morris, Trevor and Goldsworthy, Simon (2016) *PR Today: The Authoritative Guide to Public Relations.* Palgrave Macmillan.

O'Shaughnessy, Nicholas Jackson (2004) *Politics and Propaganda: Weapons of Mass Seduction.* Manchester University Press.

Palast, Greg (2002) *The Best Democracy Money Can Buy: An Investigative Reporter Exposes the Truth about Globalization, Corporate Cons and High Finance Fraudsters.* Pluto.

Parsons, Patricia (2016) *Ethics in Public Relations: A Guide to Best Practice*, 3rd edn. CIPR/Kogan Page.

Pitcher, George (2003) *The Death of Spin.* John Wiley and Sons Ltd.

Pratkanis, Anthony R. and Aronson, Elliot (2001) *Age of Propaganda: The Everyday Use and Abuse of Persuasion.* W. H. Freeman.

Robinson, Dave and Garratt, Chris (2008) *Introducing Ethics: A Graphic Guide.* Icon Books.

Ross, Irwin (1960) *The Image Merchants: The Fabulous World of American Public Relations.* Weidenfeld & Nicolson.

Seib, Philip and Fitzpatrick, Kathy (1995) *Public Relations Ethics.* Harcourt Brace.

Stauber, John and Rampton, Sheldon (2004) *Toxic Sludge Is Good for You: Lies, Damn Lies and the Public Relations Industry.* Constable & Robinson.

Stimson, Sarah (2013) *How to Get a Job in PR.* Sarah Stimson.

Thaler, Richard (2016) *Misbehaving: The Making of Behavioural Economics.* Penguin.

Theaker, Alison (ed.) (2020) *The Public Relations Handbook*, 7th edn. Routledge.

Tye, Larry (2002) *The Father of Spin: Edward L. Bernays and the Birth of Public Relations.* Owl Books.

Fiction

Buckley, Christopher (2003) *Thank You for Smoking.* Allison & Busby.

Dezenhall, Eric (2003) *Jackie Disaster.* Thomas Dunne.

Lancaster, Graham (1996) *Grave Song.* Hodder & Stoughton.

Larsson, Stieg (2008) *The Girl with the Dragon Tattoo.* MacLehose Press.

Michie, David (2000) *Conflict of Interest.* Little, Brown.

Price, Daniel (2004) *Slick.* Villard.

Priestley, J. B. (1996) *The Image Men.* Mandarin.

Thebo, Mimi (2002) *The Saint Who Loved Me.* Allison & Busby.

Torday, Paul (2007) *Salmon Fishing in the Yemen.* Weidenfeld and Nicholson.

Waugh, Daisy (2002) *The New You Survival Kit.* HarperCollins.

Wilson, Sloan (2002) *The Man in the Gray Flannel Suit.* Four Walls Eight Windows.

Films and TV

Absolutely Fabulous www.bbc.co.uk/comedy/abfab/
Absolute Power www.bbc.co.uk/comedy/absolutepower/
Babylon www.channel4.com/programmes/babylon
Bridget Jones Diary Universal Studios, 2001, dir. Sharon Maguire, 132 min.
The Century of the Self www.bbc.co.uk/bbcfour/documentaries/features/century_
    of_the_self.shtml.
The China Syndrome Columbia Pictures, 1979, dir. James Bridges, 117 min.
Days of Wine and Roses Warner Brothers, 1962, dir. Blake Edwards, 113 min.
Four's a Crowd Warner Brothers, 1938, dir. Michael Curtiz, 91 min.
The Hills www.mtv.co.uk/shows/the-hills
The Ides of March Columbia, 2011, dir. George Clooney, 97 min.
In the Loop BBC Films, 2009, dir. Armando Iannucci, 106 min.
The Man in a Gray Flannel Suit 20th Century Fox, 1956, dir. Nunnally Johnson,
    152 min.
Phonebooth 20th Century Fox, 2003, dir. Joel Schumacher, 77 min.
PoweR Girls www.mtv.com/ontv/dyn/power_girls/series.jhtml
Primary Colors Award Entertainment, 1998, dir. Mike Nichols, 143 min.
Scandal http://abc.go.com/shows/scandal
Sex and the City http://www.hbo.com/city/
Sliding Doors Intermedia Films, 1998, dir. Peter Howitt, 99 min.
Spin City www.tv.com/spin-city/show/220/summary.html
Starsuckers S2S Productions, 2009, dir. Chris Atkins, 100 min.
Thank You for Smoking Room 9 Entertainment, 2005, dir. Jason Reitman, 92 min.
The Spin Crowd http://uk.eonline.com/on/shows/spin_crowd/index.html
The Sweet Smell of Success Metro Goldwyn Meyer, 1957, dir. Alexander Mack-
    endrick, 93 min.
The Thick of It www.bbc.co.uk/comedy/thethickofit/index.shtml
Wag the Dog Baltimore Pictures, 1997, dir. Barry Levinson, 97 min.
Waikiki Wedding Paramount, 1937, dir. Frank Tuttle, 89 min.

Websites

Trade Organisations

Chartered Institute of Public Relations (UK) www.cipr.co.uk
Council of Public Relations Firms (US) www.prfirms.org
International Association for the Measurement and Evaluation of Communica-
    tion www.amecorg.com
International Association of Business Communicators www.iabc.com
International Communications Consultancy Organization www.iccopr.com
International Public Relations Association www.ipra.org
Public Relations and Communications Association (UK) www.prca.org.uk
Public Relations Society of America www.prsa.org

Trade Websites and Papers

www.odwyerpr.com
www.provokemedia.com
www.prweek.com
www.warc.com (World Advertising Research Center)

Critical Sites

www.corpwatch.org
www.prwatch.org
www.spinwatch.org

Index